DANIEL WILLARD AND PROGRESSIVE MANAGEMENT ON THE BALTIMORE & OHIO RAILROAD

DANIEL WILLARD AND PROGRESSIVE MANAGEMENT ON THE BALTIMORE & OHIO RAILROAD

David M. Vrooman

Ohio State University Press
COLUMBUS

Library of Congress Cataloging-in-Publication Data

Vrooman, David M.
    Daniel Willard and progressive management on the Baltimore & Ohio
Railroad / David M. Vrooman.
        p.   cm. — (Historical perspectives on business enterprise series)
    Includes index.
    ISBN 0–8142–0552–6
    1. Baltimore and Ohio Railroad Company—Management—History.
2. Railroads—United States—Management—History.   3. Corporate culture—
United States—History.   4. Organizational effectiveness—History.   5. Willard,
Daniel, 1861–1942.   I. Title.   II. Series.
HE2791.B3U76   1991
385'.06'574—dc20   91–18717
                                                                           CIP

Text and jacket design by Donna Hartwick.
Type set in Times Roman by G & S Typesetters, Austin, TX.
Printed by Braun-Brumfield, Ann Arbor, MI.

The paper in this book meets the guidelines for permanence and
durability of the Committee on Production Guidelines for Book
Longevity of the Council on Library Resources. ∞

Printed in the U.S.A.

9   8   7   6   5   4   3   2   1

CONTENTS

ILLUSTRATIONS

MAPS

PREFACE

During the preparation of this study, I have had to endure a certain amount of good-natured ribbing from some of my friends and colleagues about my spending hundreds upon hundreds of hours writing a "choo-choo book," likely to be read only by a handful of people with interests as bizarre as my own. Although I suppose that there is an outside possibility that they are right, I trust that they are not. If the nature of the story that I am trying to tell is fully understood, its appeal should be very broad. This is a book about many things: about leadership, about management programs, about corporate culture, and, yes, about railroading during the later years of its Golden Age. I believe that it has something to offer to people of many different backgrounds and interests.

Certainly I anticipate that academicians in the various management-related disciplines will find something of value here. Equally I hope that this book will be read and appreciated by academic historians. Daniel Willard's B&O is deserving of special historical status for a number of reasons, notably its active interest in welfare work, its unparalleled (in the United States) commitment to union-management cooperation, and the broad similarity of its managerial approach to that which two generations later gained great attention as the "Japanese management style." Even so, the company has received only the slightest attention in the academic literature; this work may fill a significant gap. I would be further pleased if this book were read and enjoyed by amateur historians, especially those with a particular interest in railroads. Despite the intentional dearth of steam locomotive photographs, I believe that they will find it interesting. It presents a side of railroading as a business that conventional railroad histories tend to pass over quickly or ignore altogether.

It is my deepest hope, though, that this study will be read, and its lessons then applied, by present or future practicing managers. Those are the people for whom Willard's B&O has the greatest significance—as an example of how it is done right. Daniel Willard was the embodiment of the principle that managerial effectiveness is, in its origin, a function not so much of technique as of character. There is no more important point for the manager to understand.

I would not be in a position to make that point, or any other point associated with this study, were it not for the help that I have received in completing my research and working it into publishable form. I must offer my profuse thanks to those who gave me that help. Foremost among them is Austin Kerr, whose guidance and encouragement led me beyond my initial preference for simply telling the story without much attention to context or interpretation. I received further valuable suggestions for improving my manuscript from Mansel Blackford and from their outside reviewer, and I would not have received any of their direction had it not been for Ohio State University Press editor Alex Holzman's interest in my project. Great help in tracking down and copying both archival and secondary sources of information was forthcoming from Martha Hodges of the Labor-Management Documentation Center at Cornell, Katherine Vogel of the George Meany Memorial Archives, James Quigel of the Pattee Library at Penn State, the staffs of the Pratt Library in Baltimore and the Manuscript Division of the Library of Congress, and Don Gordon of the Thomas Library here at Wittenberg. Uniquely insightful and personally most gratifying to me were the recollections and documents supplied by a cadre of retired members of the B&O family, especially Stanley Gearhart, John Bliss, Mildred Drechsler, the late William Howard, Jervis Langdon, Paul Mobus, and Albert Gibson. I thank Herbert Harwood, formerly of Chessie System and the B&O Museum, for leading me to these people. Thanks are due also to Ann Calhoun and John Hankey of the B&O Museum, and to Joseph Beckman, D. R. Shawley, and William Wick of CSX, all of whom helped as best they could in the absence of a real corporate archives.

I am grateful to the Procter & Gamble Foundation, to the Wittenberg Faculty Research Fund, and to our Department of Business Administration for covering most of the expenses of my research. I thank Norma Kettler for her splendidly accurate and timely typing of my manuscript, and Hansi Minnig for her excellent maps. Finally, I thank my wife, Raelynn, and my sons, Geoffrey and Michael, for their good-natured tolerance of my inaccessibility and frequent grumpiness throughout this undertaking. I trust that it has all been worthwhile.

INTRODUCTION

The practice of management at the turn of this century does not qualify to be called pervasively and remarkably enlightened. Although some individual managers led and rewarded their employees capably and equitably, and many more tried to some extent to do so, the manager who carefully and consistently set a course that met the long-term needs of both workers and company was not common. Many a boss saw his job as being simply to coerce indifferent workers into some sort of productive effort by whatever means seemed immediately effective—usually a mix of cash and intimidation. The manager oriented in this direction tended to be rigidly authoritarian, remote, at times arbitrary and unfair, and in some instances truly exploitive. The key element in his relationship with his workers was power: "I have it, and you don't."

However widespread this inclination, it was not really defensible in moral terms. Reactions against it grew in the early years of the century: "welfare work" against its dehumanizing qualities, "scientific management" against its arbitrariness and inefficiency. These alternate approaches, and the other more specific programs or actions to which they led, may be loosely labeled "progressive." Although not directly tied to the Progressive wing of the Republican party, progressive management did share with Progressive politics a concern with the human and economic costs associated with the unenlightened exercise of corporate power. It was very much concerned with doing the right thing, not the conveniently self-serving thing.

This book is about a major American corporation that, under the leadership of one man, attempted to align its management practices with progressive ideals: to treat its employees as valued individuals whose initiative and intelligence, if properly encouraged, might be enlisted voluntarily to increase the

Daniel Willard, president of the Baltimore & Ohio Railroad,
1910–1941. (Courtesy of the B&O Railroad Museum)

company's efficiency and to improve the quality of its services. It is an extended case study, focusing on the management programs and approaches that
began with Daniel Willard's appointment to the Baltimore & Ohio presidency
in 1910 and continued in some form until the early 1960s, twenty years after
his death. It is not intended to be a Willard biography, or a comprehensive
history of the B&O during this period, or a full summary and analysis of the
various programmatic elements of progressive management. Although it includes aspects of each, it is primarily intended to be a story, told in its context, with enough analysis to make clear the story's meaning.

What is its meaning? It is the thesis of this study that the successful implementation of the management approach herein termed progressive is inex-
tricably linked to the character of the leader. The programs that Willard introduced on the B&O, especially the union-management Cooperative Plan, were

successful: they returned benefits both to workers and to the company. Yet they did not really take hold across the American economy. Why not? It will be argued that the missing factor in companies that tried such programs and failed, or that rejected them altogether, was a leader like Daniel Willard. They were successful on the B&O because of Willard's patience, sensitivity, and firm moral view of their basic rightness—as well as his thirty-one-year tenure, which allowed time for those qualities to be amply demonstrated.

To put it more broadly, under a leader like Willard, a program becomes more than a matter of mere tactics. It becomes an integral part of corporate culture—the company's "set of shared, enduring beliefs," or "the way we do things around here"[1]—and its impact becomes widespread and lasting. Unless that happens, the best-conceived program in the world cannot work.

Understood at the simplest level, this book is about a particular management approach, and the management practices and programs that it entailed. That is the direct focus of most of the narrative. On a deeper level, though, it can be seen as an affirmation of the precept that management approaches are only the middle link of a chain, or the intermediate stage of a three-part process: from leader's values and character to management approach to corporate culture. The leader is important, because he is the principal source of mission and direction, or he is not much of a leader. Corporate culture is important because it is the broad outcome, the pervasive force that really shapes employee behavior and corporate success. Management approach is most important not because it has any intrinsic direct short-term influence but because it links leader and culture.

This is hardly the first volume to note such a linkage. Corporate culture and the role of the leader in shaping it have been the object of fairly intense scholarly interest over the past decade. Still, this study may offer something modestly different to our knowledge of the matter. Most published corporate culture case studies tend to be classifiable as either "good leadership shaping good culture leading to great success" or "bad leadership shaping bad culture leading to dismal failure" stories. The case of Willard's B&O is neither. Willard's leadership created a "good culture," but the company's overall performance, although it did benefit, could not be considered overwhelmingly successful. Forces beyond his control were too formidable for great success; for both institutional and technological reasons, then as now, the railroad industry was slowly failing. The B&O was never extraordinarily profitable; during the Depression it had a close brush with bankruptcy. Nonetheless, Willard was clearly successful in improving his company's relative position among eastern railroads. His case thus stands as an example of a phenomenon not widely noted: good leadership shaping good culture postponing decline or averting disaster in an environment of generally diminishing prospects.

To provide a more specific introduction to the story, with reference to those key conceptual elements, what should be said about the character and values of the leader? First, Daniel Willard was a sincerely religious man, a childhood-fundamentalist-turned-mature-Unitarian for whom the Golden Rule was a governing principle, not just a nice sentiment. Second, he was an up-from-the-ranks railroader with a good memory, who could recall exactly what it was like to be in the position of those who worked for him. Third, he was by nature compassionate and perceptive, and by that nature and his background modest and open to the opinions of others. Fourth, he possessed extraordinary energy coupled with the desire to do good work: to learn all that he could, to do the best job that he could, to have his company do the best job that it could.

What specific management programs and practices did he adopt? First, he used both welfare work and scientific management. The former was the more fully developed and abiding. B&O employee outings, athletic activities, musical groups, safety committees, and the like, were pushed hard during the early years of Willard's presidency, and they continued to be vital throughout his tenure and beyond. His embrace of scientific management was more tentative and limited, but he never rejected its basic concern for efficiency. Second, there was the Cooperative Plan. The Baltimore & Ohio Railroad Cooperative Plan was the foremost union-management cooperative program of its day. In contradiction to prevailing industry wisdom, the plan recognized that the company and its organized labor actually had many mutual interests and that both could be better off if they worked together. Its local cooperative committee meetings were forerunners of "quality circles," reimported to the United States some fifty years later as an allegedly Japanese invention. Third, there was the Cooperative Traffic Program, an amalgam of welfare work, the Cooperative Plan, and general company boosterism that helped to pull the B&O through the Depression. None of these was Willard's original idea. All were products of his determination to keep his office door and his mind open to other people's ideas.

What was the subsequent nature of the B&O culture? Like all corporate cultures, it was not determined exclusively by its president; company history, geography, employee demographics, general characteristics of the railroad industry, and outside social values had their influence. However, to a remarkable degree, it was a reflection of Daniel Willard. B&O courtesy, helpfulness, and friendliness were unexcelled anywhere in the country. Employees understood that they were to value the customer, and each other, as themselves. B&O timekeeping was extraordinary. Employees understood that their company and its customers wanted punctuality; for a division's passenger train on-time performance to fall below 95 percent for a month was an embarrassment

to the whole division. B&O employee loyalty and camaraderie were exceptional. Employees knew that they were to think of themselves as a family—a
family in which individual needs and personal justice were important, but
where the driving force was the corporate need of the family to serve the
larger community.

Among employees of the average late-twentieth-century American firm,
such espoused company values might be viewed as so much management-
serving sentimental hogwash. Among the rough, macho blue-collar railroaders of Willard's time, such notions surely were just as suspect, at least
initially. Among the B&O's sixty thousand or so employees, no doubt some
never did conform to the B&O culture. But a sufficiently preponderant majority did, to the extent that those values indeed constituted a culture, and not just
a list of platitudes. A sense permeated the railroad that although it could not
match the physical or financial resources of its competitors, the B&O was a
better company, because it worked hard and well to live by its stated values.
The New York Central was fancy, and the Pennsylvania was awesome, but the
B&O was good. And its people were proud of that. Especially during the peak
years of the late 1920s, the partisanship of the company's most enthusiastic
employees for their B&O—the "Best & Only"—rivaled that of collegiate
football fans.

So what was the result of all of this, in terms of the specifics of corporate
success? Overall it was nothing spectacular. The B&O had too many burdens
to carry: a capital structure historically too heavy on debt, routes often more
circuitous and mountain grades more difficult than those of its competitors,
and the generally hostile environment faced by the entire railroad industry
after the first decade of the century. Even so, the B&O did fairly well. During
the first ten years of Willard's presidency, the company generated an average
return on common equity of 4.6 percent; during his second ten years, the figure was 6.3 percent. Over the remainder of his tenure (1930–1941), the figure
was a mere 0.6 percent, but the Depression and the heavy interest charges tied
to the company's overleveraged balance sheet could be blamed for that. Basically, the railroad as a physical property continued to do reasonably well
through those lean years, generating a respectable pre-interest operating income and increasing its share of the eastern railroad transportation market.

To summarize and to restate the central thesis, then, Willard's principled
leadership led to the successful implementation of a set of progressive management practices, which shaped a congenial and service-oriented corporate
culture, which in turn led to that which in context must be considered corporate success. The B&O did better than it otherwise would have done. Moreover, it continued to do so long after Willard had passed from the scene.
Traces of rah-rah B&O family spirit were to be found among some of its em-

ployees into the 1970s. The Pennsylvania and the New York Central had been merged, had passed through bankruptcy, and had suffered numerous line downgradings and abandonments by the end of that decade. The B&O, albeit bereft of its independence, was still solvent and with a few minor exceptions physically intact. That should not be surprising. Willard did his job very well.

1

PRELIMINARIES

It was not until the early 1920s that Daniel Willard was widely recognized as a railroad president distinctly different from his peers. It should not be thought, though, that he was doing nothing noteworthy in prior years. In fact, he was doing a number of things of significance, all valuable in their own right, but more importantly, serving as groundwork for the programs and accomplishments that would make his reputation later in his career. From the very beginning of his presidency in 1910, he did and said things that gave his employees a firm sense of what sort of man he was, and of how and where he would lead them. Two culture-shaping themes were made clear: "We are a family" and "We have a job to do." The former was given tangible managerial expression in his tolerant approach to unions and in his establishment of an employee welfare department; the latter, in his physical rebuilding of the railroad and his dalliance with scientific management. Both themes were explicit in the establishment and conduct of safety committees and the company magazine. These and similar secondary managerial actions are described in some detail in this chapter, after a setting of the stage and a synopsis of the background of the leading player.

When Daniel Willard became president of the Baltimore & Ohio Railroad, he did not assume the leadership of a smoothly running, highly efficient organization. The B&O was no longer the dilapidated, chronically undependable laughingstock that it had been during the early 1890s; considerable progress had been made since the company's tumble into receivership in 1896. But serious problems remained. In fact, to a degree the B&O was suffering from the success of its own resuscitation. Although normal maintenance had been resumed and a number of notable improvements to the property had been completed, the railroad was incapable of handling the large increase in traffic that it had generated after its emergence from bankruptcy protection in 1898. Revenue per mile of road operated had increased almost 59 percent by the end of fiscal 1907, and track capacity had not been increased sufficiently to handle the new business. The results, especially in winter when operating conditions were more difficult, were frequent long tie-ups of freight trains waiting to get into or out of terminals or sitting in sidings out along the main lines. On numerous occasions, the company had to impose brief freight embargoes while it unclogged itself.[1]

The B&O was not the only railroad to be hard pressed by heavy increases in demand for its services during the first decade of the century. As the American economy recovered from the extended depression of the mid-1890s, the railroad industry in general was subjected to a traffic surge of unprecedented size and duration. By the winter of 1906–1907, the capacity of existing trackage and rolling stock was insufficient to cope with the flow. A Northern Pacific executive likened the situation to "attempting to force a three-inch stream through a one-inch nozzle." The situation might have continued to worsen had not the Panic of 1907 and subsequent recession relieved some of the pressure. Railroad capital improvements, although slowed by the downturn, were slowed less than the flow of traffic, and most of the industry was able to catch up a bit on its inadequacies of capacity before traffic levels resumed their rise. By 1910, across most of the system, serious bottlenecks were relatively uncommon.[2]

Unfortunately, they were not uncommon on the B&O. The company had not made the same progress in improving its property as had most of the other large carriers. The B&O of 1910 was a noticeably better railroad than the B&O of 1896, but its speed and reliability still left much to be desired.

The failure of the B&O to make adequate capital improvements to its property was not a function of any lack of profitability. The company's return on equity averaged 8.26 percent from 1900 through 1909[3]—not an outstanding figure, but a respectable one. Rather, the failure appears to have sprung from two other factors: the preferences of principal B&O shareholders, notably the Pennsylvania and Union Pacific railroads, and the interests and talents of Willard's predecessor, Oscar Murray. Murray's forte was not in physical operations, where the company's greatest difficulties lay. As for B&O shareholders and the board of directors that represented them, their primary concern late in the first decade of the century seemed to be dividends, not reinvestment of profits in capital improvements to the railroad.

Retention of at least half of annual net income for reinvestment was a widely observed industry norm.[4] The B&O adhered to that norm early in the decade, paying out only 45.4 percent of net income as dividends on common stock during the years 1901 through 1906. In 1907, though, the company shifted its dividend policy in favor of greater payout: dividends were increased despite a drop in profit. The next two years' nets were even lower than that of 1907, but the higher dividend was maintained, resulting in a three-year payout ratio of 80.9 percent.[5] Internal reinvestment was reduced to a trickle, and "construction and betterment" expenditures fell from $11.5 million in fiscal 1904 to $4.8 million in fiscal 1909.[6]

The 1907 change in B&O shareholder attitude appears to be traceable to the weakening of the pattern of intercorporate relations that characterized the railroad industry during the immediately preceding years, a pattern that had yielded greater stability and coordination than the industry had ever known. To repair the corporate wreckage caused by the depression of the nineties, the industry, with the active encouragement of its investment bankers, gradually had grouped itself into regional "communities of interest." Through common ownership and interlocking directorates among formerly competing lines, it was the intent of these groupings to eliminate the cutthroat rate competition that had plagued the railroads for decades. So, during the first years of the new century, most of the nation's major carriers had aligned themselves into seven clearly identifiable communities of interest, one of which was the Pennsylvania Railroad (PRR) group.[7]

The principal step in the formation of the Pennsylvania group was the acquisition of controlling interest in the Baltimore & Ohio; roughly 40 percent of the B&O's common and preferred stock was purchased by the PRR between 1899 and 1901. In the latter year, the Pennsylvania was able to install one of its own operating executives, Leonor F. Loree, as B&O president, and to begin running the B&O almost as a subsidiary. Loree's three-year tenure was generally good for the B&O. As the PRR now viewed its southern neighbor more as an adjunct to its own operations than as a competitor, significant property improvements were made, and dividend payouts were kept moderate. Then in 1904 Loree left the B&O, passing the presidency to Murray; the same year, the Supreme Court handed down its decision in the Northern Securities case. That decision, which found holding-company ownership of the parallel Northern Pacific and Great Northern systems to be a violation of the Sherman Act, had a chilling effect upon the whole notion of communities of interest. The Pennsylvania, concerned about facing similar litigation, sold off approximately half of its B&O holdings to the Union Pacific (UP) in 1906, and abandoned any further prospect of operating the PRR and B&O as a semi-integrated system. Thenceforward, the PRR, the UP, and other B&O shareholders seem to have viewed the company simply as a "cash cow." During the latter half of Murray's presidency, the B&O was milked hard.[8]

Oscar Murray was not a bad president; he just was not the right president.

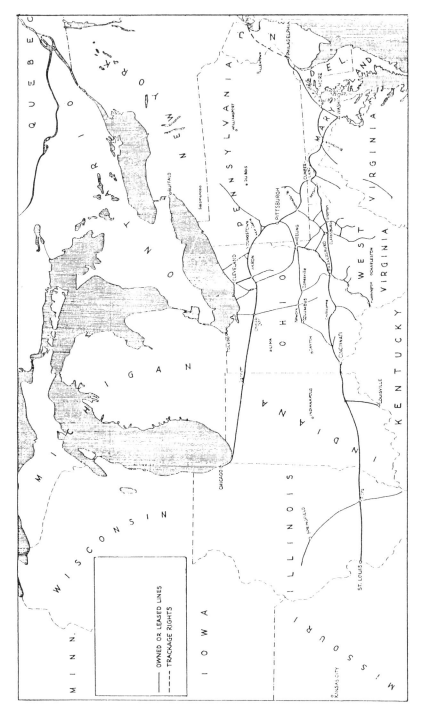

Baltimore & Ohio Railroad in 1908, before Daniel Willard's arrival

As the B&O's coreceiver during the 1890s and as traffic vice president until his elevation to the presidency, Murray had established a reputation as a salesman of the highest order: a "traffic genius, perhaps without a peer in the country." He clearly understood how to get traffic. Whether he had a similar understanding of how to develop and to operate the physical plant and equipment necessary to accommodate that traffic is less clear. The weakness of Murray's presidency, if not a failure to comprehend the nature and magnitude of the company's operating inadequacies, was at least a failure to convince a majority of the board of the pressing nature of those inadequacies and of the need for major remedial investment. By late 1909, at least one board member (Union Pacific executive Robert S. Lovett) had become convinced of such a need on his own. The long-term health of the cow was a matter of increasing concern. Either on his own initiative or with the encouragement of the board, Murray made plans to retire, and a search for his successor began.[9]

Obviously, the B&O needed a leader thoroughly schooled in the operations side of the business. Such a man was Daniel Willard. Willard had started his career at the very bottom of the blue-collar ranks, as a track laborer, and he had worked his way across and upward through practically every segment of the railroad operating department. In on-train service he held all four positions: fireman, brakeman, engineer, and conductor. In on-the-ground service he held the positions of agent, tower operator, and enginehouse foreman. As he advanced into the white-collar ranks, he served successively as trainmaster, assistant division superintendent, division superintendent, assistant general manager and purchasing agent, and operations vice president. He moved between organizations as well as within them, gaining personal contacts and exposure to different ideas and operating approaches along the way. Before becoming B&O president, he spent in succession three months on the Vermont Central, four years on the Connecticut & Passumpsic, one year on the Lake Shore & Michigan Southern, fifteen years on the Minneapolis, St. Paul, & Sault Ste. Marie (Soo Line), two years on the B&O, three years on the Erie, and six years on the Chicago, Burlington, & Quincy. With this last company he served as operations chief for the great railroad entrepreneur James J. Hill. Willard brought to the Burlington an exceptional level of operating efficiency, in so doing winning a position as one of Hill's most valued and trusted subordinates.[10]

With his great breadth and depth of experience and success in the area where the B&O needed help most, with the favorable impression that he had left during his brief tenure as B&O's assistant general manager, with his ties to one of the industry's most prominent movers and shakers, and with his pleasant and personable yet businesslike demeanor, Willard was nearly the ideal choice to lead the Baltimore & Ohio out of its inefficient and increasingly demoralized state. He assumed the presidency, with his work cut out for him, on January 15, 1910.

Willard engaged his task immediately. During fiscal 1910 (ending June 30), the B&O placed orders for 284 new freight locomotives and 15,000 freight cars, costing roughly $23 million, to be used largely on heavily congested and backlogged West Virginia coal lines. An additional $20 million in track capacity improvements was begun. Maintenance expenditures on existing plant and equipment were increased 30 percent over those of fiscal 1909.[11]

Willard continued the intensive upgrading of the property throughout the first half of the decade. By the end of fiscal 1915, $41.9 million had been spent on new equipment, and $47.3 million had been spent on construction and betterments. The notorious Doe Gully Tunnel bottleneck, on the Main Stem east of Cumberland, had been removed entirely. New double-track tunnels had been opened at Sand Patch on the Chicago main line and at Kingwood on the St. Louis main line, eliminating constrictions in the crossings of the Allegheny Mountains. The thirteen-mile Magnolia Cutoff had been built, bypassing nineteen miles of curving line in the upper Potomac Valley. Numerous grades and curves had been reduced in severity, multiple main line running tracks had been added, sidings had been added or lengthened, and terminals and classification yards had been expanded. With the capacity of the fixed plant increased, and with faster and more powerful locomotives moving the trains, the B&O's efficiency and reliability improved dramatically.

In one sense, though, Willard was no wiser or more successful than was Oscar Murray, who served as the chairman of Willard's board of directors until his death in 1917. That was in the matter of finance: the B&O's dividend payout ratio remained imprudently high (86.0 percent for the period 1910– 1915), which meant, in the absence of a new stock issue, that the company's capital expenditures had to be financed almost entirely with debt. Accordingly, the B&O's secured debt rose $83.7 million from 1910 to 1915, a 26.6 percent increase. Its ratio of total debt to common equity rose from 2.15 to 2.64 as its already burdensome debt load became even more so.[12] Continually rolled over and never really retired, the B&O's debt, and the interest charges that went with it, would nearly force the company into bankruptcy during the Great Depression. But Willard had been hired as an operating man, not as a finance man. His task was to develop a railroad and to run its trains, and he did so with distinction.

If he was not hired as a finance man, it is equally certain that Daniel Willard was not hired as a personnel theorist. Personnel matters really were not considered to be at issue when Willard was hired. If a personnel problem existed, it was assumed to be one of general morale, which might be corrected simply by fixing up the property and running it efficiently. Willard did not consider himself a theorist of any sort; later in life, when he heard himself described as "a great philosopher," he retorted that he was "no such person," just "a plain down-East Yankee . . . [of no] unusual or outstanding abilities or qualifications."[13]

Yet it was in the field of personnel relations—if not as a philosopher, then as a man with a clear, right-minded, and rigorously followed philosophy— that he made his most significant and enduring accomplishments. That is the thesis of this book: that Willard's bedrock respect for the intrinsic value and dignity of his employees led to the creation of a set of personnel policies and programs that made the B&O much more than an improved physical property. Willard treated his subordinates, all the way down to the level of car cleaner and track laborer, as people who might know something about the proper functioning of the company that he did not know. That was his starting principle. It is summarized in the sign that he had printed and placed in his office as a trainmaster for the Soo Line in 1890, and that he kept prominently displayed in his office throughout the remaining fifty-one years of his career: "SUGGESTIONS ARE ALWAYS IN ORDER."

This exceedingly simple statement of managerial philosophy gave rise, appropriately often at the suggestion of others, to a series of steps that would transform the B&O into an organization that was, for its time and its industry, exemplary. The company was by no means a textbook example of managerial perfection. But in its explicit pursuit of labor-management cooperation, in its efforts to involve workers more fully in the life of the company, and in its creation of a sense of family among its employees, Daniel Willard's B&O by the 1930s was in a class by itself among major American corporations. It is only in the past decade that his programs and approaches have been copied extensively in the United States, many of them in emulation of the remarkably similar (and subsequent) "Japanese management style."

How did it come to pass that an up-from-the-ranks operating man in an industry as hard and unyielding as railroading should be a leader in the field of personnel management? The answer surely is complex, and no comprehensive and certain answer will be attempted here. In general terms, though, it seems reasonable to look for the answer in his upbringing and in his early career experiences.

Willard was born on January 28, 1861, in North Hartland, Vermont, a tiny community in the Connecticut River valley. He grew up on a large, extended-family farm, of which his father farmed 250 acres. The Willards were financially secure but not wealthy. They were occasionally able to afford the temporary services of a hired hand, but for the most part they did their own work. Daniel, as the only boy in the family, was given heavy and de-

manding chores from early in his childhood. His duties as a child were particularly difficult during the harsh Vermont winters. Edward Hungerford,
Willard's biographer, records his remembering those childhood chores "rather
sadly." But they were "part of the discipline of the beginning of a life that was
based upon discipline." [14]

Willard's father, Daniel Spaulding Willard, had experienced a fling with
adventure during his youth, having run away to sea and having sailed twice
around the world. But when he returned from his last voyage, he settled com-
fortably into the life of the successful farmer and family man. Typical of that
time and place, he ran both farm and family in firmly authoritarian fashion.
Willard's acceptance of his father's authority evidently was inculcated, not in-
nate. In Hungerford's words, "He was full of mischief, and a good whaling
now and then on the part of a fond but just parent was merely part of the routine of life." [15]

Willard's mother died of pneumonia when he was five. He clearly was
affected by the loss, but not crippled by it, with his grandparents, various
aunts and uncles, and later a kind and dedicated stepmother to compensate for
the lost nurturing. The family member to whom he was closest during those
years was his younger sister Maria; her influence was significant and continuing throughout much of his career, as she lived with him and his wife from the
mid-1890s until her death in 1934. [16]

The Willards were devout fundamentalist Methodists, and religion was an
essential element in the shaping of Daniel Willard's character. The Bible was
read regularly in the Willard home, and Sunday mornings and afternoons
were spent in church. During his youth, Willard frequently attended revival
meetings; he answered his first altar call and personally accepted Christ at the
age of fourteen. A year later he was superintendent of the local Methodist
Sunday School and teacher of its Old Folks Class. [17]

Also at age fifteen, he was appointed teacher in the local public school. It
was customary in such small, rural, cash-short districts for the teacher to receive compensation in the form of free room and board in the homes of district residents. One local citizen with whom Willard boarded, who would have
a significant impact upon his life, was an elderly widow named Sarah Taylor.
She was a woman of intense literary interests, and she and her library created
in Willard both a first appreciation of culture beyond his own and a desire to
know more about the world outside rural New England. After nearly two years
of Mrs. Taylor's encouragement and of reading the weekly Joseph Cook lec-
tures in the *New York Tribune*, Willard left to prepare for college at the high
school in Windsor, seven miles downriver. It was his wish to enroll eventually
at Dartmouth, only ten miles upriver on the New Hampshire side, but he
lacked the money to do so. He enrolled instead, financed by the few hundred

dollars that his father could scrape together, at the Massachusetts State Agricultural College in Amherst.[18]

Willard's experience at "Amherst Aggie" was a brief and troubling one. While he was there, he had to confront three crises: one vocational, one spiritual, and one physical. First, it became clear that he never really wanted to be a farmer. He had always been intrigued by the passage of the trains of the Vermont Central, which cut through his father's farm; although farming might be a reasonably satisfying way to spend one's life, the excitement and adventure of railroading appealed to him much more. Second, he discovered that he could not reconcile his literal understanding of the Bible with the rationalist thinking and scientific knowledge to which he was being exposed; it was his faith that gave way. He was not to return to firm faith and active church participation until midlife, and then as a Unitarian, not as a fundamentalist. Third, his eyes could not tolerate the heavy regimen of reading. His astigmatism was later corrected by glasses, but there was no such help available to him in 1879. He left school in the spring of his freshman year and returned to the family farm. He worked there for a month, then went railroading on the Vermont Central.[19]

When the opportunity arose, he left his job with the Vermont Central track gang to become a locomotive fireman in northern Vermont with the Connecticut & Passumpsic (C&P). Within two years he had been promoted to engineer. A year later, at the age of twenty-one, he did an unusual thing for a young railroad man of some ambition to do back in the nineteenth century: he joined the Brotherhood of Locomotive Engineers. In 1882 a person could be fired for joining a labor union, and the superintendent of the C&P was rumored to be inclined to take such action. Willard did so anyway. Operating crew hours were long—sixteen-hour days were common—and the work was demanding and dangerous. Even so, in later years Willard insisted that it was not any sense of exploitation that led him into the Brotherhood. It was, he said, as nearly as he could tell the result of his ingrained Vermont independence; he simply did not like the idea that management could tell him not to join.[20]

In 1883, in pursuit of higher wages, he moved west to the Lake Shore & Michigan Southern. He was hired as a freight engineer working out of Elkhart, Indiana; he prospered briefly, then was furloughed as business turned downward in the spring of 1884. The experience of being on his own and jobless was among the most significant of his career. He often spoke of its impact, especially when labor relations issues were being discussed. The Willard Memorial issue of *Baltimore & Ohio Magazine*, published just after his death in July 1942, commented, "He never forgot the humiliation and discouragement of being out of work—and work just could not be had then in the railroad

Daniel Willard as a Soo Line engineer. (Courtesy of the B&O Railroad Museum)

town of Elkhart, Ind., in which he was then living. He often said that he envied the men he saw sweeping the streets. That most men want more than anything else, a steady job, and the assurance of a steady job, later became a fundamental part of Willard's labor philosophy." [21]

Willard was not long out of work, though. By July his letter to the nascent Soo Line in Minneapolis had secured him a job as a construction train brakeman. That job represented a considerable reduction in status and pay from his Lake Shore job, but before a year had passed he had been promoted twice, to engineer and then to enginehouse foreman at the newly created division point at Turtle Lake. In the latter job, Willard performed an amazing variety of tasks: engine crew supervisor, blacksmith, machinist, carpenter, car cleaner, furnace tender, relief engineer, relief conductor, and relief station agent. His successful performance of those duties brought him to the attention of top management in Minneapolis, particularly Frederick D. Underwood, the general manager. He was offered the position of chief clerk to the division mechanical officer; he declined in favor of the opportunity to return to his first love, running a locomotive. Then, despite his testing of management patience by his refusal to handle Burlington Route cars when his union struck that railroad, in 1890 he was offered the position of trainmaster at Minneapolis;

he accepted. He resigned from the union and took his first real middle-management position.[22]

Willard had returned briefly to Vermont in 1885 to marry Bertha Leone Elkins, a young woman whom he had met while he was working for the C&P; their two sons were born in 1890 and 1894. During this period he became Underwood's protégé. Underwood found Willard personally congenial, rigorously honest, efficient, and thorough. Under his mentorship Willard advanced from trainmaster to assistant superintendent to superintendent on the Soo Line. Then in 1899, when Underwood was brought to Baltimore as vice president and general manager of operations for the B&O, Willard went with him as assistant general manager. In 1901, Underwood was appointed president of the Erie; again Willard accompanied him, as vice president of operations.[23]

By this time, Willard's managerial skills had acquired some sophistication. He was determined, as indicated previously, to be active in soliciting suggestions on operating improvements from his subordinates; he also was determined to pass suggestions upward. His immediate superiors on the Soo Line, however, were not always receptive to ideas from underlings. Accordingly, he often found it necessary, in the course of discussing his ideas with a superior official, to ascribe those ideas to that other person. The artifice served him well as he rose through the ranks, but the discomfort that he felt in doing so reinforced his resolve not to force his own subordinates into similar behavior.[24] His "SUGGESTIONS ARE ALWAYS IN ORDER" sign was the most consistently visible outward reminder to the people around him to be creative and to take credit for their creations.

As would any good mentor, Underwood knew when to push his protégé on to a greater opportunity than he could offer in his own company. Underwood had been acquainted with James J. Hill when the former was with the Soo Line, in the Hill lines' home territory of Minnesota, and he had grown to know Hill better as Hill developed a financial interest in the Erie. He saw to it that when Hill made his frequent trips east over the Erie, he was accompanied by Daniel Willard. Hill was impressed, and when he acquired control of the Chicago, Burlington, & Quincy in 1903, he offered Willard its operating vice presidency. Willard was "a little staggered" at the size of the offer ($50,000 per year and a $100,000 cash bonus), but before accepting it, he made certain that he had Underwood's blessing. When that was enthusiastically given, Willard became an officer in the service of James J. Hill, "the Empire Builder."[25]

Hill had the reputation of being a tough, hard-driving taskmaster. Willard in his years at the Burlington proved that he could be the same. He treated Hill's expansion and major upgrading of the property as if it were a war of survival, and he exercised discipline accordingly. He devoted practically every waking hour to the effort, and he expected his subordinates to do likewise. For those who did not, he had little use; he replaced his secretary almost on the spot when he balked at accompanying Willard and Hill on a seventh consecutive sixteen-hour day of inspecting and directing the improvements. These years saw Willard at his toughest, but he did not lose his appreciation of the perspective of the men out on the line. As he pushed the capital program, he replaced the railroad's traditional punishment-by-suspension disciplinary system, under which an operating employee with an otherwise perfect record would be suspended without pay if found guilty of any rule book infraction, with the "Brown system," a merit/demerit arrangement under which the employee might work off the punishment without loss of pay. He won the respect of his people, and even a measure of affection; it was on the Burlington that he first was referred to as "Uncle Dan." More critically, he was successful. The railroad was upgraded, and speed and efficiency greatly increased; car-miles per car per day rose 50 percent during Willard's tenure. His reputation as an operating man was made, and through it came the offer of the presidency of the Baltimore & Ohio.[26]

At the B&O, Willard reported to a board of directors that included some forceful and influential people, Samuel Rea of the Pennsylvania Railroad and Robert S. Lovett of the Union Pacific notable among them. None, however, had either the ownership position or force of personality of James J. Hill. At the B&O, Willard was much more his own man. Free of Hill's dominance, his management style became a bit less intense, and his concern for the human side of the business began to grow.

Willard always had believed in promoting from within; as he moved from the Erie to the Burlington to the B&O, he did not take any retinue of subordinates with him. He had been known, however, to promote (and demote) somewhat abruptly, as in the cited example of his secretary. At the B&O, he seemed to move somewhat more sensitively. His handling of the Potter problem was a case in point. When Willard returned to Baltimore, the vice president of operations was George L. Potter, a former Pennsylvania Railroad official installed at the B&O by the PRR in 1903. Potter had hurt morale in the company's eastern region prior to Willard's arrival by discharging, for no apparent reason other than jealousy, the highly popular regional general superintendent, Thomas Fitzgerald. Willard did not fire Potter immediately. Arthur W. Thompson, head of maintenance of way engineering when Willard became president in January 1910, had just distinguished himself in his speedy and efficient replacement of the Susquehanna River bridge above Havre de Grace. In April Willard created the position of consulting engineer for his chief engineer, and he promoted Thompson to the latter position. Thompson continued his impressive performance, planning and building the Monongahela River bridge at Lumberport in only three months. Then in December Willard quietly asked for Potter's resignation and replaced him with Thompson.[27]

Of broader import was Willard's handling of a threatened strike by the conductors' and trainmen's brotherhoods during his first month in office. Unlike many of his counterparts at other companies, he did not approach the threat as if it were an act of hostility toward the railroad by some illegitimate outside entity. No doubt with his own time as a blue-collar union man in mind, he did not question the right of his employees to bargain collectively. Although in those pre–Railway Labor Act years he was not legally obligated to do so, he recognized the brotherhoods as legitimate bargaining agents for their respective crafts, and he sat down to negotiate. He met with union representatives and listened to their demands. He countered with an explanation of the B&O's limited resources, in light of the capital improvement program about to begin. The union men persisted, so Willard suggested mediation. The brotherhoods gave their assent, and the issue was turned over to Martin W. Knapp, of the Commerce Court, and Charles P. Neill, of the U.S. Labor Commission. Their efforts were successful: B&O conductors and trainmen received a wage increase, but one smaller than they had sought originally. The B&O settlement set the pattern for subsequent wage scale increases on most other eastern railroads. Willard's approach—firm about meeting the needs of his company, yet understanding of the needs of his employees—was noted positively by union leaders, and his credibility with organized labor grew markedly.[28]

Establishing his credibility with blue-collar union men was not Willard's only personnel concern, of course, as he began his presidency. He could not direct an extensive rebuilding of the railroad alone; he needed the dedicated efforts of his middle- and upper-level managers as well. To spur their dedication, to improve morale, and to begin to build a sense of common purpose among them, Willard in the summer of 1910 arranged an operating management retreat. Held at the resort hotel in Deer Park, Maryland, near the summit of the Alleghenies on the B&O's St. Louis mainline, the conference was attended principally by officers of the operating department. Working sessions were devoted primarily to discussion of Willard's policies and plans for the railroad and to reports of initial progress thereon.[29]

The Deer Park retreat evidently was a success, but it was not repeated until September 1913. Under the direction of Arthur Thompson, the gathering then was substantially expanded to include managers in all departments that reported to him (operating, transportation, engineering, and mechanical). Attendance was approximately 250. The conference lasted two full days. Formal working sessions were held in the mornings; afternoons and evenings were left open for informal discussions and recreation.[30] Willard delivered a lengthy and mostly extemporaneous opening address; in it, he alluded to the lack of unity that he had found to be characteristic of B&O management in the years back to his first association with the company in 1899:

> I found one thing much in evidence here that I never found to the same extent on any other railroad. I found Cowen men, Murray men, Underwood men, Fitzgerald men, etc., but there was not much said about Baltimore & Ohio men. There were too many different cliques among the men in the Baltimore & Ohio service. That is why, today, I appoint you all, Assistants to the President, and by doing so I wish to wipe out or supersede every other allegiance you may have. You are all Baltimore & Ohio men, not Thompson men, or Galloway men, or Bankard men, or Willard men, but Baltimore & Ohio men. So far as I am concerned, every man in this room is my man and is on my staff, and every officer of this railroad is my officer. If he was accepted before I came here, I accepted him when I came, and if he had been appointed since I came here, his appointment had my approval. Every officer and employe of this Company is my man today, and all are Baltimore & Ohio employes, whatever else they may be. Let us try to operate this railroad and carry on its affairs in such a way that we would prefer to have it said that we are of the Baltimore & Ohio rather than Smith, Jones, or Brown men. We should all be proud of our connection with the Baltimore & Ohio Railroad.[31]

Insufficient unity and loyalty among management were not Willard's only personnel concerns. In the same address, he devoted even more time to a discussion of difficulties in the blue-collar ranks. He noted that in the past, the B&O might not have been very scrupulous in its honoring of contracts with its employees; those days, he said, had better be over. Contracts would be made as satisfactory as possible both to the company and to the employees, and then the company would honor them uniformly and rigorously. Only under those circumstances was the company "entitled to the honest, intelligent, and loyal service of our employees." He touched upon the matter of discipline, stating firmly that it must be both strict and fair. That subject led him to reiterate his stand against "union bashing":

> It has been contended by some that the labor organization has destroyed discipline. I have never been willing to admit that. I believe that labor organizations sometimes mistakenly press matters too far. They seek to get men reinstated, for instance, who have been discharged for cause, and they press matters so hard that officers sometimes yield against their better judgment. Practices are allowed to go on that should not be permitted for a moment. For that reason I admit that the labor union at times makes it more difficult to preserve discipline. But it

does not make it impossible. I have no sympathy with the officer who says "I cannot maintain discipline because of the labor unions." [32]

Willard went on to discuss the importance of discipline to safe operation, arguing that the B&O's unionized operating employees generally would accept tight discipline when lives depended upon it. The remainder of his address—indeed, the preponderance of it—was devoted to matters of operating efficiency, cost control, general finances, regulation, customer relations, and so forth. However brief his comments on personnel issues may have been, they do provide a measure of Willard's thoughts on such matters at age fifty-two, in the fourth year of his thirty-one-year presidency.

How did his subordinates react to all of this? What were their personal estimations of their new president? Firsthand impressions are difficult to find, but two published reactions reveal something of the opinions held by those whom he struck favorably. The first of these was written by a staff correspondent for *The Baltimore & Ohio Employes Magazine* assigned to cover the 1913 Deer Park conference. It must be interpreted cautiously, as the correspondent, unprotected by any union contract, surely was aware that he was describing to the entire company the person who signed his paycheck. Nonetheless, the following impression of Willard's address, purged of the most blatant sycophancy, is of some value:

with engaging smile . . . of medium stature, spare and wiry, straight as an arrow and poiseful, it is perhaps in the flash of his wide-seeing eyes that we get best the physical revelation of the mind and soul beneath.

With nervous energy balanced by deliberate judgment, with the clearness of the logician minus the verbiage of the pedant, with the orderliness of procedure peculiar to the seasoned debater, with sharp enunciation and penetrating but well-modulated voice, President Willard's profound mind reveals itself in words of one syllable. The opposite of oratorical in his style, his gestures few but telling, his command of language large and of uncommon clarity, with the exactness of a great lawyer and the vision of a prophet, he carried those two hundred and fifty hard thinking, practical, and experienced railroad men for the better part of two hours by the sheer strength of his intellect and the earnestness of his appeal. [33]

The second reaction, written by a fireman working at Riverside Yard in Baltimore, was printed in one of the company's safety bulletins during the fall of 1912. It is less elaborately descriptive than the preceding statement, but it is also probably more reliable, insofar as a blue-collar worker protected by contractual seniority rights almost certainly would not be fired for what he said about the president. In response to Willard's talk to the assembled Riverside employees on the subject of safety, the fireman wrote of the impact of Willard's presence and persona upon the development of loyalty to the company: "and it was just such a meeting as was held when Mr. Willard, through his earnest and sincere appeal directly to the men concerned, created a sentiment which will materialize in a concrete form when occasion requires. How much more that spirit of loyalty would expand were it possible for him to make such appeals more frequently, and thus give the thousands of Baltimore and Ohio employees the pleasure of meeting him personally, is beyond imagination." [34] Even here, the rhetoric may seem overblown, but it still may well reflect the way that Willard affected people. Surely there was some grumbling and cynicism among some B&O employees, but generally it would appear that "Uncle Dan" was off to a good start with them.

So what, aside from rebuilding the railroad, recognizing national labor unions, and making at least a modestly inspiring personal impression, did Daniel Willard actually do for his employees during the early years of his presidency? Wages and salaries, although above national manufacturing and agricultural averages, were essentially commensurate with those of other eastern trunk lines: there was no great financial advantage to working for the B&O. The actions or approaches described above involved intangible rewards: pride in the railroad, and a sense of acceptance and belonging and individual worth, however hard-nosed.

Those rewards were not completely new to the B&O. Toward the end of the presidency of John W. Garrett (1858–1884), the company was characterized by a certain iron-fisted paternalism; the relief (hospitalization and death benefits), savings, and pension features of the Relief Department dated from 1880, 1882, and 1884, respectively. Perhaps from this, in the context of the ingrown management of the B&O during the balance of the century, grew the first sense of "family" among B&O employees. Whatever the cause, in the years before Pennsylvania Railroad control, some employees believed that the B&O "was in reality a great big family." [35] An attempt to recreate some of that sense led to the founding of the B&O Veteran Employes Association, for any employee with twenty-one (later, twenty) or more years of service, in 1908. Pride and mutual commitment were remembered and valued, at least by some older workers. Hence, Willard had a base upon which to build loyalty to the company through such intangible means.

Pride in the railroad and a sense of family commitment were the rewards that he sought to provide. Before he was to relinquish the management of the railroad to the federal government temporarily during World War I, Willard and his management team added two new benefits to the pride-and-sense-of-family package: the company magazine and the Welfare Bureau.

Publication of the *Baltimore & Ohio Employes Magazine* commenced in October 1912. It was not the first railroad employees' magazine, but it was a very good one: carefully edited, professional in its layout, varied and interesting in its content, and friendly and upbeat in its tone. Its purpose and perspective were clear: in a congratulatory letter, the editors of *Santa Fe Employes' Magazine* welcomed it as a "new exponent of non-factionalism and the brotherhood of man . . . a publication of good fellowship and fraternity." [36] The first issue contained the following:

Page 1: a photograph of the B&O Shenandoah Valley line and a poem, "The Way Home," by the editor
Pages 2–3: "From Stage Coach to Passenger Train," an interview of Judge Gephardt of Cumberland, Maryland
Pages 4–5: an article on "Train Handling: Practical Hints on Starting and Stopping without Shock," by O. C. Cavins (B&O engineer, Ohio Division)
Page 5 (bottom): a poem, "Our Magazine," by C. A. Wright (B&O operator, Carlyle, Illinois)
Page 6: "Men I Wish I Had Known: Robert E. Lee," by the editor
Page 7: a commendation of a heroic employee by Daniel Willard and a recounting of the incident that prompted it
Page 8: "Handling the Public," by D. M. Fisher (B&O freight agent, Washington, D.C.)
Page 9: "Caboosetalk," a continuing series of brief railroad vignettes, by the editorial staff
Page 10 (top): a poem, "The Night Train for Pittsburgh," by Folger McKinsey (from the *Baltimore Sun*)
Pages 10–11: news of the Veteran Employes Association
Pages 12–13: an article on safety of operation
Page 13 (bottom): an article on facilitating office paper flow, by G. B. Clifton (B&O supervisor of office service)
Pages 14–15: The Editor's Turntable, editorials on matters pertinent to the company and the railroad industry
Pages 16–18: The Home, topics of interest to the families of B&O employees:
    —"The Night Before," a vignette on coping with busy home life, by the wife of a B&O employee
    —"Mrs. Murphy's Baby," a vignette from the *New York Evening Mail*
    —a jelly recipe
    —"Tearless Tragedies," a poem
Pages 19–21: a summary and analysis of recent accidents and rules violations on the B&O
Pages 22–40: "Among Ourselves," reports by division correspondents on activities on their divisions (for example, the New York Division correspondent W. B. Biggs, agent in New York City, reported the names of the divisional safety committeemen and sixteen bits of local company news, such as

"Cashier F. L. Bausmith has fully recovered the use of his ankle, which was badly sprained in the three-legged race at the Second Annual Outing of the B&O and S.I.R.T. [Staten Island Rapid Transit, a B&O subsidiary] clerks some weeks ago at Grant City, S.I." [37]

Parenthetically, it should be noted that the last item contains references to two important developments on the B&O in the early teens: employee social outings and the Safety Campaign. Again, there was nothing original here; other railroads acted similarly. Nonetheless, both developments were related to the growing sense of community on the B&O. Employee social gatherings apparently grew spontaneously during the first years of Willard's presidency, presumably with the full approval if not the organized encouragement of top management. The Safety Campaign, with its general and divisional safety committees and formal bulletins, was much more intentional. When Willard joined the B&O, the company, like most railroads, had a deplorable employee safety record: dozens of crewmen were killed and thousands were injured every year. As a former crewman, Willard was concerned about this matter and said so. In response, under the direction of Arthur Thompson, in October 1911 the safety committees were created, and the campaign to reduce the carnage was begun. The B&O was the first railroad in the East to undertake such a campaign. [38]

One of the early suggestions to arise from the safety committee structure was the creation of the employees' magazine; the safety bulletins by themselves were too narrow in focus to encourage broad readership. Accordingly, the contents of the first issue of the magazine were fairly typical of early issues in that they included two safety-related articles; the average number of safety articles and reminders in the first eighteen issues was over two and a half. After mid-1914, the point apparently having been made, such articles decreased, to be replaced primarily by articles of a "what's happening around the railroad" sort. There also was a decline in the number of general literary pieces printed and an increase in the percentage of articles written by management and the magazine editorial staff. The general tone of the magazine, however, did not really change.

The employee magazine, the outings, and the Safety Campaign were pieces of a pattern of management that was of considerable interest to progressive companies of the day. This pattern was that of the "employee welfare" movement, also known as welfare capitalism or "welfare work." A humanistic movement with liberal Judeo-Christian roots, welfare work had as its goal the full development of the individual and collective human potential (nothing less than that) of a firm's employees through disciplined, energetic, socially oriented clean living. Its origins were traceable to the first paternalistic and philanthropic efforts of the earliest factory owners. By the last quarter of the nineteenth century, though not yet an organized movement, such efforts had become institutionalized at a number of American firms. Companies such as H. J. Heinz, Pullman, and Willimantic Linen boasted extensive employee benefit programs, designed to improve worker well-being both as an end in itself and as a means to greater productivity and profit. Program details differed from firm to firm, but company-sponsored libraries, social events, and recreational and educational opportunities were common elements.[39]

After the turn of the century, welfare work became more and more clearly a coherent and organized movement. With firms such as Filene's of Boston and the National Cash Register Company leading the way, the National Civic Federation formed a Welfare Department in 1904, to serve as a clearinghouse for information on successful employee welfare practices. By 1911 roughly five hundred companies were members. The programs of the most enthusiastic companies, often directed by a full-time "welfare secretary," were elaborate and comprehensive. The movement, however, did not really become dominant or pervasive; participating firms tended to be those with high percentages of women employees, and a majority of them stopped short of adopting a full program. Only forty companies (none of them a railroad) have been clearly identified as having had extensive and firmly established welfare plans between 1905 and 1915.[40] Still, along with the more technical "scientific management" movement, welfare work was at the center of progressive management thinking during the years leading up to America's entry into World War I.

Willard, by then an active member of the aggressively liberal First Unitarian Church of Baltimore, could not help but be attracted by the philosophy and promise of the welfare movement; it offered physical and spiritual benefits to the individual, social benefits to the community, and economic benefits to the Baltimore & Ohio Railroad. Some of the activities on the movement's agenda already were taking place on the B&O: company social gatherings and athletic events, for example. Hence, in May 1916, the company formally established a Welfare Bureau. The bureau's director was Dr. E. M. Parlett, a company physician who had been active in the temperance movement. John T. Broderick, supervisor of Special Bureaus and Parlett's immediate superior, in explaining the program to a conference of B&O surgeons, stated that B&O management "desires that its employes and their families shall partake of all the blessings which a wise Creator intended for them." That would be possible only through "well regulated, orderly, rational living," which would be characterized by "industry, diligence, sobriety, and thrift," which in turn implied the constructive use of leisure time.[41]

To ensure that its employees used their leisure well, the B&O through its Welfare Bureau embarked upon a wide-ranging expansion of off-the-job company-sponsored activities. These activities fell into four general categories: athletics, performing arts, intellectual and educational pursuits, and social outings.

Of these four, athletic programs were most extensively developed and most broadly successful, not surprisingly given that the majority of B&O employees were both male and modestly educated. Baseball was the most popular sport; local teams had been spontaneously organized on some B&O divisions as early as the spring of 1912. With the inauguration of the Welfare Bureau, a fairly elaborate network of teams and local leagues was set up all across the system. At Staten Island, for example, twelve teams were organized to play a ninety-nine-game schedule that first summer. The best team on each division played other divisional representatives for regional championships; the final championshp game, for the Arthur Thompson Challenge Cup, was played on the Homewood Grounds diamond in Baltimore on Labor Day (the 1916 championship, between the Ohio Division and the Philadelphia Division, was won by the Philadelphia team). For the winter, a similar if not quite so extensive set of bowling leagues was established in November 1916; the first team trophy was won by a group of Transportation Department staff members working in Baltimore. A trapshooting club for Baltimore-area employees was established that same winter.[42]

Performing arts activities organized under the auspices of the Welfare Bureau were mostly musical and nearly all located on the eastern half of the railroad, with particular concentration in Baltimore. Of these, the Men's Glee Club was the first, actually antedating the Welfare Bureau by a year and a half. Its first major performance was given in January 1915, at the dinner meeting of the Baltimore chapter of the B&O Veterans' Association. The club had fifty-four members, from a wide variety of departments and levels at various Baltimore-area installations, when it gave its first (later annual) concert and dance in April 1915, attended by over one thousand employees and guests. With the advent of the Welfare Bureau a year later, new groups were added to this nucleus. In June 1916, the Mount Clare Band was organized at the Mount Clare Shops in Baltimore, at the instigation of its superintendent, a welfare movement disciple. Directed by a machinist named H. H. Freeman and composed of approximately thirty men, mostly skilled laborers and clerical workers, the band performed at the shops every Friday lunch hour. The band also did some traveling; for instance, in August 1916 they played for the

The Mount Clare Band, 1916. (Courtesy of the B&O Railroad Museum)

joint outing of the Baltimore and Martinsburg chapters of the Veterans' Association held at Berkeley Springs, West Virginia. The success of the Mount Clare Band was followed in September 1916 by the establishment of the Baltimore & Ohio Orchestra; like the Glee Club, it rehearsed at the Central YMCA in Baltimore. Presumably because of the smaller numbers of employees at other locations on the B&O system, the Welfare Bureau did not succeed in replicating such organizations all across the railroad; still, by the summer of 1918, glee clubs had been started in the New York area, at Pittsburgh (Glenwood), and at Cumberland, Maryland.[43]

In October 1916, the performing arts wing of the welfare movement began its most ambitious undertaking: the formation of the Baltimore & Ohio Opera Club, for the purpose of staging Gilbert and Sullivan's *H.M.S. Pinafore*. The B&O Orchestra was in the orchestra pit, and the principals and chorus were drawn from the Glee Club and the Bando Club, the latter a recently formed social organization of the B&O's female employees. One hundred fifty employees participated, and over three thousand employees and family members attended the three performances, two in Baltimore and one in Cumberland. The club followed up its minor amateur triumph with performances of Gilbert and Sullivan's *The Mikado* in May 1917.[44]

In the realm of improvement of the mind, the company sponsored three activities or programs: classes on general traffic and transportation problems, the debating club, and the employees' library. The transportation classes were given primarily for traffic department employees, and were conducted intermittently in the larger cities around the system (for example, Baltimore in

April 1916, Chicago in March 1917). The Baltimore & Ohio Debating Society, centered among Baltimore-area employees, was formed in January
1917 with Welfare Bureau encouragement. The bureau had nothing to do with
the founding or operation of the Baltimore & Ohio Employes' Free Circulating Library; that institution, located at Mount Royal Station in Baltimore during the period in question, had been founded in 1885. The number of volumes
available to employees and their families across the system (carried free of
charge as company mail) stayed constant at fifteen thousand during the Welfare Bureau years, although it presumably was the bureau's position that use
of the library was encouraged, as it would foster the achievement of a dimension of the bureau's purpose.[45] Nothing else of note was done in this area; on
balance, Parlett and B&O management seem not to have been greatly interested in the intellectual development of their railroaders.

In company social outings, they were more interested, as probably were
their employees. Such gatherings more clearly fostered the sense of family
that, as an objective, preceded the more cosmic goals of the welfare movement. Accordingly, they were a matter of higher priority to the Welfare Bureau. In a statement of aims published in the company magazine in October
1916, Parlett wrote that the primary purpose of the bureau was "to foster
healthful recreation, athletics, and a closer intimacy and fellowship among
employes and officials . . ."; he barely hinted at intellectual or educational
goals. As a result, dinners, dances, picnics, and recreational outings were
fairly numerous all over the railroad (although the western region was somewhat less active), especially during the summer of 1916 and the winter of
1917. As with other activities encouraged by the bureau, many individual
events antedated its establishment, such as the New York clerks' outing and
the Baltimore-area Jennie Smith Picnic (named for a local evangelist with ties
to the railroad). In other cases, such as the Martinsburg, West Virginia Veterans' Association outings, events grew substantially in size and scope with
the Welfare Bureau's encouragement. In a third set of cases, new events were
instituted. Often these were small, local family-oriented picnics that grew as
offshoots of bureau-sponsored baseball games; in other instances, they were
major events started from scratch, such as the entertainment and dance night
of the Baltimore freight claims office and the dances sponsored by the Bando
Club.[46] Although there was no explosive proliferation of such events, the bureau obviously was successful in stimulating more company-oriented social
activity.

Was Willard's B&O different from other railroads in its embracing of
welfare work? Probably it was, but the difference appears to have been one of
degree. From present evidence, it may be argued that the B&O was the first

American railroad to adopt a thorough and comprehensive welfare program. The key words in that assertion, however, are "thorough and comprehensive." It is abundantly clear that other railroads were at least dabbling in some aspects of welfare work well before the B&O's May 1916 establishment of the Welfare Bureau.

Three welfare-oriented phenomena were fairly common across the industry by 1915: encouragement or partial subsidization of employee pension and disability insurance programs, encouragement of veteran employees' associations and their social activities, and cooperation with the national Young Men's Christian Association in the construction and operation of YMCAs on or near railroad property for employee use. In these matters, the B&O more or less ran with the pack. With respect to the first matter, through its Relief Department, the company had been a leader. However, regarding the railroad YMCA, the B&O's friendly attitude was simply typical of railroads around the country—in no way was it remarkable. In the matter of veterans' associations, the B&O was something of a laggard; the first chapter of the Pennsylvania's veterans' association was organized in 1886, twenty-two years before the B&O's association took shape.[47]

Neither was the B&O unique with respect to some other types of welfare activity. On the intellectual front, its efforts were at least matched, and probably bested, by the Santa Fe's network of reading rooms. Begun in earnest in 1898, the reading room program established small libraries and lounges at important division points (especially remote ones) around the Santa Fe system; regular individual reading opportunities were supplemented by Chautauqua-like programs of traveling lecturers and entertainment troupes. In the realm of social activity, the Southern Pacific (SP) began sponsoring employee clubs and clubhouses before 1910, and during the decade of the teens it expanded their activities substantially. Even the Great Northern (GN), under Hill management a road not noted for its concern for employee welfare, held annual halfday picnics on company time from the mid-1890s onward.[48]

More widespread among railroad work forces than broad social and intellectual activities were programs of athletics. This was so presumably for the same reason that athletics was dominant in the B&O's Welfare Bureau: the men liked sports without being told that they should. Typically, baseball was the favored game. By the summer of 1912, the Santa Fe had at least one baseball team at nearly all of its sizable installations. There was no general Santa Fe league or tournament; teams formed themselves and arranged their own schedules. Still, the best-organized teams played at least once a week from midspring through summer, and their activities were well covered by *Santa Fe Employes' Magazine*. On the Pennsylvania, baseball competition began in similarly ad hoc fashion in 1903, but by 1907, formal leagues were playing at the two largest centers of PRR employment (Philadelphia and Altoona). In June 1915 the Pennsylvania established a systemwide baseball league; that summer, sixty-six teams competed for a cup to be awarded by the formidable W. W. Atterbury, the company's vice president of operations. The league was a success, and it was expanded for the 1916 season. Its general format was copied that year by the Missouri, Kansas, & Texas (with the cooperation of Katy System YMCAs) and, of course, by the Welfare Bureau of the B&O.[49]

Many aspects of welfare work, then, were practiced by the more managerially astute railroads before the nation's entry into the world war. After the war, welfare programs resumed their expansion. During the 1920s the Southern Pacific had a band and a glee club in Sacramento, the Great Northern and the Louisville & Nashville (L&N) had extensive sports programs, and the Norfolk & Western (N&W) began sponsoring annual social outings. In addition, employee stock ownership plans (considered to contribute both intellectual and economic benefits, promoting an understanding of the functioning of the corporation and loyalty thereto, as well as dividends and long-run capital gains) were operating on the SP, the GN, and the PRR.[50] Nearly every American railroad of any size, solvency, and sophistication could point to at least a small something that it had done that qualified as an element of welfare work, and some railroads did quite a lot.

How, then, can one defend the assertion that the B&O's position in the welfare movement was special? Clearly Willard's efforts on his own road were superior to those of the L&N, the N&W, and other hard-nosed roads such as the Burlington. But what about the Santa Fe, the SP, and the Pennsylvania? Here the differences lie in the details. The Santa Fe's program did not encompass quite so many program elements as did the B&O's, and that of the Southern Pacific, although comprehensive, was not fully developed until after the B&O program was up and running. As for the PRR's welfare activities, they were different, and possibly deficient, on three counts. First, they appear to have been somewhat less comprehensive. The Pennsylvania had a superior sports program, but intellectual and artistic activities were relatively sparse. Second, much of the PRR program was administered through or in cooperation with two quasiexternal organizational units: the PRRYMCA and the Mutual Beneficial Association of Pennsylvania Railroad Employees, Inc. (MBA), the latter formed in 1913. The system baseball league, for example, was organized at the top by company officials, promoted and reported by the MBA's *Mutual Magazine* (there was no company magazine), and most often scheduled to play on YMCA fields. The employee stock ownership plan was handled by the MBA, as were most social activities. By 1916 the MBA was the focal point of PRR welfare measures, yet the company held it at arm's length. The association received a small subsidy in the form of free office space and advice from management, but unlike the Welfare Bureau, it had no full-time director or staff on the company payroll; staff members were compensated through voluntary dues from individual employees.[51]

The likely reason for this arrangement lies in the third count by which the PRR and B&O programs differed: motives. The official story was that the Mutual Beneficial Association resulted from the insistent argument of a Philadelphia-area conductor that PRR employees and management were becoming estranged, and that an intermediary employees' organization was needed to restore communication and understanding between them. In fact, according to the memoirs of *Mutual Magazine*'s first editor, Pennsylvania management— W. W. Atterbury specifically—already had decided to form such an organization before the conductor's nicely staged visit to company headquarters to present his argument. Atterbury's motive was clear to the disingenuous observer: he wished to preempt the national labor unions. "Outside" unions were troublesome interlopers, in his view; although the train-and-engine-crew brotherhoods were already established on the PRR, it was his intent both to prevent them from expanding their influence and to render other unions ineffectual.[52] Interest in an employee association might displace worker interest in the less tractable national unions. The welfare measures of the MBA thus may be seen as essentially manipulative: more as efforts to maintain control of employees than as attempts to develop them as whole and productive persons.

On the other hand, the B&O's motives in establishing the Welfare Bureau, although certainly not purely philanthropic, were not seriously tainted by any desire for union prevention. Both in public and in private, Daniel Willard by this time had made clear his willingness to deal congenially with the national unions. Workers had legitimate interests, he believed, and those interests might be served either by existing unions or by forces that could be truly destructive. In 1913, the same year that the MBA was formed, Willard stated in a letter to Seth Low of the National Civic Federation, "It is infinitely better . . . for us to try to maintain satisfactory or amicable relations with the labor unions, than to do anything which might discourage their growth and result in greater activity on the part of the Socialists. . . ."[53] Willard's acceptance of unions and empathy with their members were given quiet expression by his custom of asking labor leaders to dine with him, on the road in his private business car or in his hotel suite, or at home in his unostentatious house in the Roland Park neighborhood of Baltimore. Among most of his peers, such small gestures of respect and hospitality toward union men were regarded as inappropriate.[54] Even more irritating to some of his fellow railroad presidents, though, was his conciliatory approach to the eight-hour-day controversy.

During the summer of 1916, the operating brotherhoods made a determined push to reduce the standard workday from ten to eight hours. Railroad management as a group resisted the demand vigorously, and a nation-crippling strike was imminent. To avert a strike, Congress in September passed legislation submitted by William Adamson of Georgia mandating the eight-hour day. President Wilson signed the Adamson Act, but the railroad industry immediately challenged its constitutionality. By March 1917 the issue had come before the Supreme Court, but no decision had been rendered. The law was in limbo, and again a strike was threatened.[55]

Willard, meanwhile, had not been so adamant in opposing the act as his peers. His initial reaction to the controversy was to propose a compromise at nine hours, but he was rebuffed by both sides. At congressional hearings, pulled both by his sympathy for the principle and his sense of obligation as chairman of the industrial advisory commission of Wilson's Council of National Defense, he testified in favor of the eight-hour legislation. As he did not wish to place the B&O at a labor cost disadvantage relative to its competitors, he did not break industry ranks and negotiate an eight-hour contract on his own, but he continued to lobby his fellows for moderation. When the court-delay-prompted strike threat arose, he directly assumed the role of mediator, in lengthy eleventh-hour meetings trying to convince the union leadership not to strike before the Supreme Court handed down its decision and to persuade railroad executives to bow to the inevitable. He was successful; there was no strike. The Supreme Court upheld the Adamson Act, and the eight-hour day became standard.[56]

The role that Willard played in this matter did not endear him to many of his fellow chief executives, but it did increase the trust with which he was viewed by the leaders of organized labor. Certainly it should have removed any suspicion that his Welfare Bureau had anything to do with undercutting the unions. Willard, of course, was interested in the welfare of his company as well as that of his workers, but his motives in promoting welfare work surely came closer to being right-spirited than did W. W. Atterbury's.

During this period Willard's inclination toward progressive management practices manifested itself in another way, one that from a certain perspective appeared to run counter to his approach to welfare work and labor unions. He decided to take a look at the promised benefits of "scientific management." Scientific management, cold and technical in comparison to the welfare movement, had as its goal the maximization of work efficiency and general productivity. Delineated around the turn of the century by Frederick W. Taylor, its principal tools were such things as time and motion study, detailed record keeping, and cost analysis. It was generally opposed by organized labor; union leaders considered it to be basically a speedup technique, forcing workers to work harder and faster without commensurate wage increases.[57] Willard himself was initially skeptical of scientific management. It had been used as a stick with which he and other railroad executives had been beaten for their alleged lack of efficiency (by shippers' attorney Louis Brandeis and his expert witness, engineer Harrington Emerson) at the 1910 Interstate Commerce Commission (ICC) rate increase hearings.[58] Even so, in May 1914, the B&O, through operations vice president Arthur Thompson, retained the services of a scientific management consulting firm—the firm of Harrington Emerson, no less.[59]

Emerson was an efficiency engineer of modest ability and a self-promoter without peer. Although he was certainly not incompetent in the matters that his firm addressed, his primary professional talents were securing contracts and hiring capable technical people to carry out the actual work. He and his colleagues were responsible for the principal prior application of scientific management among American railroads, the reorganization of the chaotic and technologically obsolescent Topeka shops of the Santa Fe between 1904 and 1907.[60]

The Emerson Company's work on the B&O consisted of a thorough investigation of all phases of the road's operation, and of the development of a set of recommendations for remedial action. By the end of 1916, critiques and suggestions had been offered with respect to shop work methods, shop scheduling, shop machinery and tools, locomotive fuel efficiency, parts and materials inventory control, train schedules, locomotive utilization, hiring policies, refrigeration of perishables, maintenance of way piecework standards, cross-tie conditions, car painting, record keeping, and cost accounting. In all of this, Emerson's people evidently produced mixed results. Some of their labors clearly bore fruit. In the area of fuel efficiency, for example, the consultants developed an explicit and detailed set of recommendations for proper fueling, firing, and handling of locomotives; these recommendations then were passed on to employees through local meetings and the company magazine. Attributed savings in 1916 were over $1.4 million. In other areas, though, results were not so good. The consultants' shop work methods suggestions, for example, apparently were met with considerable resistance by both workers and foremen, and the B&O denied Emerson's request to put his own people into the shops full time "to supervise the application of these plans until the regular employees have also mastered their application."[61]

Consultant-imposed scientific management thus being demonstrated to be no panacea, Willard and his executive team backed away from it. It was not really compatible with the Willard style: outsiders with stopwatches did nothing to further the B&O family spirit. Still, although Willard lost interest in the method of scientific management, he maintained his enthusiasm for its basic goal of operating efficiency. He shied away from those of its techniques that threatened to disrupt employee relations, but he adopted many that did not, and he kept his eyes open for alternate means to deal with the more sensitive problem areas identified by the Emerson consultants. One of those areas was shop efficiency. That problem was addressed in more characteristically Willardian manner by the 1923 Cooperative Plan, the subject of the next chapter.[62]

While scientific management was waxing and waning on the B&O, a similar if somewhat less negative cycle was becoming discernible in the welfare program. After a great burst of activity during the Welfare Bureau's first year, the program began to lose some of its vitality. Parlett may not have been the right man for the job. He was, after all, a physician; judging from the articles that he had published in *Baltimore & Ohio Employes Magazine* in 1917 and 1918, he was far more interested in hygiene and general health than in picnics, operas, or bowling.[63] He apparently left the service of the B&O early in 1919.

The formal entry of the United States into World War I in April 1917 was an even more important factor in the weakening of the program. As many of the railroad's younger employees joined the armed forces (just under seven thousand, of roughly sixty thousand total employees in 1916), to be replaced by women and older men, the pool of interested potential participants in some of the bureau's activities shrank. By the summer of 1918, some of the smaller points on the B&O were no longer fielding their own baseball teams, and the Glee Club was down from sixty to twenty-one members. Moreover, there had been a loss at the top of the hierarchy as well as in middle and lower ranks. Pursuant to President Wilson's invoking his wartime powers to take over and to operate the national transportation system, the federal government assumed control of the B&O and the nation's other railroads on December 28, 1917. Daniel Willard remained as president of the Baltimore & Ohio Railroad Company, but the company no longer controlled the railroad; the United States Railway Administration (USRA) did. Willard remained active in the industry as chairman of the industrial advisory commission of the Council of National Defense, and he retained some de facto influence over the railroad, but he was no longer in charge of operations.[64]

Two of Willard's top subordinates, Arthur Thompson and Charles W. Galloway, were named federal managers of the B&O eastern and western regions, respectively, in June 1918. Although their appointments signaled continuity as well as change, the whole notion of federal takeover was managerially unsettling. Some parties, notably agricultural interests and the national rail unions, saw it as a test of or step toward some eventual form of railroad nationalization. This threat diminished somewhat as the USRA—under both its initial director-general William Gibbs McAdoo, formerly President Wilson's Treasury secretary, and under his successor, former Santa Fe board chairman Walker D. Hines—proved to be fairly sympathetic to traditional railroad corporate viewpoints. Thompson and Galloway, like other B&O people, understood that if they stayed on that property, they almost certainly would work for Willard again when the war and its aftermath were past. But for the time being, they took their orders from the USRA.[65]

Any sense of disorientation that may have resulted from all of this probably diminished in proportion to one's distance from Baltimore and lowliness of status in the railroad hierarchy, but it still had an impact. As the months passed, the Welfare Bureau became nearly invisible. In the summer of 1919, there were local B&O baseball teams, but there was no systemwide championship. The opera club disappeared, as did the bowling league. In general, it appears that some momentum was lost from Willard's efforts to shape the B&O into a cohesive unit. The railroad was not returned to his control until March 1920.

The war ended the first phase of Daniel Willard's stewardship of the Baltimore & Ohio. The period from mid-1918 through 1922 was not so positive and upward in its thrust as the first period. During the war, the heavy utilization of the property, coupled with inadequate maintenance, wore down the railroad physically; in March 1920 it was in poor shape. In addition, major wage increases and work-rule changes granted by the McAdoo regime had saddled the B&O (and all other railroads) with greatly increased labor costs and a larger and somewhat self-satisfied work force. Willard spent nearly all of his energies during the first three years after his resumption of leadership simply returning the company to where it was in 1917.[66]

In one sense, though, the war had a positive impact: it opened up to women positions on the railroad that previously had been staffed exclusively by men. Neither the B&O nor railroads in general were unique in this respect, of course; necessity arising from the lack of available men made equal opportunity employers (at least at certain levels) of many companies. However, perhaps more than some other firms, the B&O accepted female newcomers graciously. The B&O had employed women since 1855, but almost exclusively in clerical positions; as the wartime labor shortage increased, such limitations were removed. Willard was not the least interested in seriously changing traditional gender roles, but equally he was not at all disturbed by a broader definition of "women's work." At the Deer Park management retreat in June 1917, two months after the declaration of war and a year before his exile, he stated:

There are, no doubt, many places in the railroad service where the work is of such a nature that it can be done by women equally as well, and in some cases perhaps better, than by men, and owing to the great demand for manual labor, due to conditions created by the war, there is no reason why women cannot or should not perform work of that character. I simply urge that when they are so employed by the Baltimore & Ohio Company, they be treated at all times with the respect properly due them, and they should not be permitted to attempt to do work for which they are physically unfit.[67]

Accordingly, no women were hired to shovel ballast, or to hand-fire a steam locomotive, or to lay rail—but they were hired as crew dispatchers, and as drill press operators, and as station agents. Many more replaced male clerks.

By all surviving indications, they performed very well. If the company magazine was an accurate reflection of the reaction of B&O men to their new colleagues, they were accepted with something between respectful appreciation and bemused tolerance. Most articles on the newly hired, transferred, or promoted women were straightforward and enthusiastic, but one was revealingly ambivalent: in a feature story on the Ladies' Rifle Club, organized at B&O division offices in Cumberland in January 1918, a photograph of Elizabeth McNeill's nicely punctured target paper (thirteen of fifteen shots within the circle) was displayed on the same page as a cartoon that depicted club members throwing down their rifles and standing on chairs to escape a mouse. However capable they may have been, when the war ended, most of them—but not all of those in white-collar positions—were replaced by the men whose jobs they had filled. Like the rest of the country, the B&O in 1920 sought a return to normalcy.[68]

The Welfare Bureau, having been absorbed into a combined Safety and Welfare Department during federal control, reemerged as the Welfare Department, with W. W. Wood as superintendent. Activities rebounded from their moderately depressed state. A full baseball schedule was played in the summer of 1920, with local leagues playing in May and June, then sending their champions to play in the System Leagues in July and August; the two regional winners met to decide the system championship on Labor Day (the Baltimore Division defeated the Ohio Division, 3-0). Musical activities increased: the B&O Orchestra and Opera Club were not revived, but the Glee Club regained most of its former strength, and the Mount Clare Band came to be rivaled by similar groups across the railroad, the Cumberland Shops Band in particular.[69]

The greatest expansion came in the realm of social activity, often sponsored by recently formed local B&O welfare leagues or associations. In February 1921, for example, the Welfare League of Akron hosted their counterparts from Cleveland at an entertainment and dance at the local armory; the company suspended certain operations to ensure high attendance. New chapters of the Veterans' Association were formed, as were Ladies' Auxiliaries, especially in the western region, where they had been sparse. During the

B&O System baseball league champions, 1920. (Courtesy of the B&O Railroad Museum)

spring and summer of 1921, a large number of "first annual" social events were held, again often with company support. Perhaps the most impressive of these was the first annual Cincinnati Terminals outing in August, held at Chester Park. Attendance was approximately thirty-five hundred, as employees were granted a halfday off work; only operating employees whose jobs were scheduled during the picnic hours were unable to attend. The events of the afternoon included a popularity contest, egg and peanut rolling contests, hop-skip-and-jump contests, sprints, marksmanship contests (all of the preceding with separate men's and women's divisions), sack races, a fat man's race (won by the visiting superintendent of the Ohio Division at Chillicothe), and a baby beauty contest. Attendance of white-collar workers seems to have been somewhat higher than that of blue-collar workers, but most levels of the company were represented fairly well.[70]

The large, family-oriented social outing apparently had such widespread success that it came to supplant athletics as the top priority of the Welfare Department. During the winter of 1920–1921, a weak attempt at reviving a systemwide bowling league fizzled and was cut back to the Baltimore area. During the summers of 1921 and 1922, while local baseball teams continued to play each other, there was no System League. However, B&O social events generally continued, in many cases growing in size and in scope.[71]

All of these activities went on despite a national railroad labor situation that was not especially good in 1921 and 1922. The postwar recession cut railroad traffic substantially, and railroad employment went down with it; the B&O's total number of employees fell from seventy-two thousand in March 1920 to fifty-nine thousand a year later. Then in the summer of 1922 came the shop crafts strike. The strike on the B&O lasted for two and a half months, an experience not likely to enhance company camaraderie.[72] It was, however, the impetus for Willard and the B&O to transcend that which might be called the mature paternalism of the welfare movement. Many of the pieces were already on hand for the formal adoption of "cooperative management": a genuine concern for the dignity of the worker, a sense of company as family, recognition of the unions, and some tentative experience with local meetings among labor, staff, and management. The strike was the catalyst that brought them all together and led to the establishment of the Baltimore & Ohio Railroad Cooperative Plan.

2

1 9 2 3 – 1 9 2 6

THE COOPERATIVE PLAN

"We are a family" and "We have a job to do" remained central and clearly articulated themes across the B&O during the twenties, as they had been during the preceding decade. Beginning in 1923, though, a principle that previously had been just a corollary of those larger precepts was pushed up to independent and equal status. "Suggestions are always in order" acquired the power of an expectation: employees not only *may* make suggestions but *should* make them. Himself responding to the suggestion of others, Willard established a program to encourage employees to become more actively involved in the business—to help the family to do its job better both by offering ideas for improvement and by participating, through their union officers, in evaluating those ideas. The program was called the Cooperative Plan.

This chapter begins with a broad definition and overview of the Cooperative Plan (or more simply, the Plan), followed by a discussion of its origins. Internal antecedents and both general and specific external factors in its creation are discussed; particular attention is paid to the role of consultant Otto Beyer and to the catalytic impact of the Shopmen's Strike of 1922. The initial cooperative experiment at Glenwood Shops and the subsequent adoption of the Plan in all B&O shops are described; perceived early benefits and some early problems are recounted. Typical local cooperative meetings are outlined in some detail. The spread of the Plan to other departments of the B&O and to other companies, and its attendant publicity, are described. Finally, the first four years of the Plan are assessed in terms of tangible results.

What was the Baltimore & Ohio Railroad Cooperative Plan? The short answer is that it was a systematic program of representative quality circles, jointly sponsored by unions and management, developed primarily in company repair shops. As such, it was a major step forward in labor relations—sufficiently important in itself to justify the writing of this book. Everything accomplished by Daniel Willard's presidency up to this point simply qualified him to be considered an excellent railroad executive, in the highest echelon of his profession but not necessarily alone there. With the Cooperative Plan, Willard set himself apart.

Before the origin and development of the Plan are discussed, the term *quality circle* must be defined. As it came to be understood in the 1980s, a quality circle is a formalized group of workers and managers who meet regularly to attempt to find ways in which the quality of their firm's products or services may be improved. As a rule, any proposal directed toward this end is a proper matter for discussion by the group. Most commonly, proposals or issues raised in the meetings fall into the categories of product or service design, machine design, machine or plant layout, plant and equipment maintenance, work methods, productivity-related working conditions, work scheduling, materials or product flow, materials waste control, and quality control standards and techniques. The majority of the circle's membership normally is drawn from the ranks of labor; the remainder includes the workers' department or plant manager and plant staff representatives. Recent practice has been to establish numerous circles within a given facility, involving as many workers as possible. However, a single representative circle (for which workers elect peers to represent them) follows the same form and, it may be argued, serves essentially the same function. Quality circles typically operate in a context of substantial employee job security, which contributes to the achievement of higher-quality output by improving employee morale.[1]

The quality circle concept is commonly associated with a set of management approaches and techniques ascribed to the Japanese. The "Japanese management system," credited by many for the substantial gains of Japanese manufacturing firms against their American competition since the early 1970s, is discussed more fully in chapter 5. Here, it is sufficient to note that those who work in or under it (generally the full-time male employees of large corporations) enjoy great job security, advisory participation in decision making, and a broadly supportive corporate climate evocative of a sense of family. Quality circles are practically standard to the system.[2]

Therefore, it has been widely assumed that quality circles are a Japanese innovation. It is understandable that this should be the case. Until Japanese quality circles began to be noticed and copied by American corporations during the early 1980s, there were no large, well-organized, and highly visible post–World War II American examples of quality circle programs, and the Japanese were generally not hesitant to take credit for their existence. A book on quality circles published in Tokyo by the Asian Productivity Organization in 1972, for example, states, "Quality circles are an innovation peculiar to Japan,"[3] dating from about 1960; it contains no reference to William Edwards Deming, the American statistician and quality control specialist who helped the Japanese to establish their quality circles during the 1950s, nor of successful efforts to establish similar programs in other countries before that time. Because most American businesses and business schools are not especially historically minded, there were no noteworthy efforts to probe corporate records or memories of older employees for American antecedents of the Japanese development. Had there been such efforts, it might have come to be understood that the Japanese properly may take credit only for the full development and widespread application of the concept, not for its first use.

Present evidence indicates that the B&O Cooperative Plan was adopted earlier and lasted longer than any other major American antecedent of the late-twentieth-century quality circle. It began in 1923, and some of its remnants remained in effect until 1962. Directly involving thousands of employees over the years and indirectly involving tens of thousands, it certainly qualifies as a major effort. Whether Deming and the Japanese knew about it, and then copied and improved upon it, is an open question; there is no question that Willard's B&O had the concept first.

The Cooperative Plan was born as a small, tentative pilot program at the B&O's equipment maintenance shops at Glenwood, on the south side of Pittsburgh, in February 1923. It was brought into being and developed jointly by the B&O and the Baltimore & Ohio System Federation No. 30, the latter representing the B&O local chapters of the shop crafts unions (the International Association of Machinists; the International Brotherhood of Boilermakers, Iron Ship Builders, and Helpers; the International Brotherhood of Blacksmiths, Drop Forgers, and Helpers; the Amalgamated Sheet Metal Workers' International Alliance; the Brotherhood of Railway Carmen of America; and the International Brotherhood of Electrical Workers). The purpose of the program was to improve the service and efficiency of the company, hence the returns to shareholders and to employees. The preamble to the agreement between B&O management and Federation No. 30 that formally sanctioned the Glenwood experiment, signed in May 1923, stated:

The welfare of the Baltimore & Ohio Railroad and its employees is dependent on the service which the railroad renders the public. Improvements in this service and economy in operation and maintenance expenses result chiefly from willing co-operation between the railroad management and the voluntary organizations of its employees. When the groups responsible for better service and greater efficiency share fairly in the benefits which follow their joint efforts, improvements in the conduct of the railroad are greatly encouraged. The parties to this agreement recognize the foregoing principles and agree to be governed by them in their relations.[4]

Joint worker-manager meetings were to be held biweekly to raise and to evaluate service-quality-related issues and suggestions. The primary specific subjects to be entertained were shop, yard, and engine terminal operations; materials supply, distribution, care, and saving; work methods; job analysis; quality standards and control; coordinating, scheduling, routing, and planning of work; work group and overall shop performance records; conditions of shops, grounds, tools, machinery, and buildings; and department and shop morale. Not to be discussed at these meetings were individual grievances, work rules, wages, or any other matter normally handled in contract negotiations between company and union.[5] These biweekly shop meetings, or cooperative conferences, were to be attended by the shop superintendent, a few of his immediate subordinates, and the six local union representatives who constituted the regularly functioning federated shop crafts committee. Management dominance in terms of numbers of attendees was to be avoided. As the program evolved at Glenwood, meetings usually were attended by five managers or staff people and the six union men. It was encouraged and expected that the bulk of the ideas considered at the meetings would come from workers on the floor of the shops, channeled through their respective craft representatives.[6]

After a rough start, the pilot program produced results that were judged to be satisfactory by all parties to the agreement. On February 24, 1924, the program was extended to all forty-five of the B&O's shop facilities, and the Cooperative Plan was firmly established.

What was the origin of the Cooperative Plan? It did not spring full-blown from nothingness; it was the culmination of a number of preliminary steps and prior forces both inside and outside the company. Within the B&O was an evolving corporate ethos: sense of family, concern for the worker, service to customers, pride in the railroad. Such notions of what the B&O was about were intertwined with the Relief Department, respectful relationships with the unions, the safety committees, *Baltimore & Ohio Magazine*, the Welfare Department, and two somewhat narrower programs not discussed in chapter 1: "cooperative claim prevention" and division superintendents' open staff meetings. Of these elements, three were in particular respects precursors of the Cooperative Plan: safety committees, cooperative claim prevention, and open staff meetings.

The safety program was the B&O's first comprehensive effort to obtain a

Daniel Willard at his desk. From a safety campaign poster,
early 1920s. (Author's collection)

desired result through local labor-management committees. From their beginning in 1911, the safety committees had been a forum for discussions between
company officials and their blue-collar subordinates. Although chaired by a
fairly senior local manager, often the division superintendent, the typical
committee was composed in the majority of trainmen, enginemen, firemen,
shop employees, and maintenance of way workers. The safety program evolved
and grew over the years, through the "No Accident Campaign" of the federal
period, the formation of a separate Safety Department with traveling agents,
the publication of detailed results and a "Safety Roll of Honor" in the company magazine, and, in January and February 1921, the staging of mass safety
rallies featuring entertainment by local employees and the company safety
film, *Bulletin 70*. Nonetheless, the local labor-management committees re-

mained the ongoing heart of the program, and they undoubtedly helped convince B&O management at all levels of the utility of such structures.[7]

The cooperative claim prevention program established the second major set of local committees on the B&O. Created in October 1917 in an attempt to reduce loss or damage to freight shipments, it was supervised by C. C. Glessner, the company's general freight claims agent. Its committees differed somewhat from those of the safety program in that their meetings and activities tended to be dominated by local station agents. Nonetheless, all departments were represented and all employees received its bulletins. Its activities were well publicized in *Baltimore & Ohio Magazine*, and employees other than committee members were encouraged to attend committee meetings as guests. As with the safety committees, the cooperative claim prevention committees were quite successful; both were able to point to measurable improvements in their respective areas of responsibility. It was with regard to the claims program that the B&O first formally used the term *cooperative* to refer to a continuing program of mutual effort by top-level and middle- to lower-level employees to resolve a managerial difficulty.[8]

The third major internal precursor of the Cooperative Plan was the opening of division superintendents' Monday morning staff meetings to blue-collar employees. This policy began on the New Castle (Pennsylvania) Division in February 1921, on the initiative of the local superintendent, D. F. Stevens. The goals of the policy were to improve information exchange and mutual understanding, and to establish a broader range of perspectives from which to identify problems and opportunities and to recommend changes. The first meeting was chaired by Stevens and was attended by the usual division officers and staff, plus three engineers and a conductor. Willard and Charles W. Galloway, the recently named operating vice president, apparently liked the idea immediately. Less than two months later, the New Castle plan was ordered into effect over the entire railroad.[9]

The forces at work outside the company that led to the adoption of the Cooperative Plan were numerous and complex. A broad background factor was, during the first two decades of the century, a rising interest in the concept of "industrial democracy." Industrial democracy, simply defined, is a system in which substantial amounts of managerial authority are delegated all the way down to the level of the production worker. There were sporadic efforts to implement portions of the concept by some American unions in contract negotiations before World War I—the agreement signed between the United Garment Workers of America and Hart, Schaffner, & Marx in 1911 is perhaps the earliest successful example—but most of the action in the sphere of industrial democracy was in Europe during and after the war. It was a wartime event, the publication in Great Britain of the Whitley Committee report (which recommended that joint worker-management councils be established at the industry, district, and plant levels to guide managerial decision making in British industry after the war), that provided the American labor movement with both encouragement and a blueprint from which to pursue a share of managerial authority. In 1918 the executive council of the American Federation of Labor adopted as its own the basic tenets of the Whitley Committee report.[10]

That report, triggered by wartime mobilization and its attendant industrial upheaval in Great Britain, only reinforced parallel forces operating in the United States. Mobilization for the war effort had led directly to the establishment of the United States Railroad Administration, which in turn led to the possibility of changes in some basic relationships in the railroad industry. The simple fact of government control prompted many people concerned with railroad policy and operations to note that an opportunity had arisen: an opportunity for a fundamental restructuring of the industry, toward greater efficiency and "harmony of interests" among labor, managers, shippers, and the general public. On a narrower and more concrete level, rail union leaders saw the chance to increase their own power, to the benefit of themselves and their members. They seized that chance, and they were successful: under the aegis of the USRA, especially during the highly sympathetic McAdoo administration, the rail unions gained higher wages, standardized and favorable work rules, and considerable growth in membership.[11]

Encouraged by their successes, they determined to push for more. In a drive spearheaded by the train-and-engine-crew brotherhoods, railroad labor by 1919 was actively campaigning for government-sponsored industrial democracy, in the form of the Plumb Plan. Under that plan the federal government was to purchase the nation's railroads and consolidate them into a single system, operated under the authority of a board of directors composed equally of representatives of labor, management, and the public. The campaign for the Plumb Plan was abortive, but it did serve to intensify interest and to stimulate thinking, both among union leaders and among their rank and file, about participating in some fashion in managerial decisions.[12]

Throughout this period, one of the most active and visionary leaders of the American Federation of Labor (AFL) constituent unions was William H. Johnston, president of the International Association of Machinists (IAM). An ardent believer in the promise of industrial democracy, Johnston in November 1918 met and enjoyed a lengthy conversation with Captain Otto S. Beyer, Jr., an army ordnance officer and former railroad mechanical department official who held similar views on the subject. That conversation and the association that followed were to produce the first attempt to establish a program of union-management cooperation—prospectively the first step toward industrial democracy—in the shops of the railroad industry.[13]

Capt. Otto S. Beyer, Jr. (Courtesy of the Labor-
Management Documentation Center, Cornell
University)

Beyer was thirty-two years old when the war ended, but he had already
acquired considerable breadth of experience. Having received a degree in mechanical engineering from Stevens Institute of Technology in 1907, he had
worked first in the engineering department of an iron and steel firm, then
moved in 1911 to become a technical assistant to the superintendent of the
Erie Railroad's mechanical department. In 1912 he moved west to become
special motive power engineer for the Chicago, Rock Island, and Pacific Railway; in 1913, still with the Rock Island, he became general foreman of
medium-heavy and heavy repairs at the locomotive shop in Horton, Kansas. It
was at Horton that he first was able to observe extensively and to work directly
with the railroad rank and file. Then in 1916 he left railroad employment to do
related engineering research, assuming directorship of the locomotive testing
laboratory at the University of Illinois. When the United States entered the
war in 1917, Beyer joined the army; he soon received a commission as
captain, and he was placed in charge of technical training in the ordnance department. In this capacity he became involved with an experiment in indus-

trial democracy at the arsenal in Rock Island, Illinois, wherein joint labor-management committees were given authority to review working conditions, production methods, and piecework rates.[14]

During the spring of 1919, Beyer took the initiative in pushing the concepts of industrial democracy beyond the Rock Island arsenal. In March of that year, he prepared a rough draft of a union-management cooperative program that might be applied across all unionized industries. Over the succeeding months, in contact with Johnston and other AFL rail union officials, he refined his program into one directed specifically at the government-controlled railroad industry. In the meantime he was given the opportunity to put his principles into practice. Appointed director of Army Ordnance's newly created arsenal orders department, Beyer pushed successfully for the creation of joint advisory committees at five of the army's arsenals, and he posted two arsenal union representatives to advisory positions on his staff. His principal spare time activity was pursuing the railroad cooperative plan, both with the AFL and with Director-General of Railroads Walker D. Hines. Both parties supported the Beyer proposal, and on November 10, 1919, preliminary action was taken. Hines sent a letter to the regional directors of railroads, requesting that they favorably call to the attention of their subordinate railroad managers the Beyer plan for labor-management cooperative committees in their lines' mechanical departments.[15]

The Beyer plan, the essence of which closely corresponded to the B&O Cooperative Plan of three years later, basically went nowhere. By the end of 1919, it was clear that the USRA soon would go out of existence, and that federal managers soon would become or would be replaced by returning private managers. Accordingly, they were not much interested in long-range program suggestions from Hines. The great majority of federal managers never even held a serious conversation concerning the plan with their shopcrafts federation representatives.[16] It then sat in limbo for a little over two years.

During this interlude, important pertinent developments were taking place. William Johnston maintained his attachment to the program, trying several times without success to have variants introduced at manufacturing firms with which the machinists' union had contracts. His approach to selling the program to top management, however, may have shifted subtly—and critically—during the period. The status of the shopcrafts unions deteriorated markedly during 1920 and 1921, suffering both from the abolition of the sympathetic USRA and from labor surpluses that accompanied the postwar recession. Those unions, therefore, were generally on the defensive and inclined to want "to disprove the claim that they were uninterested in production."[17] It may be inferred that by the spring of 1922, when he and Beyer approached Daniel Willard on the subject, Johnston was more inclined to present the co-

William H. Johnston. (Courtesy of the Labor-
Management Documentation Center, Cornell
University)

operative program deferentially, with greater emphasis on benefits to the railroad than on benefits to his men.

Beyer and Johnston did not approach Willard and the B&O first. It was
clear to Beyer that the choice of a recipient for their pitch was critical, but he
did not immediately see a single obvious option. Late in 1921, after they had
decided to make a determined effort to revive the 1919 proposal, Beyer wrote
to Johnston, "The thing to do is to get some railroad president who is not
bitten by the Atterbury bug and who appreciates the latent value of cooperative assistance from [the unions], to go into this matter in a sincere whole
hearted way." He saw three such men: S. Davies Warfield of the Seaboard Air
Line, Alfred H. Smith of the New York Central (NYC), and Daniel Willard.
Of the last two he had one reservation: they both were involved in the Association of Railroad Executives, an industry group dominated by the Pennsylvania's W. W. Atterbury and like-minded officials.[18] His inclination was toward Warfield, despite the Seaboard's relatively small size and southern
location.

By early in 1922, though, Beyer and Johnston had worked beyond any guilt-by-association reservations to consider Smith and Willard on their own merits. Both presidents had records in labor-management relations indicating a predisposition toward the program, and the shop workers of both of their roads were sufficiently company-oriented to raise no serious objections to the program. Moreover, their roads were large and highly visible eastern trunk-lines. Warfield was dropped from consideration, and the choice was between Smith and Willard. As Johnston and Smith had a long-standing and very cordial relationship, and as the New York Central enjoyed a somewhat higher status than did the B&O, Alfred Smith was chosen to receive the proposal first.[19]

After hearing the Beyer-Johnston presentation, Smith declared himself in sympathy with it. However, when he relayed the proposal to the executives and staff of his operating department, he encountered considerable resistance. Rather than fight that resistance down the line, Smith and the NYC demurred, leaving Beyer and Johnston with their second choice: Willard and the B&O.[20]

Daniel Willard by then had a broad and solid reputation for "fairmindedness on labor issues, and for the scrupulous care with which he had endeavored to adhere to the letter of [union] agreements."[21] Some people thought that he should have been Beyer and Johnston's first choice. Interstate Commerce Commissioner Mark Potter, when asked by Beyer through Louis Brandeis to broach the subject to Willard, remarked that Willard was the one man among all American rail executives to give the proposal thoughtful consideration and to follow through with action.[22] Even so, when Beyer and Johnston sat down with him in his office for preliminary discussions, Willard was initially quite skeptical. As he recounted the conversation five years later:

Well, I was suspicious of Mr. Johnston; I didn't know Mr. Beyer, and I was curious to know just a little more about what they had in mind, and I asked Mr. Johnston to tell me a little more specifically what he wanted to do. I said, "If it is your thought to introduce some sort of a Soviet arrangement on the B&O, I am opposed to it." And he asked me very properly what I meant by Soviet.

"Well," I said, "I don't know, candidly, what Soviet does mean, but I know what I think of when I use the name, and what I am thinking of is this: are you expecting to put into existence agencies, committees in our different shops, with the understanding that matters of management and shop details shall be referred to those committees to be voted on and decided, and then we are to accept their decision?" And he said promptly and finally, "By no means; they don't propose to interject themselves into management at all."

They saw that that responsibility rested on me, and they had no desire to remove it. What they wanted to do was to help us. They felt that the men who were doing the actual work, many of them, would be the foremen and the master mechanics and officers of the road in the future; many of them were men of intelligence; they had behind them many years of experience; they were not being encouraged at that time to make suggestions of a constructive character, and they felt that they could make [through cooperative committees] such suggestions as would be helpful. Well, I was perfectly agreeable to that sort of a program, and so I told them, I'd put them in touch with the officers to work it out.[23]

Then came the nationwide Shopmen's Strike, and the plan was put in abeyance.

The Shopmen's Strike of 1922, perhaps the most significant railroad labor-management showdown of the era, was the bubbling over of worker frustrations that had been rising for some time. Its underlying economic cause was the monetary deflation that accompanied the serious postwar recession. Deflation and increasing unemployment since the fall of 1920 had created considerable downward pressure on wages. That pressure had been recognized and transformed into shop wage cuts by the carriers through the front-line institutional cause of the strike, the decisions of the Railroad Labor Board.

The Railroad Labor Board—established by the Transportation Act of 1920 to settle controversies regarding wages, hours, and work rules that the carriers and their employees could not resolve themselves—was not very popular with organized labor. Its problem was not so much a promanagement bias; the board often sided with the unions in matters that came before it. Its problem lay mainly in unequal implementation of board decisions. As those decisions were not legally binding, some railroads (notably the Pennsylvania) were given to flouting board pronouncements that did not serve their interests. Prolabor judgments on such roads could be enforced only by labor's calling a strike; promanagement judgments such as a wage reduction could be implemented simply by management's issuing smaller paychecks. Thus the weight of promanagement decisions accumulated, without any consistent balancing with effective decisions serving the interests of labor.[24]

The sequence of decisions that directly precipitated the strike began in the spring of 1921, when the railroads petitioned the board for a wage cut. The petition was granted; effective July 1, 1921, the wages of shopmen and other blue-collar employees were cut 12 percent. At the same time, subsequent to another decision by the board, the shopcrafts unions' 1919 national agreements were abrogated; those agreements had standardized, across all railroads, shop wages and work rules in a manner generally considered favorable to the unions. Then early in 1922, the railroads proposed another wage reduction. Sensing that they were about to be abused for a third time, the AFL shopcraft unions at their federated convention in April 1922 began to prepare for a strike. A few convention delegates argued that the strike should be against only those companies that had been most aggressive in their opposition to AFL shopcraft union positions, a group led by the Pennsylvania Railroad through General Atterbury. This was the minority view. The convention decided to authorize ballots for a nationwide strike of all carriers, regardless of their individual records in union relations; in this manner could the larger issue of the Railroad Labor Board and its one-sided ineffectuality be addressed most forcefully. On June 5 the board mandated a shop wage cut similar in size to that of the prior year. On June 8 strike ballots were distributed; 95 percent of the returned ballots favored a walkout. On July 1 the strike began.[25]

For the unions, the strike did not go well. On July 3 the Railroad Labor Board opined that the striking shopmen had voluntarily left the service of their employers, surrendering their seniority rights, and that they could be replaced by the carriers at will. Many roads did so with alacrity, thus reducing to minimal levels the strike's disruptive effects upon their operations. The unions' leverage was not destroyed, but it was greatly diminished. As July passed, with more and more strikebreakers reporting to work, and with some of the most strongly antiunion roads claiming near-normal operations, the unions were in trouble.[26]

Beginning to fail in the use of direct economic pressure, the shopcrafts organizations might have looked for help in the political realm. There was not much to be found. The Harding administration had been sharply split over the strike. Secretary of Commerce Herbert Hoover and Secretary of Labor James Davis tended to sympathize with the strikers, whereas Attorney General Harry Daugherty, and increasingly President Harding himself, viewed the strike as a serious and inexcusable threat to governmental authority and economic recovery, especially in the context of the simultaneous national coal strike. The unions' most influential administration ally, Hoover, gradually was losing the argument to their opponent, Daugherty.[27]

One of the few things that Hoover could do to help the unions was to encourage his fellow moderate Republican, Daniel Willard, to break with the Association of Railroad Executives (ARE) and to sign a separate and moderate agreement. The potential for such a breakaway clearly existed. The ARE, firmly under the control of the Atterbury party, by late July had taken the position that the seniority rights of strikers were forfeit. The hard-liners were going to insist upon levying punishment. Willard, on the other hand, had adopted a conciliatory approach from the beginning. At considerable cost in traffic lost to the B&O, he had held the strikers' jobs open for nearly a month; the B&O had not yet begun actively recruiting strikebreakers. Willard was not comfortable with the hard-line position, so he needed little prodding from

Hoover. The B&O commenced separate negotiations with the shopcrafts federation on July 25.[28]

Willard's basic offer to the strikers certainly was not everything that they might have wished. Essentially, it was this: union shopmen not found guilty of strike-related violence (of which there was none to speak of on the B&O, unlike on some other roads) were to be restored to their former positions at their July 1 wages and seniority, with seniority disputes vis-à-vis nonstrikers and the few incidental new hires to be resolved by a committee composed equally of union and management representatives. The offer, presented during the course of four days of negotiations between union officers and operations vice president C. W. Galloway, from the strikers' perspective reduced the strike to roughly the status of an unpaid vacation. The unions declined the offer, and it was withdrawn.[29]

The following week President Harding, swayed one last time in Hoover's direction, offered a similar proposal as a framework for a national settlement. This time the unions accepted, seeing in a national agreement the opportunity to save the jobs of their members on antiunion roads. But the ARE rejected Harding's initiative over the seniority issue: the hard-line faction did not wish to be denied its total victory. Harding, apparently not wishing to side with inevitable losers, then began to distance himself from the unions, aligning himself increasingly with Daugherty and the ARE. Their economic and political strength having largely evaporated, and with the active support of the more firmly established operating brotherhoods ever more doubtful, the shopcrafts unions were in serious trouble.[30]

By late August the strike was disintegrating. Caught between General Atterbury and a hard place, the unions were desperate, and willing to settle with anyone under almost any conditions that would preserve their seniority rights. This change of attitude was called to Willard's attention, and soon there was formed a committee of the ARE conciliatory faction, with Willard as chairman, to seek a separate peace. After an initial failure following an ARE meeting in New York on August 25, discussions were reopened on September 2 in Baltimore. Willard, Smith of the New York Central, and Warfield of the Seaboard were the principals on the management side; Bert Jewell, president of the Railway Employees' Department of the AFL, led labor. On September 5 they agreed upon the outline of a settlement. Announced officially on September 13, the Baltimore Agreement or Willard-Jewell Treaty, as it was variously known, contained the same basic provisos that Willard had offered the unions at the end of July. The B&O, the NYC, and the Seaboard were immediate signatories, followed quickly by the Southern. By the end of September, fifteen additional roads (the largest of which were the Chicago & North Western and the Chicago, Milwaukee, & St. Paul) had come to terms under the agreement. Together the nineteen initial Willard-Jewell Treaty carriers and their subsidiaries constituted 23 percent of the nation's railroad mileage.[31]

During the weeks that followed, other roads, most of them small ones, hopped on the bandwagon. Eventually, 176 of the roughly 310 railroads operating in the United States at the time settled with the AFL unions under the agreement or some close variant. The hard-liners, led by Atterbury and the Pennsylvania, never did; they were perfectly happy with their strikebreakers.[32]

The Willard-Jewell Treaty simply gave the shopcrafts unions nearly all of what they had when the strike began. By normal labor standards, then, it represented a union defeat. Even so, it prompted many unionists to look on Daniel Willard with a measure of gratitude. The explanation of this response lies in the immediate fate of AFL shopcrafts federations on those carriers that did not sign the agreement: they were either seriously weakened or obliterated. Until government-supervised union representation elections were mandated by the Railway Labor Act of 1926, much of the railroad industry dealt either with a broken and demoralized shop federation or with a "company union," a management-dominated union substitute best exemplified by the organizations on Atterbury's Pennsylvania (Atterbury did not succeed Samuel Rea as president of the PRR until 1925, but he was responsible for shaping and executing operating labor policy during the period). Across the country the AFL shopcrafts unions appeared to be on the run, and management was triumphant. *Railway Age*, the industry's principal trade publication, editorialized about the strike with faintly concealed praise for those roads that had not signed the Willard-Jewell agreement, stating that "railways such as the Pennsylvania, the Illinois Central, the Burlington, the Union Pacific, and the Southern Pacific . . . have fought truculent labor unions to a finish and completely whipped them."[33] In comparison to those who would completely whip them, Daniel Willard was the unions' friend.

That is not to say that Willard was an ardent booster of the AFL. His view of unions during the period seemed simply to be one of diminishing wariness and a growing sense of mutual interest. As he put it himself:

Some of my friends who don't exactly approve of my views are apt to refer to me as somewhat pro-labor and socialistic and Bolshevistic and all the terms that are used in that connection. Really nothing was further from the truth. It doesn't matter whether I like labor unions or not. I may not like a slippery sidewalk or a rainy day, but I don't get mad at it; it is there, and is something to be put up with. . . .

[Before 1922, the B&O] tolerated labor unions. They came into my office; they wanted to see me. I always arranged to see them as quickly as possible and have it over with. We talked it over, and as soon as the conference was done, I made it my business to lead the way to the door and help them out as quickly and as promptly as possible, hoping it would be a long time before they came again. I told the men that our conferences were friendly and all that, but it was simply toleration.

Well, then, the next step was cooperation. During the strike I had opportunity to do some reflecting. I looked at it this way. The B&O in the last fifteen years had spent almost a quarter of a billion dollars—nearly two hundred and fifty millions of dollars along its property, and then all at once sixteen thousand men didn't want to work, and they didn't work, and I believe that the other men of the service were sympathetic with the men and not with me. It was surprising how many things would happen to an engine during such a period as that that never thought of happening at any other time, indicating that sympathetic feeling between workers in all classes. And so this problem presented itself to me: what good does it do to raise money and improve a railroad if you cannot get the men to work efficiently after you have done it all, and what is wrong about our kind of management on the B&O which has brought about a condition where sixteen thousand men don't want to work and all the rest are sympathetic with them?

So it seemed to me that inasmuch as there was an influence of some kind, whether it was the influence of the labor leaders, as some said, or whether it was a feeling of sympathy that would have been there even if there had been no labor leader, isn't worth while discussing. The feeling was there and found expression through their leaders. So I thought if there is such a movement, such an influence, and they are going to stay here, why not work with them instead of against them? and so it seemed to me that it was a wise and intelligent thing to do, to try and get on some basis of cooperation. . . .[34]

The Shopmen's Strike of 1922 had three important effects upon the development of the B&O Cooperative Plan. First, it further weakened the already struggling shopcrafts unions. As their leaders (particularly Johnston and Jewell) were earnest and flexible, not manipulative and rigid, they saw that the path to strength lay in proving their worth to society, not in instigating class warfare. Their defeat in the strike simply strengthened their resolve to prove themselves. Second, it boosted Daniel Willard's stature in the eyes of most union people. He was a good cop in a room full of bad cops. Third, as the preceding quotation indicates, it was a consciousness-raising experience for Willard. His prestrike disposition was to think that his upgrading of the property and his welfare programs had pretty well solved the old problem of employee commitment: that union-management cooperation would just make a generally good situation a little bit better. The strike dissolved that illusion. He came to see the Beyer-Johnston proposal as a potentially effective solution to a problem that was deeper than he had thought. His commitment to give cooperation a serious trial increased accordingly.

The product of these factors was greater mutual enthusiasm for pushing the proposal to fruition. The unions were more eager to work with Willard, and he was more eager to work with them. As described in chapter 1, the origins of the Cooperative Plan antedate the strike and its origins; the strike was not a root source of the Plan. The strike was a catalyst, triggering reactions that pushed the Plan ahead more quickly and surely. Without it, the Cooperative Plan probably would have been tried on the B&O anyway, but its chances of success would have been much lower.

So Willard sat down again with Beyer and Johnston to pursue the matter of a union-management cooperative program in B&O shops. Since Willard was even more amenable to the idea than he was before the strike, it remained only to select a site at which to try the plan, and then to work out preliminary details. Beyer's preference was for a site where the work force was conscientious and labor-management relations were good, arguing that such a favorable setting would enable them to work out any problems with program details before applying the plan across the entire system. Willard was not so sure. He recalled later: "Perhaps it was sort of a joke in my mind; I do not say what the actuating motive was, but I knew without hesitation where the worst shop was, and I suggested they try that first, and if it worked there it would be pretty apt to work any place else. So they took Pittsburgh." [35]

Beyer and Johnston were in no position to argue the point, but Glenwood Shops in Pittsburgh, in the fall of 1922, certainly was an inauspicious place to begin an untried program of labor-management cooperation. The facility was rife with conflict among its various ethnic groups. It was located in Pittsburgh's notorious second ward, and the ward bosses and their henchmen in the shops almost constituted a second management structure, diminishing the authority of company officers. The bad situation was compounded by the mixing of returning strikers and remaining strikebreakers after the September strike settlement. Breaches of discipline by the various gangs in the shops were common; Willard observed that the "throwing of nuts and bolts and such things" was a frequent occurrence. The local union organization spent nearly all of its time and effort trying to settle grievances and to resolve disputes between its own members. Morale was terrible; productivity was approximately two-thirds that of comparable facilities. [36]

After the strikers returned to work, some eight hundred men were employed at Glenwood. As the near-chaos continued into November, the company in frustration temporarily shut down the facility, prepared to engage in

Glenwood Shops Cooperative Committee. (Courtesy of *Railway Age*)

the common postwar practice of outside subcontracting, if necessary. By January, the situation having cooled off a bit, the shops had been reopened with a work force of roughly 125.[37]

The first step taken by Willard and his mechanical department management toward the implementation of the Beyer-Johnston plan was to hold out to the men at Glenwood the promise of stabilized employment. On February 9, 1923, Willard's executive committee approved the recall of three hundred furloughed shopmen, to be effective the day after approval of the program by the membership of the Glenwood shopcrafts locals, with more men to be called back as the program gained effectiveness. On February 12 a mass union meeting was held near the shops, at which the plan was explained and endorsed by local union officers and national officials of the IAM, Johnston's union. The plan was approved by the men by standing vote.[38]

Beyer then was placed under contract to Federation No. 30 as an on-site consultant to coordinate the implementation of the project. The B&O gave him a desk and clerical help at the shops complex, where he moved in late February. His initial task was simply to help the local shop managers and union people to understand each others' complaints. Beyer's personal style was well suited for such a job: his "casual, homely manner" and "draggy way of speaking"[39] had a calming effect on the tense and occasionally rancorous early committee meetings, attended usually by him, four shop officials, the six local federation committeemen, and the federation secretary. He functioned at the beginning more as a grievance arbiter than as a program coordinator; he spent considerable time on the shop floor, listening patiently to both sides of a long series of petty disputes and misunderstandings, then offering his thoughts on the relative merits of each side. His technique of "letting himself be kicked back and forth between management and men" gradually uncovered a few items that were understood to be problematic by both sides. For example, within the shops certain machines needed to be overhauled, and certain tools needed to be replaced; both management and men could agree upon that. So the necessary overhauling and replacing was done, and the possibility of some common interest began to dawn upon both parties. Then the workers suggested the addition of a footstep-saving satellite tool room, and the tool room was added.[40]

As the credibility of the program thus gained strength, suggestions began to flow in greater volume. Discussions moved beyond personal grievances, which thenceforth were ruled to be a contract matter outside the program. A regular biweekly meeting time for the cooperative committee was established, on company time, and a simple three-category framework for evaluating ideas was developed: accept, reject (with explanation forwarded to the originator), or defer pending collection of further information. The union committeemen began to draw from their coworkers ideas for the improvement of physical working conditions, machine layout, machining jigs and fixtures, and repair methods and fixtures—just as had been hoped. Beyer was elated. On July 26 he wrote to Johnston:

> Especially during the week of July 16, further very significant developments have taken place at Glenwood, which confirm more than ever the wisdom of carrying forward the policy inaugurated on the Baltimore and Ohio. Many new improvements to the physical plant have been authorized and started. Several locomotives to be rebuilt and modernized are now in the shop, and the rank and file is responding with ever increasing enthusiasm. At the last regular biweekly meeting between the management and craft shop representatives, the latter came primed with suggestions, proposals and matters to discuss for the improvement of the shop and the welfare of the men so that the conference had to be continued way into the afternoon. It was very apparent that the men in the shop are beginning to attach great significance to these meetings, that they are thinking about ways to improve things and consequently going to their representatives to present suggestions made by them for action at the conference. The matters considered were very vital indeed and very much to the point. One could not help but be impressed with the spirit which prevailed. I am glad to say, also, that the disposition on the part of the management to act promptly and energetically to effect the betterments discussed is increasing every week. The conviction that the policy being developed on the Baltimore and Ohio is wise and sound thus receives added confirmation.[41]

Those workers who failed to catch the spirit of the program were subjected to appreciable peer pressure, both informal and formal; union committeemen were given the authority to request of shop management transfers of recalcitrant coworkers to less desirable jobs around the shop, an authority that they frequently exercised. The plan was working, and the company responded by recalling, in accordance with the promised timetable, the remainder of the furloughed workers.[42]

Most importantly for the future of the program, productivity at Glenwood rose dramatically, achieving a level that Willard and his mechanical department officers considered entirely satisfactory. This was critical to the credibility of the program among Willard's subordinate managers, who tended to be more skeptical of any alleged positive influences of unions than was Willard, and especially jealous of their own power and perquisites. The union-management cooperative program was a threat to some aspects of that power, especially for shop superintendents and master mechanics out along the divisions, who in past decades across the industry had wielded an almost feudal authority. Many of them, therefore, had no strong inclination to uphold their half of the cooperative arrangement. The Beyer letter hints at this, and Willard himself acknowledged it directly: "Now, the problem isn't all [with] the men, by any manner of means. It was just as hard, probably, for me to get our officers to accept this idea of listening to suggestions from the men as it was to get the men to accept some of the things that came to them from management."[43] Such officers presumably were less inclined to argue with their president, or to subvert his wishes, in the face of hard economic evidence.[44]

The Glenwood experiment was a success, and there was no real debate as to whether it should be extended across the entire B&O mechanical department. For Willard it vindicated his belief that a right-minded empathy among management and workers could improve productivity; his executive committee concurred without notable dissent. For the unions it confirmed the practical value of being supportive of company success. The experiment was not industrial democracy as outlined in the Whitley Committee report, but it worked: the AFL shopcrafts executive council, meeting early in February 1924, endorsed the Glenwood format as a goal to be sought in all future negotiations with all carriers. Everyone was at least tentatively happy. So on February 24, 1924, the B&O and Federation No. 30 signed an agreement establishing joint cooperative committees at all forty-five of the company's shops, and the life of the Baltimore & Ohio Railroad Cooperative Plan officially began.[45]

In the following weeks, the Glenwood joint committee and biweekly conferences were replicated around the system. Beyer, still in the employ of the

Glenwood Shops, c. 1925. (Courtesy of the Pattee Library, Pennsylvania State University)

unions, was given responsibility for directing the development of the full program. The company, to ensure speedy implementation of adopted suggestions and to spread those with broad applicability to the cooperative committees at other shops, established the Shop Practices Bureau. The larger shops, such as Mount Clare, Cumberland, and Glenwood, had their own Shop Practices staff; smaller facilities, such as Newark (Ohio), Garrett, and Washington (Indiana), shared a traveling representative. A member of this department was one of the regularly designated management members of the committee, the others being the top manager of the facility (shop superintendent or master mechanic) and the storekeeper or stockroom supervisor; another staff member or two might be assigned to the committee as seemed appropriate. As in the pilot program, the shopcrafts union committeemen were to be the labor representatives, serving as conduits for suggestions from coworkers in their respective crafts. The federation leadership, for its part, stepped up its efforts to promote the plan among its members. Instructions sent by Federation No. 30 headquarters to each of its local lodges and shop federations stated:

> Proposals, ideas, suggestions, etc., by the local shopmen for consideration at the joint local co-operative conference will naturally come to life through our

daily observations in and around our jobs, benches, machines, departments, and shops. Such ideas, suggestions, and proposals on the part of our men should be referred to their local craft committees for handling. In this connection we would suggest that the local shop committee of each craft get together occasionally at noon time or some other time convenient to all concerned and acquaint itself with various matters and suggestions referred to it by our local members for submission to the next local joint co-operative committee meeting.

We suggest, further, when each craft holds its local lodge meeting, that individual members bring their ideas for bettering things, jobs, output, conditions, etc., to the lodge room for consideration, discussion, and subsequent reference by the lodge to the proper craft committeeman for handling at the next co-operative meeting, provided, of course, the ideas receive the endorsement of the lodge.[46]

The shop-level meetings were the heart of the program. In addition, however, corporate-level meetings were scheduled once per quarter to monitor the progress of the Plan in the field. The first of these upper-tier meetings was held in Baltimore on April 1, under the chairmanship of chief of motive power George H. Emerson, the company's top mechanical officer. Other attendees were William J. McGee, president of Federation No. 30; the six general chairmen of the federation's constituent unions; three officers of the Motive Power Department; the supervisor of shops; and seven inspectors from the Shop Practices Bureau. The main items on the agenda were the recapitulation of the minutes of the first round of local meetings (a total of 421 suggestions had been introduced) and the specification of a standard suggestion numbering scheme and minutes format for all local committees. The consensus of the group was that "the Cooperative Plan had had a very auspicious beginning and that a general good feeling prevailed."[47]

As the year passed, suggestions continued to flow in all over the system. On October 30 Willard offered the first official company assessment of the Plan in an address to company employees and local dignitaries at the Chicago Division shop town of Garrett, Indiana. After briefly describing the genesis of the program and lauding the conscientiousness and cooperativeness of his men and their union representatives, he presented some statistics on the program's progress. In the eight months since systemwide adoption, 657 meetings had been held. Average attendance at these meetings was twelve; average meeting length was one and a half hours. At these meetings 5,272 suggestions had been submitted for discussion; of those suggestions, 3,810—72.2 percent— were adopted. Of the remainder, 972 were still under consideration, 85 were postponed because the associated expenditures were not yet justified, and 405 were dropped after full discussion as impractical. Willard pronounced himself pleased with those results alone, but then went on to say that particular suggestions and consequent service improvements probably were the least important accomplishments of the program. The real benefits, he felt, would be long term. He elaborated:

It may almost be said that the Baltimore & Ohio labor plan or policy which has been developed in conferences between the management and the men is little if anything more than an earnest determination on the part of each to deal honestly, fairly, and sympathetically with the other, at the same time making use of such agencies or methods as seem most likely to secure the results mutually desired. When I speak of sympathetic understanding or relationship, I do not use the word sympathetic in any maudlin sense, but rather as indicating a mutual desire to maintain a relationship based upon a friendly understanding.

Now, what is the effect of such an understanding and of such a relationship? It seems to me that there can be only one answer to that question. It gives to every employee an enlightened and enlarged view of his own worth and importance as a part of the great organization known as the Baltimore & Ohio Railroad. It emphasizes to each man the importance of the work which he himself is doing, and the responsibility which goes with his job or position, and which rests upon him personally to do good work, to do honest and dependable work, not just because it is really his duty as an honest man to give good work in return for good wages paid in good money, but because, realizing the responsibility which he shares with the management for the safe and proper operation of the railroad, he *wants* to do good work; he wants to do thorough and dependable work in order that he may fulfill the enlarged conception which he has of the responsibility which properly rests upon him as a part of the railroad organization. In fact, I think it has come about that the workmen themselves in greater degree than ever before are doing and doing happily the best that is in them, not just because they feel they are *obliged* to do it, but rather because they *want* to do it, understanding and knowing that it is the right and creditable thing to do.[48]

Morale and productivity continued to rise as the Plan matured. As local shop management grew to understand how the program should work, the Shop Practices Bureau was reduced in size and visibility. Bureau representatives in the local meetings were replaced by an increased number of foremen; at the quarterly system meetings, their places were taken by officials of the car department, and by Beyer, who became a regular attendee as he was needed less by local committees.[49]

The benefits of the Plan to the company were obvious: increased productivity, lower unit costs, higher profitability. But what was it doing for the unions and their members? The February 24 agreement had stipulated three

governing principles whereby the unions would benefit from their cooperation. First, the unions of AFL Federation No. 30 were recognized by the company as "necessary, constructive, and helpful agencies in the running of
shops, repair yards, and roundhouses." Second, the company agreed in principle to the "equitable sharing between shopmen and railroad of the gains
of cooperation." Third, the company agreed to seek actively to increase the
employment of union members by the curtailment of outside subcontracting, and to stabilize month-to-month employment through better maintenance
planning.[50]

As the preceding discussion of the 1922 strike may suggest, the first principle was significant in the context of the times. The AFL shopcrafts unions
had been beaten badly. The B&O's dominant rival, the Pennsylvania Railroad,
did not recognize the AFL unions at all, having established its own "company
unions." Under the circumstances for Federation No. 30 merely to be recognized was something of an accomplishment; to be recognized as a positive
force was a victory.

The second principle was significant in any time, addressing as it did the
"Who gets the money?" issue. Although the agreement made only the very
general statement that the workers would receive their benefits "through improvements in working conditions and wage income," without any reference
to specifics of calculation. Willard could be trusted to ensure that more than
token rewards were provided. The wage component, though, would not be
conspicuously large. With the exception of the B&O's later (1926) restoration
of the McAdoo-era time-and-a-half rule for Sunday and holiday work, well
in advance of similar concessions by the rest of the industry, hourly wage
rates generally were pegged closely to those of other major eastern carriers.
Willard made it clear that although the results of the Plan were gratifying, they
were not so phenomenal as to justify paying wages much higher than those
paid by the B&O's better-situated competitors. Working conditions, however,
were improved markedly; Willard reported that by the end of 1926, staff
analysis of cumulative recommendations indicated that "33% of all the suggestions tend to fix things that the men want, no special advantage to the company, but are desirable from the standpoint of the men, and we have been glad
to do those things because they helped bring about a state of mind which made
the men satisfied."[51]

To the rank and file, the third principle may have been the most important. With the possible exception of safety problems, which often were at least
partially created by the worker himself, the lack of assurance of a steady job
for any but the most senior workers was the greatest source of dissatisfaction
among railroad blue-collar employees. Through both the expansion and improvement of shops, and the creation of a system of long-range plans, bud-

gets, and reserves in the mechanical department, the B&O pledged to work toward the goal of steady employment of a full complement of shop workers. During 1924 the company diverted a substantial amount of heavy upgrading work on locomotives and cars from outside firms to its own shops; the wage component of the shifted work amounted to $347,303. The 1925 equipment maintenance budget provided for an even more substantial diversion to company shops; the 1925 wage component increase was to be $2,722,316, approximately an 8.5 percent wage pool increase over the prior year.[52]

The cost of this to the unions was relatively small. The Plan did require some time and effort of union officers at local, system, and national levels, but this was substantially offset by a reduction in union time spent on grievance cases. It was Bert Jewell's estimate that through 1925, the number of local grievance cases initiated by B&O shopmen dropped by more than 50 percent, while grievance appeal cases (those not settled on-site) dropped by 75 percent.[53] The only regular variable costs assignable to the program were Beyer's salary and expenses. These were not exorbitant: his 1924–1925 contract was for $9,000 per year, to be paid as monthly salary and expenses of $600 and $150, respectively. These sums were prorated among the six unions on the basis of membership, so the bulk of the expenses was carried by the carmen and the machinists, by far the largest of the six (the specific monthly breakdown was carmen, $341.86; machinists, $213.71; boilermakers, $68.37; electricians, $51.28; blacksmiths, $42.73; and sheetmetal workers, $32.05).[54] For the unions as well as for the company, the Plan's ratio of benefits to costs appears to have been fairly high.

That is not to say that those benefits were always clearly perceptible at the local level. In late spring and early summer of 1925, three incidents occurred that indicate that the expectations of B&O workers and the positions of B&O management regarding proper rewards accruing to the workers as the Plan developed may not have been precisely consistent.

The first of these incidents centered on the publication in the May 29 issue of *The Baltimore Federationist* (the local AFL paper) of an article by J. J. Tahaney, an assistant to the editor of the paper and a former carman at Mount Clare Shops. Run under the headline "COOPERATION PROVES B&O BACKSLIDER," it charged B&O management with failure to share the gains of the Cooperative Plan equitably. On June 3 George Emerson wrote to Bert Jewell of the company's surprise and displeasure over such a "mis-statement of facts," and requested that he express his opinion of the article and its contents. Jewell did so, in forceful fashion. He immediately wrote to the Baltimore Federation of Labor president, Henry F. Broening, stating that he "would very, very much appreciate it if the *Baltimore Federationist* would refrain as a part of the bona fide Labor movement, from opposing those activities being carried on by other parts of the bona fide Labor movement." The same day he fired off letters to the presidents of the six shopcrafts unions, calling the article "viciously misleading" and suggesting that they write to Broening as well; William Johnston, having heard of the matter directly, had done so already. With the reprimanding of Tahaney thus arranged, Jewell replied to Emerson that he regretted the unauthorized diatribe and that an investigation and corrective action were under way; B&O system federation president William McGee at the same time wrote to Willard apologizing for the "gratuitous piece of impertinence" and disavowing any connection between the article and System Federation No. 30. Willard and Emerson apparently accepted the union response, but Jewell continued to worry that "a rattle-brain or brainless meddler" had weakened a relationship that constituted "for the first time in history a very sound foundation upon which to conduct [contract] negotiations. . . ."[55]

The second incident arose in Philadelphia almost simultaneously with the Tahaney flap. The local shopcrafts federation there became upset with what they deemed to be the insufficiently militant posture of the system federation in contract negotiations with the company since the inception of the Cooperative Plan. On June 7 they adopted a resolution, later distributed as a memorandum to the system federation and the forty-four other local federations, charging that the former had "failed in their purpose, and seem to have substituted 'Cordial Relations' for 'Dollars and Cents. . . .'" AFL leadership, having received a copy of the memo, was not amused by this breach of fraternal solidarity any more than it had been by the Tahaney article. On July 29 Bert Jewell wrote to H. L. Alberty, the secretary of System Federation No. 30, telling him to get the troops in line: "This lack of respect for properly created authority, disregard of facts and stating of untruths, as well as indiscriminate circulating of circulars by Local Federations should be stopped by your Executive Board."[56] No more was heard from Philadelphia on the subject.

However, before this matter was settled, an even more serious controversy arose in Cumberland. In mid-July the B&O's motive power department decided to close the Cumberland heavy locomotive repair shop (the "back shop") for four days per month as a consequence of a traffic slump. The reduction in work hours came on very short notice, and only a few months after the workers had agreed to reduce their work week by a halfday to prevent junior men from being furloughed. Adding to the back shop employees' resentment was the fact that the other repair facilities at Cumberland were not cut back; comparatively junior men in the roundhouse, for example, continued to work a full six-day week, every week. A final irritant was the incompletely resolved issue of seniority rights for the 1922 strikebreakers. So in anger and frustration, the membership of the machinists' local decided to boycott the cooperative meetings. The machinists' committeeman was absent from the meeting of July 22, and the electricians' committeeman also stayed out as a gesture of sympathy. In explaining his absence to superintendent of shops John Howe in a letter dated July 23, IAM Lodge 212 president C. G. Watson complained that the company's action "takes away from us the only material consideration that we have received as a result of our efforts in the Cooperative movement." Back shop employees had done their best, he said, to make the B&O a more efficient and reliable carrier, "but when we ask for our share of the benefits that follow our joint efforts, the answer is—another vacation without pay." [57]

Watson's complaint was legitimate, but higher union officials, Jewell and Johnston specifically, were not about to see the Cooperative Plan jeopardized over a conflict that was basically a combination of insensitive management timing and local seniority grievances. IAM district general chairman C. N. Fullerton (later to become a B&O official in a subsequent new cooperative program) was dispatched immediately to Cumberland to attempt to calm the situation. He arrived in Cumberland at 2:30 A.M. on July 25, spent the later part of the morning at the shops talking with the machinists' committee and with Howe, and spent the afternoon and evening back at his hotel in conference with Watson, local federation president George Beisser, and union committee members. Fullerton's basic message was that both the seniority problems and the short-notice furlough problem were already being handled through regular negotiations at the system level, and that the local men should return to the cooperative meetings while their system and national officers took care of collective bargaining matters. Evidently he succeeded in calming the machinists, but he did not completely defuse the situation; by late August the boilermakers' union local had begun boycotting the cooperative meetings in protest over the seniority issue. Jewell and the boilermakers' national leadership were able to cajole the local into rejoining the meetings for thirty days, while system negotiations continued. To the relief of all parties a procedure for resolving the seniority issue was worked out in principle early in September, and the cooperative committee resumed its work without any apparent further unpleasantness.[58]

Such glitches must have been heartening to labor's left wing. From the beginning radical unionists had attacked the Plan as "class collaboration," traitorous and despicable. The official publications of both the Industrial Workers of the World and the Trade Union Education League had blasted the Plan as a sellout to the capitalists, doomed to end in manipulation and failure.[59] Incidents like the one at Cumberland lent credence to the leftist argument, undermining the positions of union moderates like Jewell and Johnston. AFL leaders moved swiftly and decisively in the Cumberland case so as to

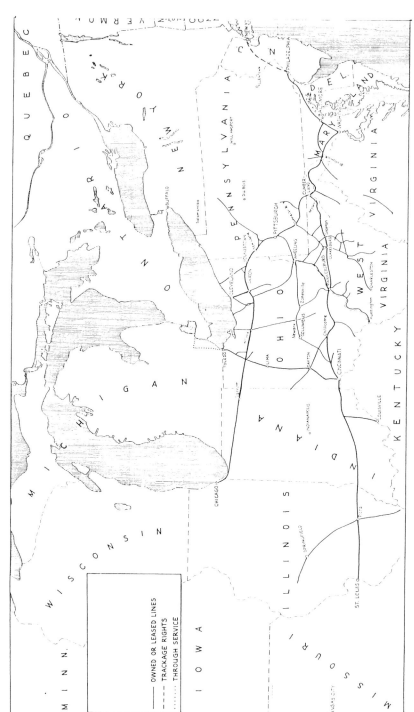

Baltimore & Ohio Railroad, 1925

shore up their positions within their own movements, not just as a gesture of goodwill toward Willard and his company.

Fortunately, such difficulties were rare, and leftist pressure probably backfired, strengthening the program instead of weakening it. Not only did it add to Jewell and Johnston's resolve to iron out problems on the union side, but also it reminded Daniel Willard and his staff that if the Plan failed and the moderates were subsequently overthrown, then the B&O could be dealing with a truly nasty element in the union movement.[60] It may be inferred that both sides thus took somewhat greater pains than they otherwise might have to ensure that the program and its meetings ran smoothly.

What were local cooperative committee meetings like? There are apparently no surviving firsthand narrative impressions of the early meetings, but the minutes of some of those meetings have been preserved. The local minutes were the official record of actions taken under the Cooperative Plan, and as such they were considered quite important; besides being kept in the shop offices, copies were sent to B&O central offices in Baltimore, to B&O regional offices (in Baltimore or Cincinnati, for eastern or western regions, respectively), to System Federation No. 30 (in Cincinnati), and to the local shopcrafts federation. The standard format of the minutes required the inclusion of place, date, and commencement and adjournment times of the meeting; management and employee attendees, with job titles; a summary list of all suggestions still before the committee at that meeting, indicating end-of-meeting status; and an item-by-item condensation of discussion of each suggestion. It may be possible, then, to capture something of the nature of these meetings from their minutes. To this end, the records of two reasonably typical local committees from the first quarter of 1925 will be examined here.

Ivorydale Shops, on the north side of Cincinnati, was a large (eight hundred to one thousand employees) facility with an active and well organized cooperative committee. The committee received 402 suggestions during its ten months of operation in 1924. By the first meeting of 1925, on Wednesday, January 7, only 62 of those items remained on the summary list, 52 unresolved and 10 to be reported as resolved at that meeting. The meeting was called to order at 1:00 P.M. in the office of the shop superintendent, F. L. Hall. Hall, five foremen (from the boiler, blacksmith, electrical, air brake, and car departments), and the storekeeper represented management; the local chairmen of the six participating unions represented the workers. Hall's secretary-stenographer took minutes.

The first item of discussion was the procurement of an emery polishing wheel for the new roundhouse, first recommended during the previous April, with amendments in August. Mr. T. H. Barker, the storekeeper, reported that he had requested and received the necessary specifications on the motor needed to rotate the wheel, and that the motor had been ordered. Second was the matter of repairs to the cracked and uneven floor of the boiler shop, dating from April and June. It was reported that the maintenance of way department had partially completed the project and was working on the remainder. Next came the final holdover suggestion from April, the construction of an employee locker room and washroom building. The structure itself was reported to be completed and ready to be opened as soon as the lockers were installed. In like manner the committee moved through the remaining forty-nine pending suggestions, concluding with the last one submitted in December: the acquisition of an air pump for testing generators in the electrical shop, referred to Paul Haaf (the air brake foreman) for action by his department.[61]

Then the committee moved to new business. Item one for the new year was the offering of personal thanks by Hall to all of the labor committeemen, and the men they represented, for the past year's cooperative efforts; his thanks were accepted. Item two was a request by those committeemen for the reinstatement of the previously mentioned time-and-a-half wage rate for Sundays and holidays. This topic was technically off limits to Cooperative Plan discussion, but Hall agreed to push the issue up the chain of command for further consideration. Item three was a suggestion by William Adams, the machinists' representative, that parts and materials from the stripping of locomotives be organized and placed in specified locations, instead of being "allowed to lay around in the shop." The suggestion was adopted, with appropriate instructions to be passed along to the proper foremen and workers. So it went through the thirteenth and last new suggestion, the repair of a drain at the crew dispatcher's office. Called to the attention of the committee by J. L. Denham, the boilermakers' representative, the matter was referred to the maintenance of way department for their action. The meeting adjourned at 2:45 P.M.[62]

The next four meetings were similar, but not exactly the same. They all began at 1:00 P.M. on Wednesday in the shop superintendent's office, but they grew progressively longer; the March 4 meeting lasted until 3:30. There were some shifts in the makeup of the group in attendance. Hall, Barker, and H. Hill, the car foreman, were the only management people to attend all five meetings. Five of the six union people attended all five meetings; R. Bauman replaced H. Grothaus in the carmen's seat after the January 21 meeting. One-time management attendees were a general foreman, an enginehouse foreman, the general boiler foreman, and a shop inspector from Baltimore, while the only single appearance from the union side was by a laborer named G. Townsend; generally, it appears that such attendees went simply to offer or to respond to particular suggestions. Management-to-labor composition of the group varied little: the ratio was seven to six for the first three meetings of the year, then six to six for the fourth, and seven to seven for the fifth.[63]

Likewise, there were at most moderate variations in the agenda. The January 21 meeting devoted considerable time to a discussion of federal defects (deviations from Interstate Commerce Commission maintenance standards) among locomotives serviced at Ivorydale, in response to a systemwide circular directive from Baltimore. The February 18 meeting included a complaint by Denham to Hall about the recent decision by the foreman at the old roundhouse not to allow mechanics to leave the building for materials under any circumstances. Denham considered the foreman's insistence that all materials be obtained by helpers excessively restrictive and occasionally counterproductive, as in cases where materials selection required the mechanic's judgment; Hall concurred, and word was sent for the foreman to modify his rule. Otherwise, the agendas were composed largely of items regarding facilities and equipment repair, capital improvements to buildings and equipment, and materials handling.[64]

Of the fifty-two items on the January 7 pending list, twenty-one remained on March 4; of the thirty-one items resolved, twenty-eight had been implemented, and only three had been dropped as either impracticable or unnecessary on further investigation. Of the eight specific January 7 agenda items mentioned, seven had been resolved by the end of the March 4 meeting. Hall's thanking of the union men was not, one would hope, a debatable suggestion, so it was cleared at the January 7 meeting. Repair of the boiler shop floor and construction of the locker and wash building were reported to be complete and were cleared from the pending list at the January 21 meeting. At the February 4 meeting, it was reported that the air pump had been installed in the electrical department, and that procedures had been worked out for the storage of parts and materials from the stripping of locomotives. The new roundhouse emery wheel finally was reported to be operational at the February 18 meeting, and on March 4, the matter of repairs to the drain in the crew dispatcher's office was dropped. The issue of Sunday and holiday overtime pay was still under advisement at higher levels; it was not resolved until the suggestion was approved systemwide in the shopcrafts' contract of 1926.[65]

Ivorydale was typical of the larger B&O shops; reasonably typical of smaller (one hundred to two hundred employees) installations was Flora, Illinois, on the St. Louis main line. Flora Shops was not large enough to have a superintendent or even a master mechanic; the highest ranking official was general foreman T. A. Dodson. Meetings followed the same prescribed format as was followed at Ivorydale, but discussions tended to be less hurried and less formal, and minutes were less professionally kept. The minutes of the January 7, 1925, meeting indicate that nineteen suggestions from 1924 were still before the committee, but there is no indication of total 1924 submissions. That meeting's summary list contained forty-six items: the nineteen unresolved holdovers, twelve holdovers to be reported as resolved, and fifteen new suggestions. The meeting, as was standard, began at 1:00 P.M. in the geneal foreman's office. Dodson, the storekeeper, and the enginehouse foreman represented management; the unions were represented by a machinist, a machinist's helper, a boilermaker, a boilermaker's helper, an electrician, and a blacksmith. The minutes taker did not identify himself.[66]

The discussion of holdover suggestions was not recorded; those suggestions were simply listed along with a summary of actions taken. The first item on the list was the purchase of an electric motor for the roundhouse turntable, submitted in August; that proposal had been sent up the chain of command for funding approval. Second was a request for repair of the fence around the property, submitted in September; that matter had been referred to the division engineering office for action. Next was an October suggestion that a partition be built between the boiler room and the machine shop; this too had been referred to division engineering. Of the sixteen remaining unresolved holdovers, the last was the December request for the purchase of a supply of twenty-four-inch Stilson wrenches, a matter being pursued by the stores department.[67]

The first new suggestion of 1925 was the proposal by enginehouse foreman H. L. Herrin to connect shop and roundhouse downspouts to the sewer system, reducing the problem of standing water around the buildings after heavy rains. This was referred to the division engineering office. The second new item was the suggestion by machinist J. F. Grabill that machinists' helpers who had been assigned lockers should share them with more recently hired helpers who had none. This proposal was adopted, with instructions to the machine shop foreman to make the necessary arrangements. Item three was another suggestion by Grabill, that form 2311 material cards be cut down in size to reduce paper costs. The idea was referred to the division master mechanic's office for consideration. The discussion continued, as Grabill made five more suggestions, followed by five from E. Williams, the electrician, and one made on behalf of absent carman L. J. Burrows. The final item came from machinist's helper C. A. George, who was of the opinion that the machine shop first aid cabinet should be moved to a cleaner location. The committee concurred, and the order was given that the cabinet be moved to the tool room the next day. Its business completed, the meeting was adjourned at 3:00 P.M.[68]

Subsequent meetings that winter were similar with respect to meeting time, place, length, and format; the composition of the committee, however, varied greatly. First, Dodson was unexplainedly absent from the shop for three meetings, possibly because of a temporary transfer; he was replaced for those meetings by the acting general foreman, G. W. Bultman. At none of the first five meetings of 1925 was exactly the same management group present. L. S. Steen, the storekeeper, attended twice, and four different foremen made either one or two appearances. On the labor side Grabill, George, and blacksmith S. H. Montgomery attended all five meetings. Williams attended four of the five meetings; no other electrician sat in for him at the one that he missed. The boilermakers' seat was occupied by three different men. The carmen's seat was vacant at the first meeting, then occupied by two different men for the next four. There was no sheet metal shop at Flora at that time, so the sixth (or seventh, eighth, or ninth) labor seats were occupied by various pipe fitters, helpers, laborers, and whoever else had an idea to present to the committee. The management-to-labor ratio of the group varied accordingly: three to six for the first meeting, then two to six, three to eight, two to nine, and two to nine again for the meeting on March 4.[69]

The nature of the agenda was fairly stable over the five meetings. The items before the committee focused predominantly upon procurement of materials, equipment and building repair, and purchase or location of tools and machinery. The discussion of federal locomotive defects at the meeting on January 21 was much briefer than that at Ivorydale: Bultman handled the matter as a short end-of-meeting blueprint-aided lecture. The only other notable deviation from the normal discussion of suggestions was a short speech by Dodson at the close of the March 4 meeting, his first session back in the committee chair after his absence. The minutes record the opening of his commentary as follows (the writing mechanics are those of the original typist):

> Well Boys I am glad to see you all living up to the instructions we received in a letter shorttime ago in attending these meeting in a neat and tidy condition. I had the pleasure of attending a meeting a short time ago and three men came to the meeting with overalls that should have been washed at least four or five months ago and I am glad to say that the Chairman of that meeting called them down strong and this probably will not happen again. I want to thank you boys for the living up to these instructions as issued.

He then spoke at similar length about his concern over recent accidents and injuries in the shop, and of the need for all employees to solicit every bit of business possible for the B&O.[70]

Of the nineteen items on Flora's January 7 pending list, all had been resolved by the start of the March 4 meeting: sixteen had been implemented, and three dropped. Even more impressively, none of the fifteen new suggestions introduced at the January 7 meeting were still on the pending list on March 4, twelve having been implemented and three having been dropped.

The eight proposals discussed individually above were resolved in the following fashion. The matter of moving the machine shop first aid cabinet was reported to be accomplished as ordered at the January 21 meeting. The locker-sharing proposal was reported to be worked out at that same session, although a laborer named C. L. Boyd suggested later in the meeting that new lockers be purchased to eliminate the need for sharing; that second-round proposal was referred to higher officials, who gave their consent before the meeting of March 4. Higher officials in the engineering department apparently raised serious questions about the building of a partition between the boiler room and the machine shop, as this idea was dropped by the committee on February 18. At its next meeting, the committee decided to drop its endorsement of a smaller material card, presumably because of discouraging word from higher places. Also on March 4, it was announced that unnamed higher officials had rejected explicitly the committee's request for purchase of an electric motor for the turntable. On the positive side, that same day both the perimeter fence repair project and the downspout-sewer connection project were officially listed as having been completed, and the Stilson wrenches were reported to have been delivered to the tool room.[71]

It was all such mundane stuff, but the Cooperative Plan to one degree or another was doing that which it was supposed to do. As a consequence, it was not long before the program began to spread, both to other departments of the Baltimore & Ohio and to other railroads.

The first application of the Plan beyond the B&O was restricted, half-hearted, and not very successful. In July 1924, at the behest of Beyer and Johnston, the management of the Chesapeake & Ohio (C&O) signed an agreement with shopcrafts System Federation No. 41 to establish a cooperative program in C&O equipment maintenance facilities. A pilot committee was formed at the company's Seventeenth Street Shops in Richmond, Virginia, and meetings were begun. C&O management soon lost interest in the program, however, and it was never extended beyond Richmond. The Seventeenth Street committee, for lack of corporate support, became less and less active, and it eventually disappeared.[72]

Later that year a much more successful effort was begun to set up a cooperative program elsewhere in the industry. On November 21 the Canadian National Railways (CNR) announced that the "B&O Plan," as it was by then widely called, would be put into effect in its shops. Discussions between Beyer and Johnston and the railroad's president, Sir Henry Worth Thornton, had been going on for several months; the November announcement capped those discussions and specified the pilot program location to be the shops at Moncton, New Brunswick. The first cooperative meeting at Moncton was held in January 1925. The CNR was a much larger and less unified property than the B&O, so the Plan was extended across the system relatively slowly. By September 1925, roughly one-third of Canadian National shop employees were covered by the Plan, but the last of them were not brought into the program until near the end of the decade. The CNR's most important American subsidiary, the Grand Trunk Western, had its cooperative committees organized by Beyer in 1926. Regional and corporate level committees were established in 1926 and 1927.[73]

The next carrier to embrace the B&O Plan was the Chicago & North Western (C&NW). The first discussion of union-management cooperation on the C&NW actually took place in the fall of 1922, between Bert Jewell and personnel vice president William Walliser, but it was not until March 6, 1925, that a program agreement was signed. Later that month Beyer was at the C&NW shops in Clinton, Iowa, to organize a pilot program. The Clinton cooperative committee held its first meeting in April; a year later, the program had been extended to all (approximately thirty) of the company's locomotive and car repair facilities.[74]

The last railroad to adopt the Plan was the Chicago, Milwaukee, St. Paul & Pacific. In February 1924 a locally sanctioned "mutual welfare committee" began meeting at the Milwaukee Road's shops in Deer Lodge, Montana, following the pattern that had been established at Glenwood on the B&O. It was not formally endorsed by top management, however, and for a time it was not replicated elsewhere. Then in 1925 the company was forced into receivership. Their financial straits having made them receptive to help from anywhere, Milwaukee Road executives sat down with shopcrafts union officers in August 1926 to discuss setting up a cooperative program. A formal agreement was signed on November 29, and committees began functioning early in 1927.[75]

Then the B&O Plan spread no further, at least among the railroads.[76] Whether for reasons of ideology, or threat to management power and perquisites, or perceived lack of necessity, no other railroad in that era was to adopt it.

During this time, however, the Cooperative Plan had been expanded within the B&O itself. The success of the Plan had become apparent to operating officials outside the mechanical department well before the end of 1924, and many of them had an interest in reaping some of the benefits of cooperation in their own departments. Labor participation in the open Monday morning divisional staff meetings had been waning; the more structured, union-sanctioned Plan appeared to be just the thing to rekindle employee enthusiasm. So the approval of the appropriate unions was sought, and a cooperative plan in the conducting transportation (CT) and maintenance of way (MW) departments began to take shape. On January 8, 1925, B&O eastern lines general manager E. W. Scheer sent a letter to his subordinates directing them to arrange monthly divisional cooperative meetings for train service, roadway maintenance, and associated support personnel "effective at once." B&O western lines management soon followed suit.[77]

The CT and MW version of the Plan was considerably less tightly organized than the original, for at least two reasons. First, it required the participation not of six unions but of nine, only five of which were tied to the AFL: the Train Dispatchers, the Telegraphers, the Signalmen, the Clerks, and the Maintenance of Way Employees unions were members of the AFL, but the train and engine crew brotherhoods (Engineers, Firemen, Conductors, and Trainmen) were independent. None of them had the passionate interest in cooperation of William Johnston's IAM. Second, and more importantly, the planning and supervision of the new program on the management side were incomplete, diffuse, and generally ad hoc. Otto Beyer—not Daniel Willard or Charley Galloway or E. W. Scheer—had worked out the details of the original plan, and Beyer was spending most of his time setting up cooperative committees in Canada. Thus there really was no strong, consistent force for standardization at the local level.

Still, it was a well intentioned effort by B&O management, and the program did function, however imperfectly and inconsistently. Each division was free to set up its own committee substantially as it saw fit, as long as it was within the spirit of the original plan. On the Charleston Division, initial cooperative committee bylaws called for the transportation and maintenance of way departments to meet separately. The Charleston CT committee was composed of the superintendent and his immediate subordinates, representatives of the company police and accounting departments, and representatives of the seven transportation service classifications: agents and station employees, brakemen, conductors, engineers, firemen, yardmasters and yard clerks, and dispatchers and operators. Each committee member or his alternate was entitled to bring one other employee, regardless of rank or department, to meetings as a guest. Potential attendance thus might be well over twenty. The chairmanship was to be rotated every other meeting, with the outgoing chairman replaced by the vice chairman elected from among the members two meetings earlier. Meetings were to be held at 8:00 P.M. on the first Monday and the first Tuesday, alternately, of successive months; meeting locations likewise would alternate between the crew bases of Weston and Gassaway, West Virginia. Business at meetings was to proceed in regular order: roll call, approval of minutes, unfinished business of the whole committee, reports and unfinished business of suggestion subcommittees, introduction and referral of new suggestions to suggestion subcommittees, review of pertinent industry data and papers, other matters of instruction or entertainment, and "open discussion of subjects pertinent to the transportation industry and good fellow-ship of employees.'' They hoped to adjourn by 10:00 P.M.[78]

The more common pattern was for CT and MW departments to meet in a single committee. With maintenance of way employees and managers added, divisional cooperative committee meeting attendance often exceeded forty. Such size could be unwieldy; when the Charleston Division adopted the single committee approach, its use of subcommittees for preliminary evaluation of suggestions surely became even more helpful than it had been initially.

Despite any unwieldiness, the committees did produce useful sugges-tions. Transportation department members contributed ideas in a wide variety of areas pertaining to train operation, including condition of cars and motive power, purchase and conservation of supplies, fuel economy, delay reduction, smooth train handling, condition and placement of signals and lights, track conditions, on-line communication, interline coordination of operations, and adequacy of freight and passenger facilities. Among the most successful in-stances of cooperative committee proposals from the CT side were the sugges-tion of a Chicago Division engineer that cylinder cock levers in locomotive cabs be moved to a less obtrusive location, where they did not obstruct the engineer's seat box, and the suggestion of a Toledo Division engineer that the hazards of road engines backing up at night be reduced by mounting a small headlight on the rear of the tender. Both proposals were tried, accepted, and made standard over the entire system. Maintenance of way employees partici-pated less actively, possibly as a result of the generally lower educational lev-els and organizational status that prevailed among track workers. They did make contributions, however, mostly in the areas of tool needs and materials economy.[79] So, although the reasonable assessment is that the Cooperative Plan as applied in the transportation and maintenance of way departments was less resoundingly successful than it was in the mechanical department, it still could be termed a success.

The success of the Cooperative Plan was not kept secret by the B&O or by the railroads that followed its lead. Although the Plan was not really at the forefront of public discussion during the period following its introduction, it did attract a decent amount of attention across the country. That attention was mostly quite favorable. There were some muted mumblings about Bolshevism from the Right and some rantings about class betrayal from the Left, but main-stream commentary on the Plan viewed it as a very promising development.

The main reason for this assessment surely lies in the virtue of the Plan itself: it was an open-minded, reasonable, and carefully executed effort to reconcile two legitimate but often opposing sets of interests. Virtue was helped along, however, by the publicity efforts of the principal architects of the Plan, especially Otto Beyer. Whenever anyone in the press showed interest in the matter of union-management cooperation, Beyer apparently was eager to tell the story. In some cases, editors were willing to let Beyer tell the story directly: during the program's first four years, articles by Beyer appeared in *Railway Age*, *The Survey*, *The American Federationist*, and *The New Republic*.[80] Willard and Johnston did not maintain quite so high a profile, but they did their parts. Each wrote a sizable article for *Railway Age*, and Willard made at least two major speeches on the subject to outside groups (to an assembly of labor magazine editors—"the first railroad president in captivity" to do so—and to the National Civic Federation).[81]

Certainly not all of the Plan's favorable publicity was self-generated. A variety of periodicals published positive articles on the subject, authored by in-house staff or independent writers. Francis Westbrook in *Outlook*, George Soule in *The Independent*, and Whiting Williams in *Collier's* all wrote of the Plan in laudatory terms. *The Nation* reported on the Plan supportively. Publications of moderate to liberal inclination generally viewed the mutual efforts of the AFL and the B&O with clear approval, and they gave the Plan a fair amount of play.[82]

The matter was of particular interest to professional engineering and management groups; as might be expected, they played an active role in noting, studying, and publicizing the Plan. At the center of these groups was the Taylor Society, named for the master of the speedup, Frederick Taylor, but by the mid-1920s the home of a more sensitive breed of scientific management proponent. Taylor Society members saw in the Plan and its offspring a means to reconcile scientific management's traditional focus on production efficiency with organized labor's concern for the needs of workers. Like Willard, they regarded union-management cooperative programs as a means to satisfy both sets of concerns simultaneously.[83] Accordingly, in February 1926 they devoted an entire meeting to a discussion of such programs. Beyer (himself a member of the society), Jewell, and Sir Henry Thornton of the Canadian National were the principal speakers. The conference, held jointly with the Metropolitan Section of the American Society of Mechanical Engineers, was very well attended and widely publicized. A transcript of the main addresses was published in the Taylor Society's *Bulletin*, and excerpts were reprinted in *Railway Age*.[84]

To reiterate a preceding summary point, then, the B&O Cooperative Plan was no secret. Indeed, by the time the Plan was four years old, an educated manager would have had to be living under a rock not to have heard of it.

If there was any time at which the Japanese might have taken note of the Plan, then it almost surely was this time. Even though they evidently did little with the idea for a generation, they certainly had an interest in such matters in general, and the opportunity to be informed about the Plan in particular. During the teens and twenties the Japanese were keen students and thorough practitioners of scientific management, especially on the government-owned railway system. Officials of that system monitored the progress of scientific management approaches and techniques in American railroad shops very closely. *Railway Age* apparently was read by more than a few, and no doubt someone at the Ministry of Railways received the *Bulletin of the Taylor Society*. Another possible conduit, albeit probably less credible than professional publications, was the scientific management consultant Harrington Emerson. He and his family, having lived in Japan early in the century, had numerous contacts and investments in various Japanese firms, including some in the transportation industry. Later in the 1920s, he made two professional speaking tours of Japan. In 1928 he tried to hustle a consulting contract from the Ministry of Railways, bragging about his role as past consultant and continuing "counselor" to the B&O. All of this, of course, is circumstantial evidence; there is no known proof of the transmission of the Cooperative Plan or its ideas directly to Japan. Still, the possibility remains intriguing.[85]

However, there is clear evidence of the transmission of the Plan, in the wake of its publicity, to a few American firms outside the railroad industry. One subsequent program was established across a group of Philadelphia hosiery manufacturers in 1927, but it was not so fully developed as another scheme begun that same year: that of the Naumkeag Steam Cotton Company of Salem, Massachusetts: the Pequot Mills program. Early in 1927, with both the company and its unionized workers under increasing economic pressure from southern competition, the "B&O Plan" was chosen as the model for a cooperative program to improve Naumkeag's operating efficiency. In return for stabilized employment, good working conditions, and wages deemed fair by local standards, members of the AFL United Textile Workers participated actively in production time studies and methods improvements, in plant layout changes, and in product sales efforts. The Naumkeag program worked quite well, until, like all other major American cooperative programs but the B&O's, it was weakened and finally destroyed by the wage and employment cuts of the Great Depression.[86]

At this point, one might ask explicitly a question brushed over previously: if the Cooperative Plan was so successful and so well publicized, why did so few companies adopt it? The answer cannot lie exclusively in industry characteristics or in a firm's position within its industry. Too many firms in too many industries held competitive positions similar to that of the B&O (or Canadian National, or Naumkeag) yet did not sit down with organized labor to work out such a program. Without stretching an argument, the most that can be said about economic determinants is that some amount of competitive pressure was a necessary condition for cooperation, but certainly not a sufficient one. Some firms probably shunned cooperation because they were already making handsome returns on their investment, and attempting to work in concert with the unions simply was not worth the bother. But other, weaker firms shunned cooperation when it probably *was* worth the bother. Why?

The answer must have something to do with personal character—the character of the individuals of power or influence on both sides of the management-labor divide. This, it may be argued, was the second and decisive determinant: that the leaders of both the company's management and the unions representing its workers be persuasive people of wisdom and broad vision, able to see beyond their own short-run self-interest, and of resolute commitment to do the right thing. Daniel Willard, William Johnston, and Bert Jewell were such people. But to find such people in control on opposite sides of a bargaining table was as rare then as it is today.

How much were firms that ignored the Cooperative Plan really missing? Just how successful was the Plan? As the B&O program settled into a steady routine, contemporary assessments of its results continued to be very positive. Cornell University economics professor Sumner Slichter, after having spent seven days late in the summer of 1926 observing cooperative committees and talking to workers and supervisors in Pittsburgh and Cumberland, judged the Plan to be very effective. Employee satisfaction was up, shop output was up, and quality of workmanship was much improved over pre-Plan levels. A steady stream of suggestions was reaching the cooperative committees, and the acceptance rate was very high.[87] Aggregate measures of the volume of useful new ideas generated by the Plan were quite impressive. Willard reported early in 1927 that through the end of 1926, roughly 18,000 suggestions had been submitted in the shop program alone. Of those submissions, approximately 15,400 had been accepted and implemented. Roughly 500 were still under investigation, and 2,100 had been rejected, 500 by management as too expensive and 1,600 by the committees as impractical. The overall acceptance rate was approximately 86 percent.[88]

Accurate and comprehensive quantitative measures of the impact of those suggestions were not developed at the time, and they are virtually impossible to develop from surviving data now. Viewing the issue in narrow terms, it is interesting to note that in 1925, the percentage of B&O locomotives required after federal inspection to be withdrawn from service for repairs was 4.0 percent, whereas the corresponding percentage for the B&O's most important competitor, the vigorously anticooperation Pennsylvania Railroad, was 8.4 percent. Moreover, the B&O's advantage with respect to this criterion increased as the decade passed.[89] Clearly, B&O shops under the Plan gained a quality advantage over those of the PRR. As indicative of the Plan's success as that result is, though, it is only one measure of the achievements of half of the program in one department. It is not the desired comprehensive indicator.

Of course, the ultimate comprehensive indicator is "the bottom line." What was happening to the profitability of the Baltimore & Ohio Railroad Company during this period? The impact of the Cooperative Plan upon corporate net income cannot be isolated precisely, as the B&O was taking other steps at the time to improve its performance. Willard was continuing his program of physical upgrading of the property; the B&O's net investment in transportation property and equipment increased by 13 percent from the beginning of 1923 to the end of 1926. However, competing carriers were doing the same thing: the corresponding figure for the Pennsylvania was 17 percent.[90] Indeed, it is defensible to declare that everything that the B&O was doing during the period to improve itself was matched or exceeded by its competition, except the Cooperative Plan. That alone was distinctive. If that is true, then a great portion of any relative improvement in the B&O's profitability may be attributed to the Plan. There was such improvement—marked improvement.

Beyer was fond of citing the B&O's absolute revenue and profit figures, but that approach was not very sophisticated: such numbers reveal little here. B&O corporate net income took a huge jump upward in 1923, from $2 million to $20 million,[91] but 1923 was a year of general industrial recovery and economic expansion, and the B&O's overleveraged balance sheet greatly amplified fluctuations in net railway operating income. If return on equity—the ratio of net income to the common shareholders' investment in the firm—is used as the profit measure, the same distortions may remain. With the use of such a ratio, however, absolute profit figures are adjusted for size of the firm, and comparisons between firms in an industry become possible. As general economic forces usually affect firms in a given industry and in a particular region more or less equally, we thus have a means of looking past the impact of those forces. Figure 2-1, then, is informative. B&O shareholders would have been gratified to see it showing B&O return on equity well below that of the Pennsylvania before the Glenwood experiment, jumping to half again that of the PRR in 1923, and holding an advantage as the Cooperative Plan went into full operation, despite the economic slowdown of 1924 and 1925. Figure 2-1 is not the most accurately revealing one, though, as it still reflects the exaggerating influence of financial leverage.

The way to remove the impact of the B&O's excessive debt is to use a net income figure computed before the deduction of interest charges, and to avoid any ratio that uses the B&O's relatively small equity base. Net railway operating income measures the earning power of the railroad, not the company; as

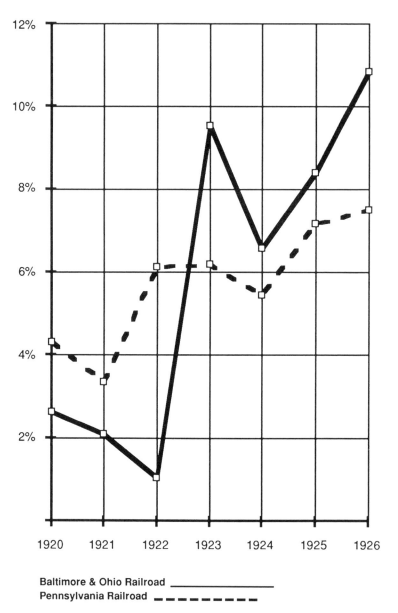

Baltimore & Ohio Railroad _____
Pennsylvania Railroad ▬ ▬ ▬ ▬ ▬ ▬ ▬ ▬ ▬

Figure 2-1 Return on Common Equity

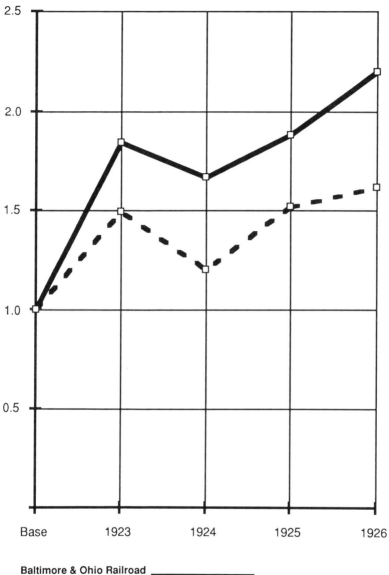

Baltimore & Ohio Railroad ─────────────
Pennsylvania Railroad ▬ ▬ ▬ ▬ ▬ ▬ ▬ ▬ ▬ ▬

Figure 2-2 Net Railway Operating Income—Index Numbers
(Base = 1921–22 average)

such, it is a proper numerator for measuring the effect of a change in the railroad. A proper denominator is again net railway operating income, but from some base period before the change in question. The result, with reference to the B&O and PRR during the first four years of the Cooperative Plan, is figure 2-2, indexed net railway operating income. It shows clearly that the Baltimore & Ohio improved the net efficiency of its railroad more than did the Pennsylvania after the base period 1921–1922. If they saw such a graph, B&O shareholders no doubt were quite pleased, as were Daniel Willard, William Johnston, and Otto Beyer.

3

THE COOPERATIVE PLAN CONTINUES

During the late 1920s, the B&O was rolling. As the company began its second century, its reputation and its people's morale were at their highest levels ever. Willard's way of doing things had taken deep root; the corporate culture that he had nurtured was triumphant.

However, it is part of the folk wisdom of management that the most dangerous time in a company's life is when everything is going well. To a degree this was true of the B&O in its golden era. Some things that had given rise to its success were ever so slightly neglected. The Cooperative Plan was foremost among these; a hint of lassitude, between both management and labor, crept into the program. Still, its strength was sufficient to ensure that when the first wave of the Depression hit, there was no falling out between company and unions. The B&O family was first just a little smug about its success, then strained somewhat by the evaporation of its financial fortitude, but it stayed a family.

This chapter looks at a variety of incidents, activities, and trends that marked this transitional period. The response of the B&O's main competitor to the achievements of the Plan, summaries of what was going on with respect to the B&O's other progressive measures (principally welfare-related activities and employment of women), and factors pertaining to the weakening of Cooperative Plan momentum are presented and discussed. The onset of the Depression, the subsequent state of union-management relations on the B&O, and the actions of Willard the statesman and strategist are reviewed. The picture painted is that of a company and its leader trying to maintain their integrity on the slide from good times to hard times.

If the preceding chapter's assessment of the impact of the Cooperative Plan upon the profitability of the Baltimore & Ohio is essentially correct, then it would have been arguably stupid of the Pennsylvania not to attempt something similar. General Atterbury and his management team were not known to be stupid. So, on November 1, 1927, the Pennsylvania Railroad established a Bureau of New Ideas. Its purpose was to achieve the same employee-stimulated productivity gains that its predecessor had. Still, the PRR's Bureau of New Ideas (BNI) was no clone of the B&O's Cooperative Plan. In both their methods and the scope of their goals, the two programs had differences, and those differences were an excellent reflection of differences in the two companies' corporate cultures.

Differences in corporate cultures are of course a function of the values of the people at the top of corporate hierarchies; that is a central premise of this book. The Cooperative Plan and the Bureau of New Ideas were not exactly the same because Daniel Willard and W. W. Atterbury did not believe exactly the same things with exactly the same degrees of relative fervor. But that is not to say that overall corporate context is unimportant. A company's history and circumstances do influence corporate values and behavior; indeed, they may be seen as fundamental, insofar as they can frame the selection of a leader, and then further shape the values of that leader once he is in place. In other words, Willard and Atterbury cannot be fully understood without reference to the history and circumstances of the B&O and the PRR.

The single most important factor in this regard was the dominance of the Pennsylvania. For five decades, there had been four railroads which upon their own tracks or those of subsidiaries ran from the industrialized East Coast to Chicago, or to Chicago and St. Louis: the Pennsylvania, the New York Central, the Baltimore & Ohio, and the Erie (not counting more recent interline routes, such as Lackawanna/Nickel Plate or Western Maryland/Pittsburgh & West Virginia/Wheeling & Lake Erie/Nickel Plate). By the mid-1920s, it had been long established that by most measures of competitive strength, the four roads could be listed in that order. The mighty Pennsy—"The Standard Railroad of the World"—was first, followed closely by NYC. The B&O was a not-so-close third, and the Erie was hopelessly out of the running in fourth place.

The B&O ran third for both geographic and historical reasons. The railroad was created by the citizens of Baltimore to maintain the competitive position of that city as a port for seaborne goods moving to and from regions inland; consequently, its main lines extended most directly from Baltimore, at the southern end of the Middle Atlantic region. That would not have posed any problem for the B&O had the Port of Baltimore achieved primacy among eastern ports; that distinction, unfortunately by a wide margin, belonged to New York City. Compounding the problem was the fact that the B&O was undercapitalized and subject to adverse political forces during its formative years; the results were many instances of suboptimal line location and engineering decisions.[1] At their worst these circumstances led to the receivership and subsequent period of Pennsylvania control discussed in chapter 1.

At their best they left the B&O with a heavy debt load and less than ideal geographic positioning, and the latter factor made it difficult to do much about the former. In 1927 the B&O served almost exactly the same major markets as did the Pennsylvania, but with few exceptions it did so in comparatively difficult fashion. The top market in the region was New York–Chicago. The B&O's route in that market began on the west side of the Hudson at Jersey City, ran over the lines of partially owned connecting roads (the Central of New Jersey and the Reading) to Philadelphia, then proceeded southwest to Baltimore and Washington before turning northwest toward Chicago. The route was 88 miles longer than that of the PRR. Less striking disadvantages characterized other important B&O routes; of the twenty-seven largest long-haul (over 250 miles) city-pair markets served by the B&O, PRR lines were shorter in eighteen instances.[2] In addition, the B&O's two main lines crossed the Allegheny Mountains on grades that were generally longer and steeper than those of its rival. On the New York–Chicago route, B&O trains had to climb 7,187 feet and 6,593 feet westbound and eastbound, respectively; the corresponding numbers for the PRR were 6,431 and 5,881 feet.[3]

The B&O, then, was a relatively expensive property to operate. It had to have employee productivity higher than that of the PRR just to prevent its operating costs from seriously exceeding those of its competition. Knowing this to be true should have encouraged a certain humility and sense of mutual dependence with respect to their employees among B&O managers. Such a company was a perfect setting for a man like Daniel Willard. The Pennsylvania, on the other hand, was subject to little pressure of that sort. With lower costs and the higher market share, it could afford a small measure of arrogance in dealing with its employees. Such a company was a perfect setting for a man like General W. W. Atterbury.

Atterbury was the embodiment of the Pennsylvania Railroad ethos: supremely self-confident, rigidly authoritarian, and aggressively antiunion. To the extent that he dealt with lower-level employees, he did so on his turf and on his terms. The AFL shopcrafts unions had been virtually run off the property in 1922, leaving in their place company-sponsored adjustment boards. The adjustment board structure, established in 1920, was a three-tier system of employee-management committees whose function was to serve as a hierarchy of tribunals for resolving wage, work rules, and discipline disputes. The company referred to this program somewhat grandly as its Employee Representation Plan. Pennsylvania management contended that the arrangement provided legitimate representation of employee interests, but the Railroad Labor Board thought differently: "While professing its acceptance and observance of the principle of employee representation, [the Pennsylvania Railroad] has set up a system which throttles the majority and establishes the representation of a coerced and subservient minority proven originally to amount to about 10½% of [shopcraft] employees."[4] Most people in the labor movement considered it to be a management-dominated sham, but the company insisted that it was "a system of collective bargaining within our own ranks."[5] Atterbury maintained that his employees did not want any unions and that his adjustment boards certainly were not "company unions": "We claim that what we have set up is a machinery of contract and adjustment, mutually established by our employees and management, and that this machinery is correctly described by the name we have given it, 'Employee Representation.' No one has to join anything to take part in it. Therefore it cannot be a union of any kind, or a system of unions. It is merely a working plan to adjust differences, and nothing more."[6] Whatever they were, they helped Atterbury to prevent the AFL unions from winning representation elections. Not until 1934, in response to labor legislation designed to eliminate company unions, did the PRR sign an agreement with a national shopcrafts labor organization—and then with an "independent" brotherhood, not the AFL.[7]

It should not come as a surprise, then, that Atterbury did not set up the Bureau of New Ideas with the consultation and aid of William Johnston and Otto Beyer. The PRR suggestion program was strictly in-house, centralized, and management-dominated. The program's purpose was narrow and specific: improvement of service and efficiency. There was no talk of building company spirit or sense of family. There were to be no joint labor-management committees nor any sort of evaluation of suggestions out on the divisions. The poster announcing the program on company bulletin boards told employees to send their ideas to assistant personnel vice president R. V. Massey at company headquarters in Broad Street Station, Philadelphia, where the proposals would be evaluated "by persons competent to pass judgment." The originators of adopted proposals were to be "accorded due recognition"; it was soon established that this usually meant cash awards, with additional cash prizes—one hundred dollars, fifty dollars, and twenty-five dollars, respectively, for the best, second best, and third best ideas—given every six months.[8] It was all neatly and impersonally bureaucratic, backed up by a few cold, hard dollars. The contrast with the B&O's approach, with its face-to-face local discussions and generalized, sometimes intangible rewards, is striking. In a microcosm, the differences between the Bureau of New Ideas and the Cooperative Plan are the essential corporate culture differences between Atterbury's Pennsylvania and Willard's Baltimore & Ohio.

One of the more revealing aspects of the PRR's different approach was its insistence upon channeling all suggestions through headquarters, and especially its rationale for doing so. The names of all suggestion submitters thus could be held in confidence within the BNI office, away from local or divisional officers who might be involved in evaluating the suggestions of their subordinates. This, according to the company, accomplished two things. First, they said, it "avoids any possible embarrassment to an employee submitting a suggestion that is found impracticable." Second, it protected the employee from any reprisals that might be prompted by questioning the wisdom of the boss; as an official company source diplomatically told *Railway Age*, "Many employees, who might hesitate to submit a suggestion to their immediate superiors, will deal with the Bureau since the name of the author is not revealed even to those officers to whom a copy of the suggestion is sent for consideration."[9] A third and unspoken reason surely was that it ensured tight central control of the whole process. If warmth and trust are definitive qualities of a family, then the PRR was not much of a family, and the Bureau of New Ideas was not set up to help the company become one.

All of this is not to say that the bureau was a failure. Atterbury was not so much interested in such fuzzy notions of company family as was Willard, so he could not have been much concerned that the BNI was of little help in that regard. It did elicit employee suggestions, and many of those suggestions were adopted. That was what PRR management wanted it to do, so it must be considered to some degree successful.

But how successful was it, particularly in comparison to the Cooperative Plan? If one looks just at simple statistics on total suggestions and acceptance rates, the Bureau of New Ideas does not measure up well. As mentioned in chapter 2, during the first thirty-four months (through the end of 1926) of the Cooperative Plan's operation, roughly eighteen thousand suggestions had been submitted and approximately 86 percent accepted. The corresponding statistics for the first thirty-eight months (through the end of 1930) of operation of the Bureau of New Ideas were seventy-two hundred and 20 percent. The disparity becomes even larger when one considers the relative sizes of the two companies. The B&O in 1925 (the middle year of the reference period) had 66,000 employees; the PRR in 1929 had 183,000 on its payroll.[10] Simple arithmetic shows that the Cooperative Plan generated one suggestion per month per 125 employees; the Bureau of New Ideas generated one suggestion per month per 967 employees. The Cooperative Plan generated one adopted suggestion per month per 146 employees; the Bureau of New Ideas generated one adopted suggestion per month per 4,757 employees. The latter pair of numbers does not mean that the Plan was 32.6 times as successful as the BNI. It does not take into account the direct dollar value to the company of each

"Making him sweat!" Cartoon from *Baltimore & Ohio Magazine*, September 1928. (Courtesy of the B&O Railroad Museum)

adopted suggestion, which presumably would be on the average higher on the Pennsylvania; the relatively intimidating formal screening process of the Bureau of New Ideas would tend to discourage small-ticket proposals, and the bureau's narrowly defined and centrally enforced purpose would provide a basis for eliminating worker-centered proposals with little tangible benefit to the company. Nonetheless, that which might be called the "constructive participation rate" was on the B&O 32.6 times higher than on the PRR.

An observer of postwar Japanese approaches to management would not be surprised even at the magnitude of that number. A sense of common interest built from face-to-face discussions must come first, he would observe; widespread constructive thinking is likely to occur only in such a context. There would have been no real question from the outset as to which was the more effective program. The Pennsylvania program was better than nothing, but it was several leagues below that of the Baltimore & Ohio. B&O partisans at the time certainly had that sense of the Plan. Their view of the matter is unsubtly depicted in an editorial cartoon from the September 1928 issue of *Baltimore & Ohio Magazine.*

The Cooperative Plan was the centerpiece of personnel programs, policies, and actions on the Baltimore & Ohio during the middle and late 1920s, but it was not the only matter of significance in that realm during those years. Programs begun before the Plan were continued, and new steps were taken as the decade passed.

The Welfare Department, still under the direction of W. W. Wood, remained alive and well, promoting company-oriented athletic, musical, and social activities. Nearly all major B&O operations centers had at least one baseball team, and bowling and basketball teams were fairly common as well. Competition among these teams generally was arranged at the local level, but there were company-sponsored tournaments, usually organized by district or region. In addition to such standard sports teams, there were a few unique sporting groups with loose ties to the Welfare Department, such as the Riverside [Shops] Gun and Fishing Club, known among Baltimore-area employees for its annual duck dinner.[11]

On the musical front, the three oldest and most firmly established ensembles—the Men's Glee Club (to which a few selected nonemployees had been added), the Women's Music Club (successor to the Bando Club), and the Mount Clare Band—continued to grow in both competence and visibility. Their growth was aided by their association with the B&O's splendid centennial celebration, the Fair of the Iron Horse. The fair, officially the Centenary Exhibition and Pageant of the Baltimore & Ohio Railroad, was held in September and October 1927 to mark the hundredth anniversary of the B&O's charter. Willard's most extravagant decision ever, the event lasted twenty-three days, cost more than $1 million, and attracted more than 1.3 million visitors. It was a public relations triumph, and it pushed the B&O's reputation to heights not achieved before or since. In itself it greatly contributed to general feelings of pride and unity among B&O employees; those feelings were magnified among those employees who participated in its focal point, the pageant. B&O employees were the great majority of the cast; most members of the Women's Music Club were involved, and the Glee Club provided the chorus. The pageant's Centenary Band included outside professionals, but the Mount Clare Band played two daily concerts between pageant performances. It was such a glorious experience that it gave rise to yet another B&O employee organization: the Centenary Association, which, among other things, staged an employee circus in February 1929. The attention and enthusiasm generated by the fair also energized the Glee Club to begin competitive singing, and very successfully. In May 1929, with eighty-two men in its ranks, it

Daniel Willard with Centenary Pageant cast member. (Courtesy of the B&O Railroad Museum)

entered the triennial competition of the Associated Glee Clubs of America, held at Madison Square Garden in New York. The B&O Club won the first-prize trophy in class B, edging the Ottawa Temple Choir of Canada; it was the only corporate glee club to win a prize of any sort.[12]

Social activities continued under the aegis of the Welfare Department essentially as before. The most common major event was the summer outing, a large departmental or huge divisional picnic featuring a wide variety of recreational activities and contests. The events in many cases were even more elaborate than those described in chapter 1, and they occurred at an increasing number of locations around the system. A good example is the annual picnic of the Cumberland Back Shop, scene of the machinists' boycott of the cooperative committee described in chapter 2. The shop superintendent, John Howe, apparently was successful in getting past his 1925 labor problem, mainly by the astute practice of MBWA ("management by walking around"—Howe made a point of spending a good portion of his day on the shop floor, talking with his men),[13] once national union leaders had calmed their local membership. The Back Shop did not have its own picnic until June 1927. It

"At the Cincinnati Glee Club Concert." Cartoon from *Baltimore & Ohio Magazine,* July 1929. (Courtesy of the B&O Railroad Museum)

was successful, and in July 1928 an even bigger one was held. Attendance was approximately two thousand; twenty-three different contests were conducted, with prizes donated by a total of one hundred Cumberland-area firms. Howe was presented a loving cup by the local shopcrafts federation president, C. J. McKay, "expressing the high esteem in which Mr. Howe is held" by local union members; the evening concluded with a dance in the fairgrounds pavilion.[14]

More modest events were begun as well. The concerts and dances of the Cincinnati B&O Glee Club are an example. The second such event was held in Cincinnati's Grand Hotel ballroom; it consisted of the glee club concert, a combined skit and square dance featuring several local officers as an apparently competent country string band, and dancing to the music of a professional orchestra. There were also less modest events. The possible record holder in this respect was the Fourth of July celebration organized by the B&O Athletic Association of Parkersburg, West Virginia, in 1929. The day's activities began at 9:00 A.M. with various races and contests, followed by a baseball game between the B&O teams of Holloway, Ohio, and Parkersburg. Then came lunch and an address by B&O general counsel, director, and former West Virginia governor John J. Cornwell, followed by round and square dancing in the park pavilion, a band concert, and a second Holloway-Parkersburg baseball game. Next were dinner and more square dancing. The evening concluded with an hour-and-a-half fireworks display, the climax of which featured a giant set-piece B&O emblem. A special train was run from Holloway and Wheeling to bring in out-of-town celebrants; presumably counting citizens not affiliated with the B&O who attended the fireworks display, total attendance was estimated at more then twenty thousand.[15]

Serving as principal reporter and cheerleader of all of this, and more, was the *Baltimore & Ohio Magazine*. That publication reached its peak in the late 1920s. The July 1929 issue, for example, contained 144 pages, of which only $3\frac{1}{2}$ were advertising; the balance was company news and family features. "Among Ourselves," the section at the end of the magazine devoted to local correspondents' reports of local activities and events in the lives of their co-workers, ran 64 pages. There were 6 pages on retirements, a 4-page women's section, a 3-page children's section, 3 pages of riddles and puzzles, 3 pages of book notes and poetry, 2 pages on promotions of officers, 2 pages on the deaths of well-known employees, 2 pages of railroad history, and a page on miscellaneous current events. The remaining $50\frac{1}{2}$ pages provided reports on recent capital improvements, employee safety, official meetings, traffic solicitation efforts, and the various employee social-musical-athletic events, as well as exhortations to greater courtesy and conscientiousness. It was an engaging magazine, upbeat in tone, professional in layout and editing, partisan in its viewpoint, and friendly and unpretentious in its style.

Robert M. Van Sant was editor of the magazine during its prime, but the tone and style of the publication may have been influenced at least as much by its associate editor, Margaret Talbott Stevens. Writing under her own byline, and occasionally as "Peggy" in the women's section and as "Aunt Mary" in the children's section and elsewhere, Stevens was the ultimate B&O cheerleader. Her folksy enthusiasm was infectious; she clearly loved people, her job, and her railroad. Associate editor since 1920, she had impressed Daniel Willard to the point that in 1927, he suggested to Van Sant that he might want to consider turning the magazine over to her for an issue. "Perhaps she has some ideas she would like to feature . . . think it over," Van Sant recalled Willard's saying. The editor later commented, "You know how you 'think over' such suggestions." The result, in May 1927, was the first annual Women's Number, written almost entirely by and for B&O women, both employees and wives of employees. The Women's Numbers typically placed greater emphasis than did other issues upon matters of home and family, but they were not exclusively domestic. They contained regular reports of company developments, as well as the "Among Ourselves" section, and their feature articles often focused on successful railroad career women, both on the B&O and beyond.[16]

One such profile was of Olive Dennis, who was along with Stevens one of the two most important women on the railroad. The daughter of a Baltimore physician, Dennis was a mathematician and civil engineer by training. After completing a master's degree in mathematics at Columbia in 1909, she spent ten years as a schoolteacher in Washington, D.C.; then in 1919, dissatisfied with teaching, she entered the civil engineering program at Cornell. When she finished her degree a year later, however, she was rebuffed in all of her first efforts to find a job in her new profession. Eventually she returned to Baltimore and contacted the B&O; finally finding a place where her credentials outweighed any anticipated disruptive effects of the presence of a professional woman, she was hired as a draftsman in the bridge engineering department. In 1921 she was promoted to the newly created position of "engineer of service," reporting directly to Willard and responsible primarily for the design of passenger train equipment and services. In that capacity she either recommended or personally designed a number of innovations and alterations, including improved reclining coach seats, women's dressing rooms in coaches, dimmable coach ceiling lights and individual reading lights, a pre-air-conditioning car window ventilator (upon which she held a patent), and a lunch counter coach for passengers who could not afford the regular dining car. She also worked in the aesthetic realm, routinely reconfiguring dining and club cars, designing carpets and fabrics, choosing color schemes, and so forth; her most notable accomplishments in this area were the design of the Centennial Blue china used in B&O dining cars and, toward the end of her career, most of the design of the 1947 streamliner *The Cincinnatian*.[17]

Both the Women's Numbers and Olive Dennis were firsts for Willard's B&O among American railroads. There was no parallel in the industry to Margaret Talbott Stevens's charge, and Dennis was the first—and for many years the only—female member of the American Railway Engineers' Association. They were two principal reasons for the reputation of the Baltimore & Ohio as an unusually progressive and fair-minded employer of women in an exceedingly masculine business.[18] There were serious limitations, of course: not even an Olive Dennis could hope to rise any higher than junior officer status. She was an officer nonetheless, and she and other B&O women were given prominent recognition in the official publication of the company. Daniel Willard's railroad family was a patriarchy, but it did not consign all of its women to anonymous slavery in the kitchen.

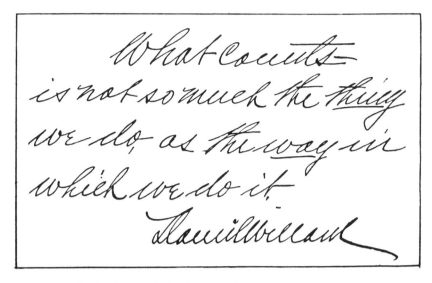

Willard epigram, 1929. (Courtesy of the B&O Railroad Museum)

Baltimore & Ohio Magazine was the central element in reinforcing the family spirit and service ideals that Willard wished for his company. Letters, memos, and personal contacts were important means of conveying the message, but in a firm employing over sixty thousand people, their impact could not be continual and pervasive. The magazine, in contrast, was sent to every employee every month. Accordingly, it was standard practice for Willard and the magazine editors to select snippets of his letters, memos, comments, and speeches, and to reiterate them in the magazine's articles, editorials, cartoons, and column fillers. This began in the magazine's early years: "Safety—above everything else" was Willard's slogan for the B&O before World War I. After the war it was "The Good Neighbor Railroad" and "The Will to Please," as well as lengthier epigrams such as "Honesty in selling our service to the public—we don't want business secured through misrepresentation" and "Not because we feel obliged to do so, but because we want to do so." The notion of right motivation was critical to Willard. Conscientious service was for him a moral imperative; moreover, he understood that action taken for moral reasons manifests itself outwardly in a certain attractive style. This point was implicit in the 1929 slogan, "What counts is not so much the thing we do as the way in which we do it." Of course, either short of or beyond such philosophizing was "Suggestions are always in order"—sometimes in the background, but still understood to be his definitive simple statement on management.[19]

With respect to matters affecting the well-being of his employees, Willard usually heard and acted upon contructive suggestions noticeably ahead of his competition. In one instance, though, in the adoption of a progressive and solidly practical program for rewarding his employees and increasing their sense that the railroad was their railroad, he was actually beaten by the Pennsylvania. That was the case of the employee stock ownership plan. The PRR had given some encouragement to employees buying company stock as early as January 1926, such purchases being financed through its Mutual Beneficial Association. In July 1929 a more comprehensive and direct stock purchase plan, through which all Pennsylvania employees were entitled to purchase company stock in proportion to their annual wages or salaries, was instituted. The stock was offered at par—less than half of its market price—and payment could be made over several months. Of the railroad's total work force, 94,863 employees, or 52 percent, took advantage of the offer.[20]

The charter of the Baltimore & Ohio forbade it to sell common stock below par, which was one hundred dollars per share. From the end of 1914 to mid-1926, the market price of B&O stock was usually under that level; it did not rise above one hundred dollars for several consecutive weeks until September of the latter year. For nearly twelve years before September 1926, then, the B&O could not legally float a new equity issue.[21] The company thereby was prevented from setting up a clean and simple employee stock ownership plan. It might have been possible to arrange for the transfer of existing stock at the market price through some third party, or to find a few extremely loyal employees willing to pay one hundred dollars each for new shares worth less than that, but it was not feasible to establish a plan that would simultaneously expand the company's equity base and reward employees financially. It was feasible after September 1926, though, nearly three years before the PRR began their full program. Why the B&O did not act is not clear. One might speculate that it had some relation to finance's being Willard's weakest area, or to possible shortsightedness among existing stockholders and Willard's board of directors, to which allusion was made in Chapter 1.

The B&O finally did announce an employee stock ownership plan, however, in November 1929, less than a month after the collapse of the stock market. If not for its awful timing, it would have been a good program. Employees were entitled to buy one share at par, on partial payments over a period of months, for each $500 of their annual compensation. As the market price of B&O stock had fallen only to $115 by the end of November, it was still a bargain, for the moment.[22] Of course, its price continued to fall—soon below $100, where it stayed for many years—and the employee stock ownership plan was finished. Willard may be faulted here for a lapse in his progressive inclinations, but it should be kept in mind that this lapse, if indeed that is what it was, prevented his employees from "taking a bath." By June 1932 the price of a B&O common share had fallen under $4.[23]

Meanwhile, the Cooperative Plan functioned substantially, though not entirely, as it had during its first years. Throughout 1927 the local cooperative committees continued to meet as they had since 1924. The program was, however, no longer really in the foreground of company consciousness. In 1926 the Plan had been given considerable emphasis in *Baltimore & Ohio Magazine*; letters from employees praising the program, often citing its Biblical underpinnings, were given prominent play.[24] In 1927 the attention of the magazine was turned toward the centennial celebration, and the Cooperative Plan became more of a background item.

A slight loss of momentum caused by this diversion of attention may have been accentuated somewhat by the B&O's 1927 financial situation and its impact upon shop employment levels. The year 1927 was a good one for the B&O, but not so good as the peak year of 1926. Company revenues were $255 million, down 3.8 percent from the prior year. Net income was $20.3 million, off 19.8 percent; return on equity was 6.55 percent, down from 10.82 percent.[25]

The decline in traffic did not really begin until June. However, the B&O ended 1926 with its rolling stock in first-rate condition; as a consequence, the company began 1927 with a reduced need for equipment maintenance work. That in turn led to layoffs, and those layoffs were predictably hard on both employee morale and confidence in the Plan. The existence of the Plan was not threatened, but the enthusiasm of its participants was dampened; in late March, System Federation No. 30 officers quashed a proposed article on the Plan in the *American Federationist* on those grounds.[26] Those officers, naturally, were complaining to the company as the furloughs, compounded by the recession-induced traffic slump, continued into the second half of the year. On July 26, operations vice president Charles Galloway replied to federation president William McGee's complaints, protesting that the company had made a serious effort to stabilize employment, with equipment maintenance expenditures for the first half of 1927 "in excess of $2,000,000 more than the budget allowance." He went on to state that if the traffic situation continued to slip, then Mount Clare, Cumberland, and Glenwood shops would have to be closed altogether for a time. That threat ended the formal complaints, as McGee and his cohorts turned their attentions toward an effort—a successful one—to talk Galloway and Emerson out of any such closing.[27]

In relative terms B&O unionists had little to complain about. The company had been delivering on its promise of employment stability in the context of the inherent instability of the railroad business—not irreproachably, but still commendably. Outside assessments seemed to support Galloway's protestation of good faith: a study published in the *Monthly Labor Review* in August 1928 showed that since 1924, when the Cooperative Plan became fully operational, the B&O had done better than either the NYC or the PRR in maintaining full-time employment for its machinists. For the period 1924–1927, B&O machinists had worked on average approximately 93.5 percent of full time; the corresponding figures for the NYC and PRR were 92.0 and 90.6 percent, respectively. For 1927 alone the B&O figure was 94.2 percent, compared to 91.9 and 87.8 percent, respectively, for the NYC and PRR.[28] The differences were small but worthy of some appreciation. Unfortunately, for the person at the bottom of the seniority list, the only acceptable number was 100 percent; 94 percent (and dropping) was not good enough.

The negative pressure on shop employment levels brought about by the traffic slump did not abate until late in 1928. B&O revenues for that year fell another 4.1 percent below those of 1927. To prevent further furloughs, McGee in June 1928 convinced Emerson to place Mount Clare and Glenwood on a reduced workweek (five and a half instead of six days) for the balance of the summer. By fall, with traffic beginning to recover, some of the furloughed men were being called back to work, but the credibility of the program had to have suffered some, especially among those relatively junior employees who had been for a time unemployed.[29] They, at least, might have questioned either the competence or the conscientiousness of those B&O officers responsible for equipment maintenance planning.

Through all of this, Daniel Willard seems to have been somewhat surprisingly remote from the frontline action: his operating officers appear to have held the initiative in making tactical personnel decisions. Having set the general direction of personnel strategy in prior years, Willard apparently left the day-to-day implementation of that strategy to his immediate subordinates—wise delegation, if one's subordinates fully understand and agree with that strategy. But as noted in the preceding chapter, Willard himself had some doubts about whether such understanding and agreement were initially present among lower-level managers as the Cooperative Plan was instituted; more critically, he might have wondered about Emerson and Galloway's level of commitment to the Plan. If he and his officers were not of one mind on the subject, then it would have been incumbent on him to continually keep an eye on the program and to probe those of their decisions that even indirectly affected it.

There is evidence to suggest that either Emerson or Galloway did not always share fully Willard's commitment to the Cooperative Plan,[30] and there is also evidence that Willard did not on his own initiative probe very deeply some of the decisions that were made concerning its administration. As might be expected, this lapse in good judgment on Willard's part led ultimately to an embarrassing situation. It occurred in August 1928, at the bottom of the 1927–1928 recession. Because of the continuing traffic decline, Willard had been exceedingly cost-conscious: throughout the spring and summer, he had been urging all of his people "to reduce expenses in every way possible." In July he was informed that the company's various committee meetings, principally those of the safety and cooperative committees, were costing four thousand dollars per month. Apparently without thinking through the issue, he ordered that a temporary but substantial reduction be made in those expenses. It is not precisely clear from surviving records what happened next, but it appears that sometime around the first of August, Galloway issued a directive that cut the frequency of cooperative committee meetings from every fourteen days to every ninety days.[31]

When they heard of this unilateral action, the union hierarchy were dismayed. They sought immediately to appeal the issue to Willard, who at the time conveniently was in Chicago, only a few blocks from Bert Jewell's home office. On the afternoon of August 6, the two men met at the Congress Hotel to try to iron out the matter. Jewell found Willard in a chastened mood. Having received a telegram on the subject from William McGee earlier in the day, Willard already had telephoned Galloway in Baltimore to have him rescind his order, and to direct Emerson to meet with the system federation executive committee to seek some less draconian solution to the cost problem. Willard accepted ultimate responsibility for the mistaken decision, and he suggested that Emerson and McGee might negotiate an agreement that the cooperative committees meet every thirty days until traffic levels recovered. This was accomplished on August 15.[32]

The agreement applied only to the cooperative committees of the mechanical department, however. In the transportation and maintenance of way departments, the circumstances and outcome were different. As noted previously, union commitment to the Plan there was lower than in the mechanical department. Also, because of greater committee size and the geographic dispersion of committee members, the costs of convening a meeting were much higher than they were for the shop committees. Accordingly, the ninety-day schedule order remained in effect for the CT and MW committees.[33]

The tendency toward penny-pinching evident in the meeting schedule misunderstanding almost caused a much more serious rupture in relations early in 1929. For some time, shopmen of the New York Central had received a base wage one cent per hour higher than B&O shopmen, as a partial offset for the latter's Sunday and holidays time-and-a-half advantage. Then in mid-January an arbitration board granted NYC shopmen a further five-cent-per-hour increase. System Federation No. 30 immediately asked the B&O for a similar adjustment. Willard was away from Baltimore at the time, on a lengthy

Electrician Raymond E. Buckheister and his air-jack wagon for generator removal: suggestion submitted to Mount Clare Shops cooperative committee in May 1928. (Courtesy of the B&O Railroad Museum)

vacation, so vice president Galloway conducted negotiations over the request without the benefit of face-to-face, day-by-day discussion with his boss. Galloway began discussions by offering four and a half cents; then he withdrew that offer and offered four. Union officials were more than mildly miffed. After ascertaining that Galloway would not budge on his own, they cabled Willard that if he would not assure them that five cents would be granted, then they would submit the four-cent offer to the membership for a strike vote. Such an occurrence probably would have blown the Cooperative Plan to pieces. So Willard intervened, the higher increase was agreed upon, and there was no public falling-out. Nonetheless, like the meeting schedule problem, the incident did not contribute much to union confidence in the consistency of Willard's management team. That, in turn, did not help the Plan.[34]

The Cooperative Plan, then, was an active but somewhat troubled program in 1928 and 1929. The problems described would have been in themselves cause for concern. There was, however, a potentially greater problem developing beneath the surface: the program simply was running out of issues with which to occupy itself. This was partly due, no doubt, to a certain slackening of employee interest in looking for issues, brought about by the company's sometimes clumsy efforts at holding expenses down. The greater reason, though, was that, in the words of system federation secretary H. L. Alberty, "This movement has developed and exhausted about all the things the program called for. . . ." The most obvious suggestions for improvement had nearly all been made; the Plan was being weakened by its own success.[35]

The solution from the union point of view was for Otto Beyer to become closely involved with the B&O program once again. Beyer during these years was spending most of his time establishing a cooperative program in the maintenance of way department of the Canadian National, and serving as the AFL's all-around railroad consultant and troubleshooter; aside from his usual attendance at the corporate-level cooperative meetings, he had little contact with the Baltimore & Ohio. McGee and Alberty, in particular, wanted Beyer to make a tour of all B&O shops, meeting with each local cooperative committee in an attempt to spark greater creativity and enthusiasm. Correspondence among Jewell, Beyer, and system federation officers implies that Beyer finally made such a tour, covering most but not all B&O shops, in the summer of 1929.[36]

Union leaders also tried to persuade Daniel Willard to go to work on the problem, in a rather unusual capacity. B&O shop forces were not 100 percent unionized; the shopcrafts unions were particularly weak, surprisingly, at Mount Clare. Jewell attributed this phenomenon to the presence, at Mount Clare and elsewhere, of "obstructors," informal leaders among the men who had no real use for unions and who influenced numerous coworkers to think likewise. Jewell further was convinced that by keeping union membership, and thereby Cooperative Plan participation, lower than it would be in a fully unionized shop, these obstructors diminished the vitality of the Plan. His solution to this problem was to have Beyer and McGee present the matter to Willard in those terms, and to have them attempt "to persuade Mr. Willard to see the necessity of taking some action which will convince these obstructors of the error of their ways." Willard was asked, in effect, to serve as a booster of union membership.[37]

Much later, in the spring of 1933, Cumberland Back Shop superintendent John Howe was so active in his concern for the betterment of his union lodges that the embarrassed local federation asked him to desist, presumably for fear of being upstaged.[38] Whatever he was doing, it was probably not something that he was directly told to do by his chief executive. There is no known evidence that Willard ever, as a railroad officer, actively supported a campaign for increased union membership, much less pressured antiunion shopmen on behalf of the AFL. He was, however, putting some effort into boosting the Plan. During the fall of 1929, the local shopcrafts federation at the Cumberland Back Shop, with the encouragement of superintendent Howe, conducted a series of evening "demonstration meetings" for the general public—operating open houses where local citizens could see just what it was that the back shop did. To the demonstration meeting of November 6, local federation chairman W. J. Jones invited Willard. Willard not only accepted, but brought the company's board of directors with him, and he took advantage of the opportunity to make a Cooperative Plan promotional speech. His address was, as

MAKING THE GRADE
VIA—
CO-OPERATION

IT'S EASIER WHEN WE WORK TOGETHER

Cooperative Plan poster, 1929. (Courtesy of the B&O
Railroad Museum)

his addresses typically were, both unceremonious and purposeful: a little of
the background of the Plan, a few didactic anecdotes from his own blue-collar
days, praise for the shopmen, comments on the importance of an honest day's
work and of consequent fair rewards by the company, and an exhortation to
further the Plan and the B&O family spirit. The speech and laudatory editorial
comment about the Cooperative Plan were featured in the December issue of
Baltimore & Ohio Magazine.[39]

Such appearances may not have been of earthshaking significance, but
they were perceived as clear evidence that Willard cared about the program
and the people who participated in it. Union leaders on the B&O appreciated
that. J. J. Tahaney, the disgruntled former B&O carman who had blasted the
Plan in the *Baltimore Federationist* four years earlier, did not see it that way:
he believed that Willard was receiving credit that belonged entirely to the
AFL. Union men of broader perspective, however, understood that even though
they had done most of the work, the Plan never would have succeeded without

Willard's unparalleled support and encouragement. The success of the Plan had not eliminated employment instability or nonunion shopmen, but it had reduced them to a degree. In 1929 as in 1922, Daniel Willard was not a hero of the labor movement, but he was a friend.

As January 1930 marked the twentieth anniversary of Willard's appointment to the presidency, the officers of System Federation No. 30, joined by those of the other unions on the B&O, decided to show their appreciation by giving him a testimonial dinner. The planning of the event was led by William McGee, working with an arrangements committee that consisted of the general chairmen of the machinists', conductors', telegraphers', clerks', boiler-makers', and maintenance of way employees' unions, plus Otto Beyer. The main banquet ball of the Lord Baltimore Hotel was secured for the evening of January 13; entertainment (the Men's Glee Club, the Women's Music Club, and the Cumberland Shops Band) was lined up, and an impressive list of speakers was arranged. The master of ceremonies was to be Edward Keating, editor of *Labor*, the rail unions' weekly newspaper; the welcoming address was to be given by Baltimore mayor William F. Broening. The first testimonial speech was to be given by William Green, president of the American Federation of Labor. He was to be followed by Senator James Couzens of Michigan, chairman of the Senate Committee on Interstate Commerce; by James J. Davis, President Hoover's secretary of labor; by Sir Henry Thornton, Willard's like-minded counterpart at the Canadian National Railways; and by Albert C. Ritchie, governor of Maryland. The evening was to conclude with the conferring upon Willard, by the unions' Association of General Chairman, of the honorary degree of "Doctor of Humanity."[40]

Unfortunately, the executive council of the AFL already had been scheduled to meet in St. Petersburg during the week of January 13, so Green was not able to attend the testimonial in person. However, he did prepare a speech for the occasion, working from a preliminary draft supplied by Beyer, to be read on his behalf at the dinner by Bert Jewell.[41] Otherwise, the evening's agenda was carried out exactly as planned, and the dinner was considered to be a great success. The unions sold tickets to the event to help defray their expenses; 1,293 people subscribed, enabling the general chairmen to cover their costs almost completely. Another 300 or so people crowded into the hall for the speeches after dinner was cleared, bringing total attendance near 1,600. Included in the assemblage were eight senators (among them such notables as Robert LaFollette and Burton Wheeler), ten congressmen (one of whom was Fiorello LaGuardia), thirteen past or present national labor officials (including William Johnston), five members of the B&O board of directors, the president of Johns Hopkins University (of which Willard was president of the board of trustees), and Robert McVicar, the locomotive engineer with whom Willard had made his first runs as a fireman fifty years earlier.[42]

Willard's "degree" was presented by C. W. Jones, B&O general chairman of the Brotherhood of Railroad Trainmen. In making the presentation, Jones said, in part:

> During our twenty years together, we have become more and more persuaded that the inner light that guides you is profound understanding of the human being as he conducts himself in railroading. You have imaginative sympathy for those who toil, for those who owe their living to the Baltimore & Ohio Railroad. You appreciate that a railroad company is only, in reality, sound when its employees as wage earners and producers enjoy protections and guaranties analogous to those of the Company's owners and patrons. Upon this bedrock of policy rest many of the accomplishments and much of the progress of the Baltimore & Ohio during the last twenty years.
>
> Through your appreciation of the part played by your fellow workers, the Baltimore & Ohio trackmen, shopmen, trainmen, enginemen, telegraphers, clerks, and officers, in the running of the railroad, you have won their hearty cooperation. Your spirit of tolerance has created in others the will to work with you.

He went on about Willard's "[understanding] that in the free and independent labor unions of its employees the Baltimore & Ohio has an asset," his "readiness to share the benefits of cooperation with all who play a part in the common project," and his general capabilities as a motivator and statesman. Then, on behalf of the assembled "workers in the University of Life and Labor," he conferred upon Willard his award.[43]

Willard opened his acceptance comments with the "plain Down-East Yankee" remark recounted in chapter 1, protesting that those who had spoken of him during the evening had greatly inflated his personal achievements and contributions. Bert Jewell, speaking for William Green, had called him the "one man in the United States who has surpassed all others in the development of the administrative affairs of the transportation industry." Senator Couzens had said that with "his genuine attitude, his lack of four-flushing, the simplicity of his courage, the humanitarian aspect sticking out all over him," he was "the greatest railroad man in America." Sir Henry Thornton had spoken of him with the words of Psalm 145: "One generation shall praise Thy works to another and shall declare Thy mighty acts. . . . They shall abundantly utter the memory of Thy great goodness and shall sing of Thy righteousness." Willard surely was pleased with such praise, but he also seemed a little embarrassed; he insisted that his family and closest friends could see that "the Daniel Willard you have been hearing about has been conjured up for the occasion."[44]

The heart of his comments was a reflective overview of the genesis and benefits of the Cooperative Plan and of B&O labor-management relations in general. Toward the end of this reflection, he said:

> I have frequently been asked for a copy of our labor policy, the implication being that we have something carefully worked out like a code of by-laws with numbered paragraphs, each to apply to different circumstances and situations that may arise. We have nothing of the kind beyond a very brief statement of belief and procedure. What have we then as a basis for our labor relations? I have tried many times to find the answer to that question. In my opinion the basis of the Baltimore & Ohio labor policy is best described as a state of mind resulting from the confidence which employees have in the fairness of management and which the management also has in the fairness of the employees. Instead of thinking of each other in terms of suspicion, a feeling of mutual respect and growing confidence exists, and this, in my opinion, is the outstanding contribution of our cooperative policy. . . .
>
> I have said that we endeavor to deal fairly with our employees, and the question might well be asked, "What do you mean by fairly?" That is a difficult question to answer because, so far as I know, there is no definite standard for determining fairness. There is no established measure of fairness such as the yardstick. Fortunately, however, there is a rule many centuries old which, if honestly followed, I believe will bring substantial justice or fairness. The rule I have in mind is to treat the other man as you think you would wish to be treated if in his place. It is a very old rule, and a very simple rule, but I have not yet heard of a better one. That rule, I like to think, is the essence of the Baltimore & Ohio labor policy.

After ascribing most of the success of that policy to the unions, to his subordinate officers, and to B&O employees in general, and after offering that which he deemed to be hopelessly insufficient thanks to those who had honored him, he sat down.[45] Thus did he receive the seventh of fourteen honorary degrees bestowed upon him in his lifetime. It was probably the most important one.

Daniel Willard, almost sixty-nine years old the evening of his testimonial dinner, was at the peak of his reputation. He was beginning to acquire a certain legendary quality, not just from grand banquets and speeches, but also from the observations and subsequent tales told by ordinary employees around the line. On two consecutive Saturday afternoons in November 1929, for example, he was seen by employees at Camden Station in Baltimore carrying burdens for fellow incoming passengers up the stairway from the lower-level platform to street level, quietly and without identifying himself—in one instance the two small children of a young woman, and the other time the suitcase of a frail, elderly woman.[46] Such actions made a greater impression on his people than any number of speeches and bulletins on the importance of humble courtesy.

His reputation and all of the qualities associated with it were to be critical in taking the Baltimore & Ohio through the years ahead. As 1930 passed recession deepened into the Great Depression, and the B&O soon was in serious trouble. The company's revenue in 1929 had recovered almost to the level of 1927, but it fell 14.2 percent in 1930. Despite the decline, throughout the year the B&O continued to honor its employment stabilization commitments to the unions as best it could. On February 10 the company and System Federation No. 30 signed an agreement designed to prevent the Depression, still thought to be a short-term phenomenon, from throwing any of the remaining 12,100 B&O shopmen (down from an average of 13,700 in 1929) out of work altogether. The principal provisions of the agreement were that all B&O shops would remain open, that all back shop forces would work a reduced (forty-four-hour) week, that a pool of junior men in danger of lengthy furlough would be designated to fill in for senior jobholders and guaranteed at least a twenty-four-hour week, and that overtime and any other costly or wasteful practice would be eliminated to the last degree possible. Management anticipated that for the year, equipment maintenance expenditures might exceed the normal budget, which was a function of both measurable need and traffic levels, by as much as $2 million.[47]

In addition, a placement service was established to aid those workers who had been furloughed or given part-time substitute status. A file containing the names of all such employees and their service records was established by the company; when a job became vacant, the employing officer was required to hire from the file, given that it contained the name of a qualified worker willing to make any necessary transfer. Beyond that, the B&O promised to use whatever remained of its purchasing muscle to secure outside employment for its furloughed employees. Finally, in October the company authorized the construction "in anticipation of future requirements" of one thousand boxcars, one thousand heavy gondolas, and forty-five locomotive tenders; all of the work except the erection of the boxcar bodies was to be done in B&O shops. The project was a considerable boon to B&O shopmen; it provided approximately sixty-five thousand man-days of work that normally would have gone to outside car manufacturers, and that, given the state of business, might not have been contracted at all. The total cost of the project was estimated to be $4 million.[48]

The result of all of this was that the number of B&O shop employees actually increased between January and October 1930, by 1.4 percent, even as the traffic decline was accelerating. In contrast, the B&O's competitors were cutting their shop forces: the Pennsylvania by 8.4 percent, the New York Central by 8.5 percent, the Erie by 11.3 percent.[49] Willard obviously was doing the good thing.

Whether it was also the smart thing might have been less obvious, especially to the B&O's shareholders and bankers. Had the economy begun a serious recovery in late 1931 or early 1932, Willard would have been seen in the long run as having been both good and smart. However, it did not: 1931 was a very bad year, and 1932 was even worse. The company's revenue in 1931 was 18.5 percent below that of 1930, and in 1932 it fell another 20.9 percent. The B&O's traffic in 1932 was barely more than half of what it had been in 1929. Spending $4 million on new equipment as an increasingly large percentage of the company's existing car fleet sat idle was a decision that might have been questioned and probably was questioned. There is no record of any link between his offer and possible criticism of the car building and employment stabilization decision, but in January 1931, citing his advancing age on the occasion of his seventieth birthday, Willard offered to resign. The offer was refused vigorously by his board, as was his similar offer the next year and every other year save 1937 until his retirement in 1941, but it still might have crossed the minds of some people that perhaps Willard's compassion and optimism had outweighed his prudence.[50]

The B&O did not place a new equipment order of that size again for the balance of the Depression, and layoffs of its employees eventually came to be commensurate with those of its competitors. Willard really had no choice; 1931 profits of $1.4 million amounted to a tiny 0.4 percent return on equity, and the 1932 loss of $6.3 million represented a negative return of 1.8 percent. By November 1932 the total number of full-time B&O employees had fallen to around thirty thousand, from an average of sixty-six thousand in 1929. Of those thirty thousand few were working the old forty-eight-hour full-time week. In the shops, to spread the remaining work around, the standard week had been dropped to thirty hours. To provide some income for men on furlough, a voluntary work sharing program was organized; many of those not among the fortunate thirty thousand thus were able to work fifteen or twenty hours per week.[51] That was about all that employment stabilization could mean in 1932.

In the midst of these difficulties, an attempt was made to develop the Cooperative Plan a step further. Late in 1929 an agreement was reached by the Canadian National Railways and the Brotherhood of Maintenance of Way Employees to establish a full set of cooperative committees within the CNR's maintenance of way department.[52] As described in chapter 2, B&O maintenance of way workers already were involved in the Cooperative Plan, but they were generally submerged in the transportation department meetings and were not very active. In December 1930 Otto Beyer wrote to Willard, proposing the creation of separate MW committees on the B&O. Willard was amenable to pursuing the possibility, and in March 1931 preliminary discussions were held between Beyer and B&O management, represented by Charles Galloway and by Earl Stimson, the company's chief maintenance engineer. Beyer reported to Bert Jewell that Galloway and Stimson both "were quite willing and ready to proceed" and that he would prepare a more formal report on the structure and staffing of the program for presentation at a follow-up meeting later in the spring.[53]

Beyer's report proposed an arrangement that was very similar to the one in effect on the Canadian National. There was to be an MW cooperative committee for each of the B&O's fourteen divisions, plus one each for the Green Spring tie plant and the Martinsburg maintenance of way equipment shops. The Green Spring and Martinsburg committees were to meet monthly; the divisional committees were to meet once every two months, because of the logistical problems and attendant costs posed by their geographic breadth. Representing management on each divisional committee were to be the division engineer, one or two of his assistants, one or two bridge and building force supervisors (master carpenters), and three to eight supervisors of road (the number depending upon the number of track subdivisions on the given division); representing labor were to be three to eight members of the track forces (one for each subdivision) and one or two members of the bridge and building forces. Composition of the Green Spring and Martinsburg committees was to be similar to those involving the shopcrafts unions. The labor representatives on the divisional committees were to be allowed one or two days per month to travel their respective segments of the railroad to receive suggestions from, and to pass information to, the local work crews. At the top of the structure there was to be a system cooperative committee, composed of Stimson and four of his subordinates, four general officers of the maintenance of way (MW) union federation, the five executive committee members of the MW federation, and William McGee of the shopcrafts federation; McGee's presence was the result of the anomaly at Martinsburg wherein the workers were members of his unions.[54]

Beyer pegged the direct costs of the program, primarily in the form of paid release time, at $7,130 per year. He recommended that before the program be implemented systemwide, a six-month trial be conducted on the Cumberland Division and the Chicago Division, both notable for the discipline of their union locals and the harmoniousness of their local management-labor relations.[55]

Bert Jewell anticipated that the proposal's recommendation concerning McGee and the Martinsburg situation might be walking into a turf battle between the two departments headed, respectively, by Stimson and by George Emerson; shopcrafts people normally reported up through the mechanical department to Emerson, but at Martinsburg they reported up through the MW department to Stimson. In a June 26 letter to Beyer acknowledging receipt of his report, Jewell observed: "I think our most difficult cooperative problem is yet to be met—that is, cooperation between the respective departments of the Railway Companies. . . . There is so much friction, jealousy, individuality—buck-passing if you will, as between the different departments of a railroad that it seems to me cooperation between them is bound to be most difficult." He went on to say that he hoped that the presence of a shopcrafts union officer on the system MW committee would "contribute to steadying the boat." [56]

In that hope he was disappointed. When Stimson met with Beyer, brotherhood president Fred Fljozdal, and officers of the B&O MW federation on July 16, the suggestion about McGee was one of three sticking points. The other two were timing—Stimson and the federation people argued for waiting for an upturn in traffic—and money. With regard to the latter point, Stimson did not wish, given the company's straits, to spend even $7,130; he insisted upon trying the program without giving the local labor committeemen company time to travel their territories gathering ideas. The four-hour session ended with only the agreement to try again in the fall, when business would be better.[57] Of course, business was not better in the fall. It did not improve much for a long time.

As the Depression lengthened, and wage cuts and layoffs began to look more and more permanent, union-management relations across the country were subjected to severe strains. The mutual good feeling that had fueled and had been fueled by cooperative programs began to run out. Cooperation was no longer even a slowly growing movement; in fact, it was shrinking fast. Seeing no future in his position with the AFL, Beyer left to become director of the labor relations section of the Office of the Federal Coordinator of Transportation in 1933. The AFL that same year quietly retreated from its official espousal of cooperative programs. Before long the B&O Plan was the only surviving major cooperative program in the United States.[58] It did not grow; serious discussions between the B&O and the MW brotherhood were never reopened. But it survived.

The obvious question now is, Why just the B&O? Why of the dozen or so sizable companies that tried a program of cooperation, and of the thousands that might have, was the B&O the only one in the country to stay the course? Why did not the economic forces that wrecked cooperation in the clothing and textiles industries and on other railroads wreck it on the B&O? One author states somewhat glibly that the B&O Plan survived "for the simple reason that it had proved profitable to the men and the company." [59] That explanation begs the question: *Why* was it profitable for the B&O, and not for other firms in the same industry? We return to the same broad answer suggested to similar ques-

tions on preceding pages: character of leadership. Leadership determined to
see the long-run benefits to company and employees in a program that for
short-run stretches might not appear profitable: if that is not wholly the
answer, then surely it is a vital part of it. It is hoped that by now the reader
has become convinced that in Daniel Willard, the B&O had such leadership.

The proof of such a judgment lies in an accumulation of small but revealing incidents, many of which have been related already. A further case in
point still may be appropriate.

The annual Glenwood shopcrafts picnic was the most important company
social event of the year for employees of that facility. Although it had to compete for employee attention with other local B&O festivities, such as the outings of the Veterans' Association and the Pittsburgh Division Athletic Association's Labor Day weekend corn roast, it was always exceedingly well
attended. Dating from the early days of the Cooperative Plan, it had grown
quite elaborate over the years. Recently it had been held at Conneaut Lake
Park, more than one hundred miles from Pittsburgh. The B&O ran special
trains to the affair, upon which employees and their immediate families of
course could ride free—at some considerable expense to the company, especially as the trains could use B&O tracks for only a portion of the trip.[60]

The Mutual Beneficial Association of the PRR had for several years run a
similar outing for its central region chapters—similar except in size (total attendance at three separate picnics in July 1930 was sixteen thousand) and in
the levying of a charge upon attendees (thirty-five cents for adults and ten
cents for children, for lemonade, coffee, and off-line handling of trains—the
PRR did not directly serve Conneaut Lake, either). Then in 1931, as a De-
pression-induced economy move, the MBA and the railroad canceled the
event. Presumably being aware of the Pennsylvania's action, and subject to
increasing pressure from Baltimore to keep costs down, local B&O officials
prepared to do the same to the Glenwood outing.[61]

When advised of this action, Glenwood shopcrafts leaders were upset. Local federation officials drew the matter to the immediate attention of William
McGee, who in turn pursued the subject up the B&O's managerial hierarchy
to Charles Galloway. Galloway stood by the initial decision: no special trains,
hence no outing. McGee did not give up. He apprised Otto Beyer of the situation, and the two contacted Willard, calling his attention to the symbolic importance of the picnic to the Glenwood cooperative program. Willard was on
an inspection trip over B&O western lines at the time, but when he returned to
Baltimore, he promptly sat down with McGee to discuss the issue. The discussion did not last long; Willard concluded that his views were "quite in ac-
cord" with those of Beyer, McGee, and the men at Glenwood. He reinstated
the picnic, with special trains, and sent McGee down the hall to work out the

details with Galloway's assistant. The only change in arrangements from those of prior years was in the advertising of the trains: they were announced as a "Baltimore & Ohio excursion Pittsburgh to Conneaut Lake," available to all area B&O employees, not as special picnic trains for the shopmen at Glenwood. So on August 29 two full trains were run, and, according to the local correspondent for *Baltimore & Ohio Magazine*, everyone had a marvelous time.[62]

The incident reinforces the conclusion that Willard was a leader sympathetic to his workers, and willing to spend some scarce money in the short run to maintain their loyalty in the long run. It also strengthens the following conclusion about the style (as opposed to the substance) of his leadership. In broad terms Willard should be judged a highly participative leader, one who delegated a great deal of authority to his subordinates, especially Galloway. Except with respect to results, he did not seek out and exercise tight control over the company's administrative details. He would note and order prompt remedy of streaks and smudges on passenger car windows, but he would not specify the means of remedy, other than that the first recourse should not be punishment. He would discuss any general issue or specific problem in labor relations with McGee, but he would not work out details of contracts or agreements, for lack of sufficient knowledge or expertise, unless forced to do so.[63] A task would be delegated; Willard would note that it was not being executed up to standard, and he would order correction, with the details left to the person responsible. A problem or an opportunity would emerge; Willard would gather opinions and information, alter or reaffirm pertinent policies, and delegate the development of technical specifics. He would step back into a matter only if policies were violated or standards not met. His essential style was this: to set general policies, standards, and tone; then to delegate, to watch that things were done properly, and to intervene if they were not. Sometimes that allowed problems to grow somewhat before they were resolved, but generally it was a very effective means of getting the most out of his subordinates' managerial talent. To have been more autocratic would have been to violate the spirit of the sign in his office.

Problems like the picnic incident notwithstanding, Willard's management team generally knew what the boss expected of them. Most disputes or performance problems were resolved in the field; Willard did not often have to serve as final arbiter or enforcer. His door was virtually always open, but not everything landed in his office. This was as true of the Cooperative Plan as of any other matter. During the late twenties and early thirties occasional problems with disagreeable or uncooperative local supervisors still arose. Such minor unpleasantness apparently was usually corrected at lower levels of the hierarchy, without any intervention by Willard.[64] Galloway and his subordinates may not have been quite so rigorously committed to cooperation as was their president, but neither were they the stumbling blocks that they at times might have seemed.

Nor should it be thought that all of the labor-management difficulties that arose during this period were the fault of management. During the summer and fall of 1931 a disagreement that demonstrated that the unions were capable of being every bit as niggling and shortsighted as the most unregenerate of operating officials occurred. In mid-June, after a lengthy period of pressuring and negotiating with Pullman Company management, the B&O succeeded in landing a contract to install air-conditioning in a number of Pullman sleeping cars at Mount Clare shops. It was highly unusual for Pullman to engage outside subcontractors, but the B&O had gone in hard pursuit of the contract anyway, seeing it as one means by which the company might honor its employment stabilization pledge under the Cooperative Plan. Perseverance paid off, and the contract was won. To complete the work—a rush order, since summer was beginning—Mount Clare management retransferred ten workers from the freight car department back to the passenger car department, where they had worked before a force reduction seven days previously. To speed the work along, the second shift was reinstated, to be worked by the returning men. Their wages were jumped back up to the passenger car rate of eighty cents per hour from the freight car rate of seventy-three cents, and ten men were recalled from furlough to fill their places in the freight car shop. Everyone should have been delighted. Instead, the local shopcrafts federation, on behalf of the ten men, filed a claim for penalty overtime.[65]

The Mount Clare superintendent, F. S. Stewart, was stunned. There was a clause in the shopcrafts contract that allowed a worker transferred from one shift to another without his request to demand the overtime rate for his first day on the new shift, a measure designed to protect the worker from frequent transfer from shift to shift at the whim of management. Stewart's subordinates, in their haste to get to work on the Pullman job, had neglected to post notice of the shift reinstatement so that the ten men could request the retransfer themselves. Because they had been working the day shift in the freight car shop and had not formally requested to be transferred, the men were technically entitled to invoke the penalty overtime clause. Stewart and his staff could not believe that the men would do that, since they were essentially getting their old jobs back at nearly a 10 percent higher wage and making room for the return of ten unemployed colleagues. On July 6 Stewart denied the claim.[66]

The shopcrafts committee did not let the matter rest; they appealed the decision up the chain of command. The issue was listed for discussion at the fall grievance conference between Federation No. 30 and headquarters management in Baltimore. It was discussed, on November 10, but to no different outcome. Conference chairman F. E. Blaser (Galloway's assistant) noted as critical to management's decision the fact that everyone knew that the ten men wanted the retransfer.[67] Subsequently, on November 16, McGee appealed directly to Galloway.

One can practically see the steam rising from Galloway's letter in response to McGee's request for an appeal conference. In essence he called the union position petty, ungrateful, and utterly unreasonable, and he made it clear that although he would meet with McGee promptly, they would be wasting their time. He also made it clear (to paraphrase) that it would be a cold day in hell before he went out of his way to land any more Pullman subcontract business.[68]

Beyer and Bert Jewell meanwhile were keeping an eye on the dispute from a distance. Beyer, probably embarrassed by his union colleagues' behavior, never did interject himself into the matter. Upon receiving a copy of Galloway's blast, however, Jewell did become involved. He sent Willard a copy of his file on the dispute, with a cover letter that, although not specifically discussing the merits of the case, called the matter to Willard's attention and offered the thought that it was "most unfortunate that the right of appeal from one officer to another cannot be exercised without the expression of undue resentment and threats."[69]

Willard's reply to Jewell, although not so emotionally accusatory as Galloway's, was uncharacteristically blunt and reproachful. He thanked Jewell for calling the matter to his attention, and he stated that since by the letter of the contract the men were entitled to time and a half, their claim would be paid. He then went on to say that he nevertheless was very much in sympathy with Galloway's position: that the ten men and their union, for the sake of a small, effortless gain ($3.20 each), were penalizing their company for its efforts on their behalf. The damage done would exceed the $32.00 benefit. "Personally," he wrote, "I think that the Company can much better afford to pay the claim than the men can afford to take it, in all the circumstances."[70] By mid-December the matter was settled: the men got their day's overtime pay, McGee got an "I guess I've been circumvented" letter from Galloway, and Jewell and Beyer got an attempted explanation from McGee.[71] There is no evidence that Mount Clare shopmen got any more Pullman air-conditioning work.

Willard by this time was the acknowledged senior statesman of railroading. His opinions and judgments were widely sought and respected outside as well as inside the industry. He was a director of AT&T, a member of the board of visitors of the Naval Academy, and the chairman of the board of trustees of Johns Hopkins University. He was held in high esteem in Washington, especially by kindred spirits in the progressive wing of the Republican party. He was much in demand as a speaker, both to trade groups and to the academic community.[72]

The judgments he offered in the world beyond his railroad were invariably those of a statesman: loyal to his own interests, but appreciative of and even defensive of the interests of potential adversaries. He was not afraid to speak up in favor of a legitimate but unheard side of an argument. His willingness to take the part of the common worker before an audience not too eager to hear it is well demonstrated in a speech that he gave in March 1931 at one of the great bastions of laissez-faire capitalism, the Wharton School of the University of Pennsylvania. In the course of presenting his thoughts on the role that Wharton should play in the world outside its walls, he stated that he could think of "nothing more deplorable" than that a man should be able and eager to work but be unable to find a job. Then he went on to say that were he unemployed, he would steal before he would starve.[73] That comment created something of a stir, both in his audience and later in the press, coming as it did from such a man in such a setting. But in the midst of a depression, it was something that the future financial elite and their teachers needed to hear.

A statesman also is willing to try to serve as a conciliator between two sharply opposing interests. One notable attempt to do so was his quiet lobbying of a number of coal mine operators, the "bad" side of an industry with perhaps the ugliest labor relations history of any in the United States, to sit down with the United Mine Workers and set up a B&O-type cooperative program on their properties. In 1933, at the suggestion of Beyer and Ellis Searles of the UMW, he took the matter up with several coal firms, but only one—a major B&O customer—indicated any serious interest in pursuing direct talks with Searles. Even that one possibility came to naught, but he did try.[74] The year 1933 simply was a terrible one to talk about cooperation, as the economic pie was shrinking and everyone was scrambling for crumbs. Besides, the Appalachian coal industry was a more hopeless place for a union-management cooperative program than Glenwood in 1923.

Of all of Willard's acts of statesmanship, though, his most difficult and, at the time, widely appreciated was his nearly single-handed negotiation of the 1932 railroad wage reduction. Throughout 1931, as the monetary deflation that accompanied the Depression deepened and as traffic nationwide continued to fall, the railroad industry's need for a general wage cut became increasingly obvious. During the first part of the year, the subject was being discussed privately by a number of railway executives, including Willard. As the year passed, the consideration of various approaches to the possibility became more intense. The hardest of the hard-line railroad executives favored posting notices of an intended 20 percent across-the-board permanent cut.

"Uncle Dan" Willard on the cover of *Time* magazine, January 11, 1932. (Copyright 1932 by Time Inc. Reprinted by permission)

Willard's preference was for a 10 percent temporary cut, with full wages to be restored as traffic levels improved. As discussions proceeded through the fall, the presidents of a group of the most powerful roads (including the Pennsylvania) settled on announcing a 15 percent cut. Willard opposed such a step. After a lengthy and heated debate at a conference of the Association of Railway Executives in November 1931, he succeeded in convincing a majority of his counterparts to give him a chance to negotiate a voluntary temporary 10 percent wage reduction. Working with a committee composed mainly of the presidents of roads of modest strength, Willard arranged for a conference with the twenty-one AFL and independent rail unions, to be held at the Palmer House in Chicago beginning on January 15, 1932. The debate at the conference was even lengthier and more heated than at the preceding executives' conference. For seventeen days Willard argued his case, with individuals, in small groups, and finally before the entire assemblage. When the matter was put to a vote, he won: all twenty-one unions agreed to an eighteen-month 10 percent pay concession. In an unusual display of respect and affection for a man who had just talked them out of 10 percent of their income, the unions sent him a basket of flowers.[75]

For his own part Willard already had cut his own salary by 20 percent from $150,000 per year to $120,000. As the Depression continued, he cut it to $60,000. He reduced the salaries of his officers—those earning at least $300 per month—by 10 percent in November 1931 and by another 10 percent when the union agreement became effective.[76] Then in June 1932 he ordered a cut that was painfully symbolic of the B&O's declining fortunes: suspension of the publication of *Baltimore & Ohio Magazine*. Its publication did not resume until March 1934.

Statesman that he was, Willard could not stop the B&O's financial slide. Neither could he halt the gradual decline in vitality of the Cooperative Plan. All of the negative forces and incidents already described gradually took their toll. Through 1926, an average of 529 suggestions per month had been submitted to shop cooperative committees; for the subsequent period through 1933, the average was only 190. The suggestion acceptance rate also fell in the latter period, from 86 to 78 percent.[77] Mutual irritation between labor and management, exhaustion of the more obvious improvements, reduction in meeting frequency, lowered interest resulting from worn-off novelty, and reduced enthusiasm caused by lower morale all slowed the program down. The most tangible reason for the declines, though—of particular importance with reference to the acceptance rate drop—was budgetary constraints, especially from 1930 on. Otherwise acceptable ideas were being deferred or rejected for lack of funds with increasing frequency as traffic levels plunged.

The impact of the company's financial exigency can be seen in the minutes of the system cooperative meeting for the first quarter of 1933. Held from 10:15 to 11:55 A.M. on January 4 at the B&O central office building, the meeting was attended by a typical complement of seventeen people: George Emerson chaired the meeting and represented management, along with the superintendent of the car department, the superintendents of motive power for the eastern and western regions, the superintendent of Mount Clare Shops, and three lesser mechanical department officials; labor was represented by Otto Beyer, William McGee, the general chairmen of six Federation No. 30 unions,[78] and an assistant general chairman. There were five items of old business on the agenda, all of which had been deferred for financial reasons. The first item, the construction of a washroom at the East Dayton shops, had been held in abeyance since the meeting of January 1927—for six years—"account necessity holding down all expenses." The second item, the addition of a washroom and lockers at Toledo, had been held up almost as long for the same reason: its cost, estimated at $3,570. The other three items were proper drainage for the floor of the car shop in Lorain, Ohio; the resurfacing and waterproofing of the pits in the Glenwood back shop; and the elevation for drainage purposes of track 20 in the car yard at Benwood, West Virginia. All of these recommendations dated from 1930, and all had been deferred because of insufficient funds.[79]

Upon only one of these five items was action taken at that meeting: it was decided to proceed with raising the soggy yard track at Benwood. The other four items were deferred again, until April. There was no new business before the committee; the balance of the meeting consisted mainly of McGee's asking Emerson about the possible reinstatement of work forces at various specific points around the system and Emerson's providing little definite encouragement.[80]

The Cooperative Plan had been more than a short-term success. In systemwide operation for nearly ten years at the end of 1933, it had built up some impressive numbers. Some 9,524 meetings (shops and CT/MW, local and system) had been held; 41,333 suggestions had been received, and 32,754 of them adopted.[81] Nonetheless, Cooperative Plan activity had slowed considerably, and its impact upon company profitability, it may be inferred, was much diminished. Such an inference is supported by Figures 3-1 and 3-2. The B&O's return on equity more or less kept pace with that of the Pennsylvania through 1928. In 1929, though, it fell well below PRR return on equity, and it stayed there; B&O ROE did not equal or surpass that of its rival again until 1941. Net railway operating income figures were less discouraging, but they still indicate that during the late 1920s, the B&O lost some of the ground it had gained on the Pennsylvania earlier in the decade. From 1930 through 1933, PRR net railway operating income fell as far as did the B&O's, but it recovered in comparative terms thereafter.[82]

As pointed out at the end of chapter 2, ascribing shifts in such general measures of profitability to the level of Cooperative Plan activity cannot be done with great confidence. Capital expenditures, and strategic decisions more broadly, are at least potentially weightier determinants of economic success. B&O and Pennsylvania percentage increases in net plant and equipment were roughly equal from 1927 through 1933: 18 and 17 percent, respectively. This apparent parity would seem to wash the factor out as a major element behind the relative performance of the two railroads. However, Willard and Atterbury did not spend their money at the same time or in the same ways. Broadly speaking, Atterbury concentrated his investments on betterments to existing property relatively early in the period, while Willard spent heavily on

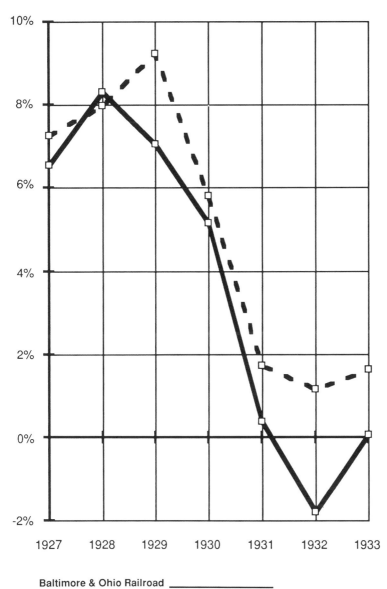

Baltimore & Ohio Railroad _____
Pennsylvania Railroad _ _ _ _ _ _ _ _ _ _

Figure 3-1 Return on Common Equity

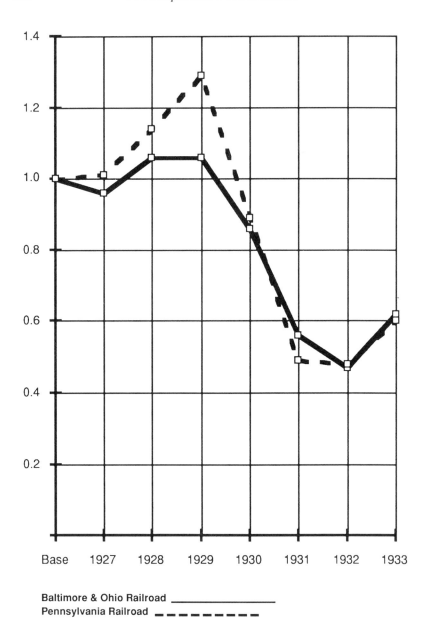

Baltimore & Ohio Railroad _____

Pennsylvania Railroad ___ ___ ___ ___ ___ ___

Figure 3-2 Net Railway Operating Income—Index Numbers
(Base = 1925–26 average)

acquisitions of new property in 1931. Nearly two-thirds of the increase in value of PRR net plant and equipment during the period was from internal investment before the end of 1929; roughly one-half of the B&O's corresponding line increase resulted from the purchase and consolidation of the Buffalo, Rochester & Pittsburgh (BR&P) Railway and the Buffalo & Susquehanna (B&S) Railroad, completed in November 1931. Willard's acquisition of the BR&P and the B&S, along with his simultaneous expenditure of $25 million for the entire capital stock of the just-out-of-receivership Alton Railroad, simply did not pay off as Atterbury's betterments did. With the Depression dragging on, the Alton proved to be more hindrance than help, and the BR&P and B&S probably were less help than a debt reduction would have been.[83] The ineffectiveness of the B&O's capital expenditures, then, distorts the profit picture by which the effectiveness of the Cooperative Plan might be judged. Figures 3-1 and 3-2 thus provide no definitive answers, but they are consistent with the conclusion that a weaker Plan was providing a weaker boost to B&O profits.

Was Willard's wisdom in personnel policy being offset by foolishness in overall strategy? To answer the question affirmatively would be unduly harsh. Neither Willard nor anyone else in 1931 expected that the Depression would continue without a full recovery for eight more years. Had there been the anticipated robust recovery by 1933, then Willard's acquisitions would have been good investments. Furthermore, his acquisitions did not spring from some impromptu expansion impulse, but from a government-encouraged master plan for eastern railroad mergers that had been gestating for over a decade. Willard had been involved in this matter from the beginning, seeing in the orderly ICC-supervised consolidation of smaller and weaker roads into larger and stronger ones the chance to achieve economies and efficiencies that would benefit both the public and the companies. Through his friendly relationship with the progressive Republican senator Albert Cummins of Iowa, he had helped to shape the portion of the Transportation Act of 1920 (the Esch-Cummins Act) that mandated such consolidation. Throughout the 1920s his long-range strategic plans for the B&O both influenced and were influenced by the ICC's evolving merger plan. He was a strong supporter of the final plan proposed by the commission in 1929, and, in concert with the Hoover administration, he worked hard to cultivate its acceptance among his fellow railroad presidents.[84]

Discussions over the next two years finally yielded a somewhat watered-down consensus on a four-system plan, submitted to the ICC in October 1931. The four systems were to be built around the B&O, the PRR, the NYC, and the C&O–Erie–Nickel Plate. In addition to roads in which it had long-standing partial ownership—Reading, Jersey Central, and Western Maryland—

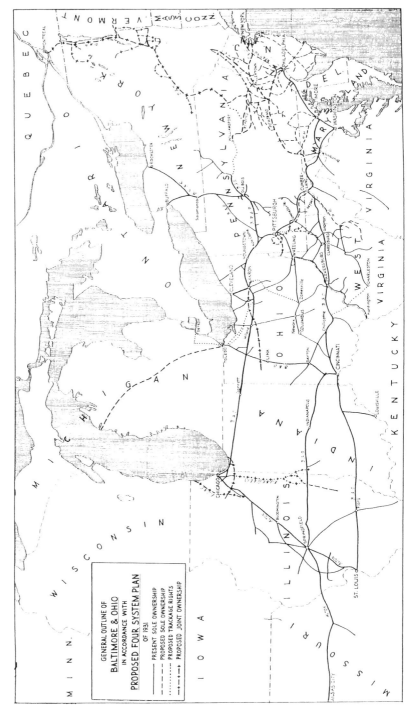

Daniel Willard's master plan of expansion of the B&O Railroad. Four-system plan presented to the Interstate Commerce Commission, 1931

the B&O was assigned the BR&P, the B&S, the Alton, and the Ann Arbor (see map). In making his acquisitions, then, Willard was moving to carry out an element of public policy that had been under development for a very long time.[85]

His conscientiousness was not well rewarded. Final ICC approval of the plan was announced in July 1932, but Willard's counterparts in the other three groups moved much more slowly or not at all, thus saving themselves precious cash and credit for other uses. Willard was out on a limb, and the Depression was weighting him down more and more as the weeks and months passed. He needed the loyalty and commitment of his employees more than ever before.

4

1 9 3 4 – 1 9 4 1

THE COOPERATIVE TRAFFIC PROGRAM

With the full realization that good times would not be returning any time soon, the B&O set about making the best of its depressed situation. Its pivotal need was for more traffic; its solution was the Cooperative Traffic Program, or CTP. An employee traffic solicitation program and more, the CTP was both a product of the B&O culture and a reinforcer of it. The CTP was the response of B&O family members to clear evidence that their company was in trouble, and it served both to remind employees of what the company stood for and to stimulate them to go out and convince others of the B&O's virtues. It was the dominant personnel-centered program of the now-aging Daniel Willard's declining years.

The chapter opens with an overview of the impact of the Depression on the railroad industry and of the consequent need for intensive traffic solicitation; a description of the B&O's pre-CTP efforts in this realm follows. Then the development of the CTP is described and discussed in some detail: its organization, its meetings and results in both nascent and mature stages, its participation rates, and its impact (or lack thereof) upon the rest of the industry. An account is given of the continuing decline of the Cooperative Plan, and observations on Daniel Willard nearing the end of his career are offered. The chapter ends with an assessment of the CTP's results, both tangible and intangible, and of its significance.

At the end of 1933, the American economy, like that of the rest of the world, was a sputtering wreck in comparison to what it had been four years previously. Industrial production had bottomed out at 59 percent of the 1923–

116

1925 average during March of that year. A recovery that began in April lasted only until midsummer; by fall, production was seriously slipping again. Optimism that prosperity was just around the corner was slipping as well. The AFL estimated that 25 percent of the unionized labor force, or some 13.7 million people, were unemployed.[1]

Less was being produced, so less was being shipped, and few people could afford much travel. The railroad industry, then as always, was hit harder than most other industries by economic slowdown. Railway operating revenues of the eastern district railroads in 1933 were only 50 percent of their 1923–1925 average and only 49 percent of their 1929 level. Freight and passenger cars sat empty and idle in yards and storage tracks. Long strings of locomotives, "white-leaded" to prevent rust, sat in dead lines outside their shops. Trains were shorter and less frequent; the industry's enormous track capacity was grossly underutilized. Half of the nation's railroad workers scrambled for lesser jobs elsewhere or sat at home. Many roads tottered on the brink of bankruptcy; some went over it.[2]

How did Willard and the B&O cope with this bleak environment? First, as already detailed, they cut costs—slowly at first, but eventually much as everyone else did. Hours were shortened, shifts and crews were cut, wages and salaries were lowered, capital expenditures were deferred, and the magazine was suspended. Second, as a positive complement to all of these negative measures, they developed the Cooperative Traffic Program.[3] An amalgam of elements of welfare work, the Cooperative Plan, and prior traffic solicitation campaigns, the Cooperative Traffic Program was an attempt to involve employees in boosting revenues: to work on the top line of the income statement, not just the cost lines below. As an innovation, it was not in a class with the Cooperative Plan. However, it served the company's greatest need at the time, and it became the B&O's highest-profile personnel-related management program for the balance of the decade.[4]

All railroads needed such a program, but the B&O needed it more than most. The reason for the B&O's greater need was not greater-than-average revenue decline. Its railway operating revenues had bottomed out in 1932; they were up slightly in 1933, to 53.7 percent of their 1929 level, nearly 5 percent better than the eastern district industry average. The reason for the B&O's greater need was its decades-old albatross: debt. Although a sales decline of almost 50 percent would pose severe problems for almost any company, those problems can be overcome to the extent that costs can be quickly reduced proportionately. The difficulty with debt is that for most companies, the B&O certainly included, it cannot be so reduced. Hence, for a company as highly leveraged as was the B&O, such a precipitous sales drop was potentially disastrous.

How bad was the B&O's debt situation? The total-debt-to-equity ratio of the Baltimore & Ohio at the close of 1933 was 2.51; the corresponding number for the Pennsylvania was 0.84, and that of eastern district Class I line-haul steam railroads as a group (in which the B&O was included) was 1.02. The B&O, then, was trying to cope with the loss of nearly half of its business with a debt burden two and a half times the regional railroad industry average and three times that of its principal competitor. In relative terms its interest charges were enormous. Despite layoffs, a penny-pinching purchasing policy, and the slight upturn in traffic, the B&O's 1933 net income was $204,772, a negligible 0.06 percent return on equity; interest and other fixed charges consumed $34.8 million of what was under the circumstances a respectable $35 million gross income. Further cost cutting could not reduce those fixed charges ($32.6 million of which were interest payments), and the company certainly was in no position to retire any of its debt.[5]

There really was only one practical course of action to pull the railroad out of its solvency-threatening situation: the rebuilding of a larger sales base over which to spread its fixed charges. The B&O needed a revenue increase fairly desperately; it could not afford simply to wait out the Depression, to wait for traffic levels to recover on their own. It needed to act aggressively to capture traffic that was already moving by other carriers. It needed to increase its market share, and it needed to do so without spending much money. Selective price cutting, the normal response of a firm facing falling sales in a deflationary economy, was inhibited by the complexity and ponderousness of railroad rate-making machinery. All rate changes were subject to ICC investigation and approval, and railroads generally maintained a united front through their regional rate bureaus when arguing for an adjustment before the commission. A road that broke away from the position of its rate bureau invited retaliation, in the form of diversion of connecting traffic by other member roads. For all practical purposes, then, price competition was out.

The firm that cannot compete on the basis of price most often relies on the alternative of product differentiation: convincing the prospective customer that the company's products or services are qualitatively superior to those of the competitor. Normally this is done through advertising. The B&O, though, had eliminated most professional advertising and promotion for the sake of cost reduction. That left only word-of-mouth advertising, which, being free, is usually the best kind anyway. The obvious word-of-mouth channel was the company's work force, the employees who actually provided the services to be sold.

There was nothing radical about this reasoning. Several railroads, the B&O prominent among them, had been at least sporadically encouraging informal employee traffic solicitation efforts for years. The Pequot Mills adaptation of the Cooperative Plan explicitly included promotion of the company's products among the responsibilities of the union and its members. With the onset of the Depression, other railroads began to try more actively to encourage such efforts. Most programs, though, were limited in scope, and some were dependent upon the use of tangible incentives. The Delaware, Lackawanna & Western, for example, offered all of its employees other than officers a cash bonus (from one dollar to five dollars) for booking individuals or groups on Lackawanna package tours. The traffic tip campaign of the Chicago, Burlington, & Quincy promised employees a variety of prizes (such as playing cards, automatic pencils, and engraved gold pocket knives) for successful traffic solicitation, the value of the prize being tied to the value of the traffic secured. Somewhat broader in scope and more dependent upon employee loyalty were the Railroad Family Clubs formed by the Southern Pacific (SP) at several major points on its system, most successfully at company headquarters in San Francisco, to which both employees and local shippers were invited to hear various speakers describe the advantages of rail transportation. Local merchants patronized by railroad employees were to be encouraged by those employees, led by the clubs, to reciprocate and to patronize the railroad. To reinforce the process, the SP placed advertisements in local newspapers, listing and endorsing those merchants who shipped or received goods by rail. A somewhat narrower reciprocity campaign was undertaken by the Missouri-Kansas-Texas Lines: MKT employees were issued gummed labels printed with the company logo and a message asking for the recipient's shipping and travel business, to be attached to personal checks written by the employee. Perhaps the most thorough and intensive program was the employee club network of the St. Louis–San Francisco. The clubs, located at sixty-four major points around the system, were credited during 1931 with having secured for Frisco Lines 6,896 carloads of freight, 9,823 less-than-carload freight shipments, and 3,003 passengers.[6]

Employee loyalty, cultivated by Daniel Willard for more than twenty years, surely was at least as strong on the B&O as it was on those other lines; mustering B&O employees into a major campaign to solicit traffic was undoubtedly feasible. Modest efforts in this direction had been exerted since before World War I. Moreover, there existed already a model of how a major campaign might be handled organizationally: the Cooperative Plan representative committee structure. It had been a highly effective means of gaining general employee involvement in improving maintenance and operations efficiency; a logical inference was that a similar committee structure might succeed in gaining general employee involvement in improving sales and marketing effectiveness.

It is not clear who first made the suggestion explicitly. The new program's first traveling "special representative" attributed the idea to Willard himself. Willard said that the idea had been brought up in the fall of 1933 at a head-quarters staff meeting by "someone," and a company pamphlet issued more than a decade after Willard's death traced the idea to a Cooperative Plan shops committee meeting. Whatever its origin, the concept was a natural one, and it was quickly pursued. By the end of 1933, the idea was being developed into an organization, with local committees, a staff, and a name: the Cooperative Traffic Program.[7]

The notion of involving employees outside the traffic department in sales efforts had been used with some small success on the B&O for nearly twenty years before the commencement of the Cooperative Traffic Program. The first notable attempt in this direction apparently began spontaneously early in 1915 at Connellsville, Pennsylvania, where the local freight agent and three en-ginemen formed a committee, later joined by the division superintendent and master mechanic, to serve as a business-generating and service-improving liaison between the railroad and the local merchants' association. Shortly thereafter, growing out of a luncheon discussion between Willard and division freight agent W. R. Askew, a more comprehensive but less personal campaign began in Baltimore. No employee committee was organized, but a handout sheet was prepared to be distributed by all Baltimore-area B&O employees to their friends and associates.[8]

Both of these efforts were strictly local, although employees in other locales were encouraged to emulate them; for a short time in 1916, a business prospect postcard was inserted into the company magazine. It was not until after World War I that a true systemwide campaign was undertaken. This time Willard assumed a more direct and public role than he had in the prior cases. The occasion for commencing the campaign was a meeting of the B&O Vet-erans' Association in Baltimore on November 13, 1920. The postwar re-cession had begun in earnest, and B&O carloadings were slipping rapidly. Willard arranged to speak at the veterans' meeting; his subject was the traffic loss and what the veterans might do to stem it. Essentially, he appealed to all members of the association to use their personal contacts to boost the com-pany's market share. He placed particular emphasis upon the opportunities that might present themselves to operating personnel who had contact with freight customers, such as local freight train conductors; he urged them espe-cially to approach and to try to regain former customers whose shipments, often of high-rated merchanise, had been directed to other carriers during wartime federal control of the railroads. He also reminded his audience of the importance of courteous and efficient service in creating favorable word-of-mouth advertising and in ensuring repeat business.[9]

Mr Shipper:

⁋ The city in which a great railroad has its headquarters, receives the greatest share of the money spent by that railroad. Baltimore, through the Baltimore and Ohio enjoys this distinction.

⁋ You who are interested in the welfare of Baltimore, know that what is good for Baltimore is good for you

⁋ Do you know that the Baltimore and Ohio Railroad, with its headquarters in Baltimore, is the largest employer in the city, paying wages amounting to many millions of dollars each year, nearly all of which is spent in Baltimore?

⁋ The Baltimore and Ohio, operating one hundred thousand freight cars advertises Baltimore in every state in the Union, the Dominion of Canada and the Republic of Mexico.

⁋ There is not a town or hamlet in the United States that boasts of a railroad that has not read the name "Baltimore" on one of these cars at some time.

⁋ Your attention is directed to the very interesting data on the following page which shows the extent to which the Baltimore and Ohio Railroad contributes towards the support of Baltimore merchants.

⁋ The Baltimore and Ohio asks that you give this careful consideration and indicate your concurrence therein by favoring it with your business.

⁋ Information as to rates, schedules, etc., will be cheerfully furnished on application, by the General Freight Office, Commercial Freight Office or Freight Solicitors.

W. R. ASKEW	J. L. HAYES
Division Freight Ag't	Commercial Freight Ag't

BALTIMORE AND OHIO
IN
BALTIMORE

Total Investment....	$30,000,000
Total Mileage in Baltimore	180
Pay roll, monthly	$ 575,000
Pay roll, yearly.................	$ 6,900,000
Total number of employes in Baltimore	8,500
Using factors adopted by U S. Census Bureau, employes at 4.54 persons to family would indicate population in Baltimore depending on Baltimore and Ohio employes of	38,590
Following same authority their expenditures annually for certain principal items would be as follows:	
Flour, meal, etc..............	$ 172,380
Potatoes and other green vegetables......'.........	$ 376,584
Meats and sausage...........	$ 803,998
Milk, cheese and eggs........	$ 470,288
Boots and shoes..............	$ 277,848
Men's clothing..............	$ 583,667
Ladies' apparel.............	$ 825,463
Purchases in Baltimore annually:	
Lumber and ties..............	$ 141,118
Stationery and printing.........	$ 545,722
Miscellaneous.................	$ 1,289,283
Total	$ 1,976,123
Total amount spent annually in Baltimore.	$ 8,876,123

Reciprocity card, 1915. (Courtesy of the B&O Railroad Museum)

The cause immediately was taken up by Robert Van Sant and *Baltimore & Ohio Magazine.* In January 1921 Van Sant sent a letter to the presidents of all Veterans' Association chapters, reminding them of Willard's appeal and urging them to lead their groups to answer it with action. In the February and March issues of the magazine, prominent display was given to the sales successes of veterans on the Connellsville and Chicago divisions. Meanwhile, the traffic department had printed and had distributed through the association ten thousand traffic solicitation postcards, carrying a request for the shipper's patronage, lines for the names and addresses of the shipper and the veteran who handed out the card, and space for a reply by the shipper as to whether he had favored the B&O with new business. In April the company began collecting and tabulating these cards in order both to evaluate the success of the program and to give credit to those employees who had secured traffic from the competition.[10]

Also in April, the decision was made to extend the campaign beyond the veterans' groups to all B&O employees and to increase its intensity. A series of major rallies was planned, covering nineteen of the most important points on the B&O in eighteen days. The local Veterans' Association chapters were to host the events, but all B&O employees and their families were invited. All local officers, of all departments, were expected to attend. Appropriately large halls were hired, and entertainment was booked. A traveling team of speakers, consisting of commercial development manager H. O. Hartzell, welfare department chief W. W. Wood, and Veterans' grand president George Sturmer, was formed.[11]

The level of enthusiasm generated by the rallies varied from location to location. When the series was over, mixed results were apparent: attendance ranged from a very impressive 1,000 at Chillicothe, Ohio, down to a dismal 50 at Philadelphia. Overall, the average attendance of 260 was deemed sufficiently encouraging to continue a high-profile campaign. The company magazine began publishing the names of employees who had successfully solicited new customers, along with a description of the traffic that they had secured; notable individual, departmental, or divisional efforts continued to be featured in front-of-the-magazine articles.[12]

Despite all the attention given it, the campaign was only a marginal success. Through August 13, 1921, nine months after Willard's appeal, approximately 1,700 carloads of new freight traffic had been credited to employee efforts—just under 200 carloads per month. The list of returned solicitation cards published in the August issue of *Baltimore & Ohio Magazine,* covering the four weeks ending July 30, revealed that the 164 carloads reported for the period had been secured by a mere thirteen people. Many of the same names appeared on the list month after month; the Connellsville duo of P. J. Harrigan and James Wardly, who jointly brought in over a quarter of the July carloads, had entered regular and major contributions into the record from the beginning. Passenger statistics, which were recorded beginning in May, were no more impressive. For the four weeks ending August 1, an inconsequential forty-nine "new" passengers were enticed aboard the B&O by a total of eight employees, one of whom was Baltimore export clerk F. W. Melis, like Harrigan and Wardly a regular contributor of large numbers of freight carloads. For all of 1921, less than 0.5 percent of all B&O employees made credited contributions to the campaign.[13] The net income generated by the new business, some of which would have moved via B&O anyway, probably did not do much more than cover the costs of the kickoff rallies.

Still, the campaign was the sort of activity that meshed well with Willard's desire to build employee loyalty and communitarian spirit across the railroad. Consequently, the idea never really disappeared. Throughout the 1920s, espe-

Traffic solicitation postcard, 1925. (Author's collection)

cially whenever traffic levels began to decline, B&O employees were asked to seek out more business. *Baltimore & Ohio Magazine*'s business prospect postcard insert was reinstituted as traffic turned downward in the second half of 1923; the magazine's listing of the names and credited traffic of "business-getting employes" resumed at the beginning of 1924, was dropped for a time, and resumed again as another recession began at the end of 1926. Local public relations committees, 158 of which were set up across the system in 1924, provided indirect aid and encouragement. Then as the Cooperative Plan gained momentum, union locals began campaigning for B&O patronage, some quite aggressively.[14] Such urging had its effect; B&O employees over the decade gradually became more involved in traffic solicitation. The securing of additional passenger business increased much more substantially than did that of freight—not surprisingly, given that the average employee was much more likely to know someone planning to take a trip than someone planning to ship a carload of merchandise. The record of returned prospect cards for July 1928, typical of those of the late 1920s, shows 325 passengers secured by 112 employees; freight entries show approximately 120 carloads, 9 carload routing orders, 3 less-than-carload (LCL) routing orders, and 8 LCL shipments secured by 38 employees.[15]

The prospect card program continued into 1932, when publication of the magazine was suspended, hampering distribution of cards and eliminating the principal means of publicity. During the last months that the program was in full operation, credited traffic was lower than it had been before the start of the Depression, but it had not fallen so far proportionately as had B&O traffic in general. The April 1932 list shows approximately 300 passengers secured by 110 B&O employees, with another 27 having secured 89 carloads and at least 14 LCL shipments of freight, plus 5 unclassified freight shipments; a total of 14 employees of the newly acquired and separately operated Alton Railroad secured 16 passengers and 41 freight carloads.[16] As with the results of the 1921 campaign, the dollar value of traffic diverted from competitors was hardly noticeable in relation to the company's total revenues. The tangible impact of any one month, or even any one year, of employee traffic solicitation efforts probably was not worth the bother. The cumulative effect, however, of twelve years of reminding employees of the role that they could play in determining the volume of business that their company received—the long-term intangible impact—probably was worthwhile. The postcard program, and its predecessors, served as one more means of making Willard's point that the B&O family would prosper only if its members did more than their minimum assigned duties. This now-familiar point, along with the similar message and essential organizational structure of the Cooperative Plan, served as the foundation upon which the Cooperative Traffic Program could be built.

Responsibility for development of the CTP, as the program quickly became known as, was given to O. S. Lewis, since 1930 the railroad's general freight traffic manager. Lewis and his superiors determined at the outset that unlike preceding traffic solicitation programs, the CTP would have full-time staff. Initially, Lewis himself devoted nearly his full attention to organizing the CTP. His first major decision was the appointment, on December 1, 1933, of a true full-time CTP staff member: C. N. Fullerton was named "special representative" of the traffic department, with duties first as an adviser to Lewis and a liaison with the mechanical department cooperative committees, then as a traveling CTP booster, helping local CTP committees to organize themselves.

Fullerton, who as a union officer had helped to end the machinists' boycott of the Cumberland Back Shop cooperative committee in 1925, was an excellent choice for the job. He was energetic, outgoing, and widely experienced, and possessed high credibility with the rank and file. He had served as president of System Federation No. 30 from 1918 to 1920, and as general chairman of the machinists' union on the B&O from 1920 to 1926. In 1926 he left the B&O for a coordinator's position in the machinist apprenticeship program of the Railway Educational Bureau in Omaha; when that program was discontinued in February 1933, he returned to his old job as a machinist at the B&O shops in Washington, Indiana, where he had begun his career in 1903. From there he was promoted to the new CTP position.[17]

The first local CTP committee met on December 5, 1933, at the B&O's venerable Queen City Hotel and station complex in Cumberland; in rapid succession, CTP committees were formed and met at all points around the system large enough to be able to muster a group of interested employees. By the end of December, plans had been laid for the organization of 185 committees, 162 on the B&O and 23 on the Alton; 95 of those committees had met and had elected chairmen. The smaller points of activity on the railroad usually had only one committee. Larger points generally had proportionately larger numbers of committees, formed around particular departments or facilities; initially, there were 6 committees in Cumberland, 10 in Cincinnati, and 34 in Baltimore. At locations with large numbers of both female and male employees, separate women's committees were set up, 12 on the B&O and 5 on the Alton at the end of December.[18]

A great deal was accomplished in a short time, and the initial success of the program was quite encouraging. During its first month, 1,007 freight carloads, 634 LCL shipments, and 439 passengers were credited to the CTP, plus 225 carload routing orders, 21 LCL routing orders, 180 miscellaneous reports and tips, and 52 traffic-related suggestions. Some 444 employees contributed to at least one of those statistics.[19] The increased success in all categories, in comparison to the old prospect card program, was appreciable. The monthly *CTP Bulletin*, in which were published the names and contributions of individual CTP participants grouped by respective committee, grew rapidly in size in subsequent months. As additional committees were organized, increasing numbers of employees went out to solicit new business. January results were almost double those of December: 1,934 carloads, 710 LCL shipments, and 821 passengers, plus various tips and suggestions, credited to 838 employees. February results were off somewhat, but those of March were up again in all categories except full carloadings: 1,650 carloads, 1,303 LCL shipments, and 1,124 passengers, plus tips and suggestions, from 1,025 employees.[20]

In April 1934 the growing number of women's committees was organized into a women's division. Under the leadership first of Margaret Talbott Stevens and then of Olive Dennis, the women's committees had expanded their membership to include not only the B&O's women employees, but also the wives of B&O men, and in so doing had become a considerable presence. With the establishment of the separate division, Dennis passed her CTP responsibilities to a new full-time CTP staff member, Helen Foreman. Foreman, formerly a clerk in the car service department, served as the counterpart to C. N. Fullerton, spending most of her time on the road speaking and helping to organize committee activities.[21]

The organization of the local committees was generally open and unstructured. Sometimes a group would gather spontaneously and elect its own officers, without help from elsewhere in the company. In other instances an individual would step forward—or be asked to step forward by his or her superior officer, or by Fullerton or Foreman—to advertise and convene a first meeting; in those cases, the first committee officer elected usually was the convener as chairman. Membership in the program was automatic for all B&O and Alton employees and their families. Local committee membership often was not much more restrictive: at some locations, as a matter of practice if not of intent, anyone who showed up at a business meeting was a member of the committee. The company generally kept an eye on committee leadership, for the sake of maintaining basic unity of purpose and reasonable efficiency, but the program was designed to be inclusive, not exclusive.[22]

To help ensure that the local committee chairmen were both purposeful and enthusiastic, a meeting of eastern region chairmen was held in Baltimore on May 14. Eastern region CTP supervisor H. O. Hartzell presided; more than one hundred attended. The meeting gave the program's field leadership an opportunity to exchange ideas, to make suggestions, to receive information from top management, and to exhort and to be exhorted to greater efforts. Discussion was neither narrowly confined nor tightly controlled from the top; during the afternoon session in particular, Hartzell was more the recipient of advice than the dispenser of it. Over half of the employees present brought problems or missed opportunities from their home offices or territories to his attention. The transcript of the meeting indicates that the group generally displayed the same wide-ranging concern for company success characteristic of the original Cooperative Plan committees. Particular matters of employee concern included the excessive centralization of decision-making authority, an insufficient number of passenger trains on certain key routes, the absence of freight pickup and delivery service for customers without their own sidings, dirty stations, early freight station closing hours, inattentive coach porters, and lack of consistent traffic department acknowledgment of all tips on customer prospects from nontraffic employees. In the course of the discussion, Hartzell promised that management would follow up immediately on all of the concerns expressed, although the feasibility of some recommendations from the group, such as adding more passenger trains in the face of a huge decline in business, he questioned on the spot.[23]

Unfortunately, it appears that no similar meetings were held in the western regions. Nonetheless, by the summer of 1934, *Baltimore & Ohio Magazine* could state accurately "The Cooperative Traffic Program is now well past the preparatory stage and moving ahead all along the line." CTP credited traffic continued to grow in all categories, and so did the employee participation rate. In July, for example, the names of 1,429 people appeared in the *CTP Bulletin*, along with their contributions. This was only 3 percent of the 42,000 B&O and 5,200 Alton employees at the time, but for a single month it was fairly impressive; even allowing for the fact that the most active employees secured traffic nearly every month, it is likely that well over 3 percent of the work force made some sort of a contribution during the year. The impact of these contributions on company revenues was of some significance. At a mass CTP meeting in Baltimore in February 1935, Willard stated that CTP credited carload, LCL, and passenger traffic for 1934 had brought in $1.4 million; when routing orders and other promises of business were added in, the total was estimated to be roughly $2 million. That was 1.4 percent of the B&O's 1934 revenue; Willard pronounced it "a splendid showing." [24]

Certainly the people responsible for the program could point to its concrete successes, however small in relative terms. However, as with Willard's other personnel-centered programs, the purpose of the CTP extended beyond direct, tangible traffic solicitation. The original Cooperative Plan was designed to have as its most fundamental objective the long-term development of mutual commitment between labor and management; the same was essentially true of the Cooperative Traffic Program. Early in 1934 Fullerton had stated that the immediate goals of the CTP were (1) to secure more business, so that the B&O could (2) provide greater job security for employees still working and (3) recall those employees who had been furloughed. It was understood, however, that broader objectives were being served at the same time. Familiar terms such as *teamwork, family,* and *goodwill* appeared frequently in formal statements presented at local CTP meetings. In December 1934 Lewis stated in an open letter prominently printed in that month's company magazine that an ultimate objective of the CTP was the increase of "good-will both on the part of the public towards the Company and good-will among ourselves." Willard made the point more explicitly at the Baltimore CTP rally mentioned earlier: "The dollars and cents result has been most helpful. But more important than that is the finer community of interest that has been established on our road, the clearer understanding of our common problems, the better teamwork, and the increased spirit of friendliness that has been developed in our own railroad family, and between the people we serve and ourselves." [25]

Unlike the Cooperative Plan, the CTP sought to achieve such objectives without the formal, active support of its unions. If the union role had been decided on the first impulse of Bert Jewell, that would not have been the case. At the system Cooperative Plan meeting in January 1930, William McGee and George Emerson had decided to establish a joint labor-management committee to investigate procedures for securing more business for the B&O. McGee apprised Jewell of their action, and Jewell responded enthusiastically with suggestions as to how they might proceed. Jewell's main recommendation was that a central committee and a network of district committees be formed to organize a canvass of every shipper and citizen in Baltimore & Ohio territory, urging them to pledge all of their business to the B&O. The canvass would be supported by arrangements for local union officers to speak before groups such as Chambers of Commerce and Rotary Clubs, pointing out the contributions made by the B&O to the community and urging community leaders to reciprocate. Jewell further proposed using *Labor* editor Edward Keating's contacts at the Associated Press and United Press International to line up extensive and favorable wire service coverage of the campaign.[26] For a national union leader to show such eager partiality toward a particular company was somewhat unusual; it was a measure, presumably, of the depth of Jewell's concern about increased highway competition, of his appreciation of Daniel Willard, and of his antipathy toward the B&O's union-busting rail competitor, the Pennsylvania.

Such a grand scheme, bearing the imprimatur of the AFL, never came to fruition. The precise reasons for this are not a part of the surviving record, but a reasonable assumption is that it ran afoul of the very factor that made Jewell's suggestions unusual: the tendency of such favoritism to reduce union employment at the beneficiary company's competitors. From the perspective of the shopcrafts unions, hurting the PRR was no problem, but the Pennsylvania was not the B&O's only rail competitor. A major boost-the-B&O program might also hurt railroads such as the New York Central, the Erie, the Nickel Plate, and the Chesapeake & Ohio, where the AFL shopcrafts unions were well established. No doubt William McGee liked Jewell's ideas; it is almost as certain that the system federation presidents on those other roads did not. Moreover, the independent train and engine crew brotherhoods, with whom the AFL at least perfunctorily proclaimed solidarity, were established on the Pennsylvania. Whether Jewell retracted his proposal in the face of pressure from his brethren, or simply thought better of it himself, the AFL did not adopt any high-profile role in the B&O's traffic solicitation campaigns in 1930, in 1933, or beyond. All that Jewell was able to give Willard in this regard—not an insignificant gift—was his unions' quiet cooperation and encouragement.

Such support notwithstanding, in comparison to the Cooperative Plan there was in the CTP a certain organizational vacuum where the unions might have been. Filling that vacuum was largely the job of C. N. Fullerton, Helen Foreman, and, beginning in the summer of 1935, Dr. G. P. Grimsley. Grimsley, a B&O industrial geologist whose position was made largely unnecessary by the depression in heavy industrial activity, first assumed responsibility for the eastern region CTP during the illness of H. O. Hartzell late in June; gradually, his oversight duties were expanded to include speaking and organizational activities like those of Fullerton and Foreman. Eventually, a pattern evolved in which Grimsley worked primarily with committees on eastern lines while Fullerton generally worked the west, and Foreman handled the women's committees over the entire system. With minor variations this organizational arrangement, a three-person traveling staff supported by clerical help, provided the central leadership of the CTP for the remainder of its existence.[27]

As a natural result of the importance of the program's intangible objectives, from the very beginning there was a social as well as a business dimension to the CTP. Drawing upon the examples provided by earlier company gatherings such as the safety rallies and welfare department activities, major CTP meetings often were heavy on entertainment. A noteworthy example was the November 1934 meeting of the combined CTP committees of Newark, Ohio, a dinner program held at the Knights of Pythias Lodge and attended by 550 B&O employees and family members. Before the start of the business meeting, attendees "were entertained by a string orchestra, courtesy of McMichael's School of Music, and by an orchestra from Somerset, Ohio, led by Section Foreman D. M. May." They then were treated to a performance by the Grotto Male Chorus, singing "Hail, the Baltimore & Ohio," the company song written by Margaret Talbott Stevens and Walter Goodwin (composer of "That Wonderful Mother of Mine") for the Centenary Pageant in 1927. The business meeting itself consisted of brief remarks by Helen Foreman, the Cincinnati regional freight agent, and six local division officers, and a keynote address by C. N. Fullerton. Fullerton ended his speech with a reminder that "suggestions are always in order," and the evening concluded with another sing-through of "Hail, the Baltimore & Ohio."[28]

This format was typical of larger CTP meetings during the mid-1930s. The most noticeable variation was a function of the size of the local B&O employment base: larger B&O points tended to have more elaborate entertainment and higher-ranking principal speakers than smaller ones. Thus Baltimore meetings might feature the B&O Women's Music Club and Charles Galloway, whereas Huntington, West Virginia, might rate only a clarinet-playing tower operator and the local passenger agent. Attendance would vary as well, of course. Baltimore might draw nearly 1,000, and Huntington only 150. Another variation was the occasional joint event; at some points CTP gatherings

The company song: "Hail the Baltimore & Ohio." (Copyright 1927 by the B&O Railroad. Reprinted by permission of CSX Corporation)

were combined from time to time with those of other B&O groups. It was not unusual for large seasonal events such as Christmas parties and summer picnics to be held in conjunction with the local Veterans' Association chapter, or with a group tied to the welfare department.[29]

Such major events seldom took place at a given location more than three times per year; the rest of the CTP meetings, usually held monthly, were somewhat less social and considerably less well attended. At Clarksburg, West Virginia, the women's committee rotated its meetings among the homes of its members; attendance was usually about two dozen. The typical meeting agenda called for a social hour and refreshments, followed by individual reports of business secured; at their November 1935 meeting it was reported that during October, nineteen of their members had secured fifty-one passenger trips worth a total of $514.91 to the company. The women's committee of New Castle, Pennsylvania, handled its meetings in similar fashion. Their September 1935 meeting, attended by twenty-eight women, began with a spelling bee, followed by lunch and the business meeting; four of those present made traffic reports, amounting to eight passenger trips. Their meeting of the following month, attended by three members of the Warren, Ohio, women's CTP as well as by the New Castle regulars, featured a skit, bingo, and refreshments before the business meeting; two of the local members reported securing a total of eleven passengers and one LCL shipment.[30]

Regular committee meetings in the men's division tended to be lighter on entertainment and heavier on speeches than were the women's meetings. The meeting of the Staten Island men's committees at the Livingston station on the evening of January 31, 1936 (unlike Cooperative Plan meetings, CTP meetings normally were not held on company time) consisted of eight speeches of varying length by various people, including Grimsley and the division freight agent. There was no entertainment, with the exception of whatever casual conversation occurred over the refreshments served after the speeches. At the men's CTP meeting at Clarksburg in February 1936, speeches were delivered by the division freight claim prevention representative, the division captain of police, and the local station services supervisor. Although attendees were offered neither entertainment nor refreshments, ninety-one men showed up; three of them made traffic reports, totaling six passengers and seventeen freight tips. At the Baltimore Terminals men's division meeting the next month, more than two hundred employees turned out in a heavy rainstorm to listen to addresses on current conditions and services by O. S. Lewis and four lesser traffic department officials. Entertainment was provided by a local orchestra and by a Dr. Gray, who did impersonations.[31]

Throughout 1935 and 1936, those meetings and hundreds of others like them continued to have the desired effect upon both morale and traffic levels.

Annual CTP credited traffic slipped slightly but remained above $1 million, with tips and routing orders pushing the probable real total higher. The benefits of the program came at a reasonably low cost: the only CTP expenses charged to the company were the salaries and expenses of Grimsley, Foreman, and Fullerton; the costs of collecting data and publishing the *CTP Bulletin;* and the rental fees of large halls for major CTP rallies.[32]

Buoyed both by the CTP and by gradual improvement of the economy, B&O traffic continued its slow rise from the 1932 nadir. Total revenues increased 2.9 percent in 1934 and another 3.8 percent in 1935. Profits, however, did not keep pace. Largely because of a sizable increase in equipment and track maintenance expense, made necessary by the distressingly large amount of deferred maintenance accumulated since 1930, losses of $3.8 million and $3.2 million were incurred in 1934 and 1935, respectively. Then, with what appeared to be real economic recovery under way in 1936, there was a sharp improvement in the company's fortunes. Revenues jumped to $178 million, up almost 21 percent. Net income available to common equity became positive again, in the amount of $4.5 million. That represented an ROE of only 1.37 percent, but it was the best that the company had done in six years. Revenues still were nearly 30 percent below their 1929 level, and cumulative net income since the end of 1930 remained negative, but the B&O was beginning to regain a measure of financial health.[33]

During this period, unfortunately, there arose for the first time a reason to be concerned about the health of the B&O's leader. On August 9, 1935, it was reported that Willard was in Johns Hopkins University Hospital, having suffered a case of ptomaine poisoning while on an inspection trip. Bert Jewell noted an article in the *Chicago Tribune* to that effect, and the same day wrote to Willard, expressing the hope "that ere this reaches you, you will have entirely recovered and are enjoying your usual good health." Willard replied on August 10 that he had become "somewhat ill" during his inspection trip of the B&O's Reading subsidiary, and that he had returned to Baltimore and checked in at Johns Hopkins (of which he still was president of the board of trustees) simply "to find out what was the trouble." He told Jewell that he felt "quite all right again" but that his doctor insisted upon his staying in the hospital for a week or ten days. Willard allowed, "I suppose I may follow his advice, but I am not certain."[34]

In fact, it was not ptomaine poisoning, but a mild heart attack that Willard had suffered. He was seventy-four years old and still working a six-day week of long days. Even on Sunday, his day off, it was his frequent practice, after church in the morning, to spend time strolling around the B&O's various Baltimore-area facilities to see how things were going. After his heart attack, he was forced to curtail some of his activities, especially in the eve-

Daniel Willard at his farm in Salisbury, Connecticut. (Courtesy of the B&O Railroad Museum)

nings. He began working a shorter day and retiring to bed shortly after dinner to read or listen to the radio.[35] Daniel Willard finally was becoming an old man, and that was not good news either to him or to the Baltimore & Ohio Railroad.

By the spring of 1936, the Cooperative Traffic Program was two and a half years old; it properly could be called mature. Around the system 368 committees had been organized, 291 in the men's division and 77 in the women's division. There were not so many monthly meetings; it had become standard procedure for multiple committees in a single city or town to meet together. The only separation routinely observed was that between men's and women's divisions. The essential fact was that CTP meetings were being held every month at every location of any significance on the entire B&O–Alton system.[36]

Perhaps the most striking demonstration of the size and momentum that had been gained by the CTP was the Baltimore Terminals mass meeting held in May 1936. Approximately four thousand people packed the Alcazar Auditorium for the event, overflowing the main hall into balconies, adjoining rooms, and stairways. The agenda for the evening was familiar and smoothly executed. A lengthy program of entertainment, largely consisting of song and

Baltimore Terminals CTP meeting, May 1936. (Courtesy of the B&O Railroad Museum)

dance numbers, was provided mostly by the children of local employees. A sizable collection of door prizes, mainly small electrical appliances, was awarded. Brief introductory remarks were made by the terminal superintendent, two local CTP committee chairmen, and O. S. Lewis. Willard was to be the principal speaker, but he was recovering from a serious episode of bronchitis; Charles Galloway acted as his stand-in, praising CTP efforts in particular and B&O employee cooperation in general. The assembly was led in song (presumably including "Hail, the Baltimore & Ohio"). Finally, the floor of the main hall was cleared of chairs, and there was dancing for those who wished to stay, to the music of a professional orchestra.[37]

As the headquarters city, with by far the largest number of B&O employees of any point on the system, Baltimore could be counted upon to turn out the largest crowds for major CTP rallies. In absolute terms, then, the CTP may have been most successful in Baltimore. In relative terms, however, its success may have been equal—or in a few instances even greater—in some other B&O towns. As the program became firmly established, a pattern of CTP participation rates emerged, a pattern similar to those discernible in earlier employee involvement programs such as the Veterans' Association, the safety rallies, and welfare department activities. Participation rates were not uniform across the railroad. They appeared to be a function of two factors: the size of the community and the salience of the B&O in that community. The degree of employee participation in the CTP tended to be inversely related to the former: the larger the town, the lower the rate, presumably because employees and their families in large cities had a wider range of entertainment or other diversionary opportunities than did their small-town counterparts, and because large-city culture generally placed a lesser emphasis on loyalty and sense of belonging. On the other hand, the participation rate tended to vary directly with the second factor; the more obviously important the B&O was to the well-being of the town, the higher the rate. Thus CTP participation, as a percentage of local employees, usually was highest, month in and month out, in small towns where the B&O was one of the largest employers. In relative terms, then, the CTP was at least as successful in turning out the troops in towns such as Cumberland, Wheeling, New Castle, Clarksburg, and Chillicothe as it was in Baltimore. Conversely, it was less successful in Philadelphia, home of the Pennsylvania Railroad, and in Chicago, where the B&O was just one of roughly twenty major railroads serving the nation's second largest commercial and industrial complex.[38]

So in the smaller towns especially, the CTP came to be a center of considerable employee attention and activity, often ranging beyond the original purpose of the program. At the New Castle men's meeting in November 1937, for example, the regular CTP business reports were followed by planning for a bowling league and a CTP minstrel show.[39] Those last items traditionally were within the purview of the welfare department. However, even if W. W. Wood objected to such incursions upon his turf, no one else seemed to mind; the same company-spirit-building purpose was served no matter whose program received the credit. Increasingly, the umbrella program under which the company's extracurricular activities were conducted was the CTP.

In that sense, the program was increasingly successful in achieving its objectives in the intangible realm. With respect to its tangible objective, traffic generation, it was holding steady at a satisfactory level. Numerical results for the CTP's first five years were in many key respects roughly quintuple those of the first year, a remarkable degree of consistency. Credited traffic for the five years ending in November 1938 totaled 108,037 freight carloads, 95,877 LCL shipments, and 167,062 passengers. Monthly averages in these categories were 1,801, 1,598, and 2,784, respectively. The first two averages were comparable to figures achieved during the program's first year. The last one, the passenger figure, was somewhat larger than the first-year average; unfortunately, it also was in gross terms the least lucrative of the three categories. In addition to reports of accomplished sales, 39,258 freight prospect tips, 16,341 passenger prospect tips, and 2,746 suggestions were received by CTP committees and forwarded to traffic department representatives. The average number of employees per month offering some kind of CTP report was 1,308, again a figure comparable to the first-year average.[40]

Given an average B&O–Alton system employment of roughly 47,000 during the 1934–1938 period, the figure 1,308 may be translated into an active CTP participation rate of 2.8 percent per month. Unfortunately, an annual participation rate was not computed, and a full set of *CTP Bulletins* was not preserved to allow such computations to be made now. Still, as suggested previously, it may be inferred that the annual rate was much higher than 2.8 percent. Fragmentary evidence suggests a rate closer to 10 percent: for example, CTP committeemen of the Cincinnati Terminals apparently were embarrassed by an active participation rate of only 3.4 percent for the first seven months of 1938.[41]

In the considered judgment of the officials who ran the program in subsequent years, 10 percent is a reasonable estimate of the average active rate. The estimate is a soft one, made decades after the fact and based upon subjective assessment of data that might have been slightly exaggerated in the field; business secured by employees was largely self-reported, and, to reinforce the desired atmosphere of trust, no verification attempts were made by CTP officials. Let it be assumed, though, that 10 percent is a correct figure. It still may not appear to be especially impressive. It raises the question, What about the other 90 percent? The answer, in part, is that many of them attempted to solicit traffic for the B&O and failed, and a much larger number at least occasionally dropped by for CTP meetings, particularly the major entertainment-oriented events. If a total participation rate is defined to include those who occasionally participated passively as well as those who aggressively went after traffic, then the number is plausibly in the neighborhood of 30 percent, a more heartening figure.[42]

Whatever the participation rate, the gross revenues attributed to the CTP were of some consequence. Lewis estimated CTP carload freight revenue for the first five years of the program to have been about $5.4 million. LCL and passenger revenues may be estimated similarly to have been $783,000 and $438,000, respectively. The total would have been more than $6.6 million, and the annual average of over $1.3 million would have been just slightly less than the first-year credited total of $1.4 million. The credited total would have constituted 0.84 percent of the B&O's revenues during the period, or more pertinently, since CTP figures included Alton results, 0.77 percent of the revenues of the B&O–Alton system. If routing orders and other noncredited promises of business materialized in the same measure that was expected in 1934, CTP revenue contribution would have amounted to approximately 1.1 percent of the B&O–Alton total.[43]

Certainly, 1.1 percent is a small figure, but it was not of negligible value, as the second wave of the Depression hit the B&O hard. Industrial output and rail traffic began falling again late in 1937, and they fell further in 1938. Largely because of precipitous declines in coal, ore, and steel traffic, B&O

revenues in 1938 were 21 percent below their level in 1936.[44] Without the CTP they might have been 1.1 percent lower yet. Whether the B&O might have been forced into receivership by marginally larger operating deficits occurring in the absence of the CTP will be discussed at the end of this chapter. The call was close.

At this point, a more thorough consideration of whether the traffic attributed to the CTP really should have been so attributed is in order. It has been noted already that most CTP business was not formally verified; thus there existed the possibility that reported traffic might have been inflated somewhat by ambitious but unscrupulous employees wishing to attract favorable attention to themselves. The chance of being discovered by peers or superiors in a position to observe whether the reported traffic actually moved, though, would tend to discourage such behavior. A more troublesome question is this: Would the traffic credited to the work of CTP participants have gone via B&O even without their efforts?

More than a small amount of it might well have. For example, the record of the November 1937 women's meeting in Zanesville, Ohio, credited the wife of signalman S. E. Cupp with two passengers from Zanesville to Chicago. The B&O was the only railroad offering passenger service in Zanesville; the town had no scheduled air service, and a trip of nearly four hundred miles by bus or by automobile would have been lengthier and less comfortable than on the B&O's direct train.[45] The same basic observation may be made about CTP business reported at any town where the B&O was the dominant transportation company—not just Zanesville, but also communities such as Cumberland, Clarksburg, Parkersburg, Wheeling, and Chillicothe.

However, even if most of such trips or shipments would have been made by B&O anyway, the CTP would not have been terribly overcredited. "Monopoly" towns such as Parkersburg and Clarksburg were much more the exception than the rule: at most of its major traffic-generating points, the B&O faced serious rail competition, as well as increasing pressure from subsidized air and highway transportation. In most cases, then, CTP-credited hauls or trips were ones for which B&O routing was one of two or more reasonable options; in some instances, the B&O would have been the less obvious choice. For example, at the November 1937 women's meeting in Lima, Ohio, the wife of tank repairman C. E. Richards was credited with securing a passenger from Lima to New York. Lima was a stop on the New York–Chicago main line of the Pennsylvania; a routing via B&O would have been circuitous and much more time-consuming, with at least one layover and change of trains. At the New Castle men's meeting the same month, yard clerk H. P. Ward was credited with a tip, forwarded to the traffic department, that secured twenty-five carloads of steel from Johnstown, Pennsylvania, to New Castle. Shippers in Johnstown presumably would have looked to the PRR first, as the town was on that road's main line, and the PRR's route to New Castle was shorter than the B&O's. At the Dayton, Ohio, men's meeting in November 1938, E. L. Marrinan reported securing fifteen LCL shipments from New York to Dayton. Again, the Pennsylvania had the advantage of a shorter and faster route.[46]

Instances of such salesmanship continued through the CTP's sixth year and beyond, even as general traffic levels recovered and the B&O pulled away from the brink of bankruptcy. At the Columbus men's meeting in August 1939, five employees (a yardmaster, a claim clerk, a rate clerk, an agent, and a chief clerk) each were credited with having secured passengers traveling between Columbus and New York. Both the Pennsylvania and the New York Central provided direct main line service over that route; the B&O again was circuitous and required a change of trains. Air service was available to the affluent, and bus service was available to those on a very tight budget. The passengers in question must have traveled B&O only through the determined and persuasive urging of the CTP participants. In a few cases, CTP participants went to unusual lengths to secure new business. The December 1938 issue of *Baltimore & Ohio Magazine* reported that agent John Fosbrink, stationed at Winchester, Virginia, on the Shenandoah Valley branch, secured the patronage of two passengers by offering to drive them personally to Martinsburg, West Virginia, the nearest B&O main line station. The two prospects had been contemplating a bus rip to Fort Worth; instead, they rode the B&O to St. Louis, where they transferred to another carrier to continue their journey.[47]

It is clear from all of these and many similar examples that some B&O employees really were energized by the Cooperative Traffic Program to go beyond their basic job descriptions to sell B&O services. But a further question might now be asked: Which employees were those? Were they evenly spread across departments and hierarchical levels, or were they concentrated in particular areas of the company? A cursory glance at CTP committee reports suggests that a somewhat disproportionate share of reported traffic came from white-collar employees or from their wives. Was the CTP dominated by higher-status employees? If it were to a degree that was seen by lower-status workers as discomfiting, then the teamwork and "company family" objectives of the program would have been undercut.

The question is difficult to answer, because surviving records are incomplete and because critical terms in the question are not very clearly definable. Assigning relative status to particular jobs, or even defining which jobs are white-collar and which are blue-collar, can be a slippery and subjective matter in the railroad company. Generally, as in most industries, employees who wore white shirts and ties—identifiably white-collar—held higher status than those who wore overalls or other coarse and heavy work clothes on the job. However, in some instances this pattern was blurred or even reversed. Passenger trainmen, for example, wore white shirts and ties on the job, yet they belonged to the same union and were essentially of the same service class as freight trainmen, a blue-collar group. Engineers wore overalls to work, yet they, especially those in passenger service, clearly enjoyed higher status and higher pay than most of the railroad's generally white-collar clerks. Other similar examples abound.

Nonetheless, if it is understood that color of collar is but loosely correlated with status, the question may be pursued. Job groups can at least be identified, and for the sake of drawing an approximate profile of CTP participation, those groups can be tagged as white-collar or blue-collar on the basis of the typical work attire of a majority of its members. Local CTP committee reports analyzed according to this scheme can yield some insight, however limited, on the issue of whether any particular group of employees dominated the program.

The most nearly complete sets of CTP records for two contrasting settings are those of Cincinnati (the Temple Bar Building offices, Cincinnati Terminals, and Ivorydale) and Zanesville, Ohio, during the fifth year of the program, December 1937 through November 1938. Cincinnati's records survive in nearly full detail (only two of eighty-one contributing employees are unidentified by job title) but only for the last seven months of the period. Zanesville's records for the entire period are extant, but considerable detail is missing from them (four of thirty-one contributing employees are unidentified by job title, and 66 of 106 traffic reports do not mention the exact number of shipments or passengers credited).[48] An analysis of those records is presented as tables 4-1 and 4-2.

Table 4-1 appears to indicate that in Cincinnati, white-collar employees did indeed dominate the program. During the period in question, of the total B&O work force roughly 25 percent would be classified as white-collar.[49] At Cincinnati, however, the group of identified employees reporting traffic was 90 percent white-collar, and 93 percent of their individual monthly reports were from white-collar employees. Such a striking imbalance might well have been cause for concern. However, to put those numbers in perspective, it should be noted that Cincinnati was the headquarters of B&O western lines, and as such had a higher concentration of white-collar workers than any other B&O community except Baltimore. Table 4-2 further shrinks the significance of the Cincinnati figures. At Zanesville the principal B&O facility was the signal shop; the white-collar proportion of the B&O work force was much

TABLE 4-1
Cooperative Traffic Program Report Summary
Cincinnati (Including Ivorydale)
May–November 1938

Number Reporting business	Position	Number of reports	C	LCL	P	T
				Reported business*		
	MEN'S DIVISION					
	White-collar					
7	Agent	16	46		21	
1	Asst. general freight agent	1			1	
1	Car distributor	1	37			
1	Cashier	1	1			
17	Clerk, rate clerk, ticket clerk	27	21	12	13	
4	Chief clerk, chief rate clerk	7	8		7	
2	Coal traffic rep., coal freight agent	3	1		3	
2	Crew caller, crew dispatcher	2			202	
2	Master mechanic	2			3	
7	Secretary, stenographer	7			9	
1	Special representative	1			1	
2	Supervisor of station services	2			6	
1	Tariff compiler	1	1			
9	Yard clerk	19	78		7	
3	Chief yard clerk	4	7			
3	Yardmaster	3	4		3	
63	Total white-collar men	97	204	12	276	0
	Blue-collar					
1	Car foreman	1		1		
1	Conductor	1			1	
2	Electrician	2	1		1	
2	Engineer	2			7	
1	Laborer	1			3	
1	Operator	1			1	
8	Total blue-collar men	8	1	1	13	0
2	Position unidentified	2			3	
	WOMEN'S DIVISION					
	White-collar					
2	Clerk	3			5	
1	Comptometer operator	2			14	
6	Secretary	7		6	4	
1	Telephone operator	1			1	
1	Timekeeper	3	1		3	
11	Total white-collar women	16	1	6	27	0

*C, carload freight; LCL, less-than-carload freight; P, passenger; T, tip.

lower than at Cincinnati, and so was the white-collar presence in the CTP. There the group of identified employees generating traffic (either themselves or through family members) was only 22 percent white-collar, and only 25 percent of individual reports came from such employees. In other cases where reasonably detailed local CTP reports survive—notably New Castle, Salamanca (New York), Wheeling, and Columbus—white-collar percentages lay between the Cincinnati and Zanesville extremes, tending toward one or the other in relation to the overall makeup of the local B&O work force. A reasonable assessment of the issue is that white-collar employees as a group indeed participated in the CTP to a greater extent than blue-collar workers, but not to such a degree as to constitute a widespread problem.

In addition to helping to resolve the white-collar/blue-collar issue, tables 4-1 and 4-2 contain at least four interesting pieces of information. First, it may be noted that during the periods being examined, no family members of employees reported traffic at Cincinnati, and no women employees reported traffic at Zanesville. The latter may be explained by a lack of traditional women's jobs at Zanesville, but there is no obvious explanation for the former. It is not likely that one group tended to drive out the other: employees and employees' family members apparently coexisted very nicely in women's CTP groups in towns such as Wheeling. Second, at both Cincinnati and Zanesville, train crew members are conspicuously scarce as CTP participants. With regard to this information, the tables indicate a pattern that characterized the CTP throughout its existence: engineers, firemen, conductors, and trainmen usually were much less active than other groups of employees. This pattern had two principal causes: all but the most senior train and engine crewmen were subject to working long, odd, and irregular hours, and they as a group tended to be more independent and less group-minded than desk-bound railroaders. This phenomenon, however inevitable, was more disappointing to the company than any low general blue-collar participation rate.[50]

The third observation that may be made is that consistent with the tendency discussed previously, the overall participation rate in small-town Zanesville was greater than in big-town Cincinnati. The B&O had fewer than 200 employees in the Zanesville area but more than 2,000 in and around Cincinnati. If the total number of employees reporting business in Cincinnati for the seven months indicated (84) were simply annualized, the resulting figure (144) would be roughly 7.2 percent of Cincinnati employment. Zanesville's 31 contributing employees, in contrast, were approximately 15.5 percent of the Zanesville base: an active participation rate more than double the estimate of the larger town's rate. A related point not indicated in the table is that 70 men attended Zanesville's regular CTP meeting in November 1938, a total (active and passive) participation rate of over 35 percent;[51] the Cincinnati CTP seldom did that well even at its major social events.

TABLE 4-2
Cooperative Traffic Program Report Summary
Zanesville, Ohio
December 1937–November 1938

Number Reporting business	Position	Number of reports	Reported business*			
			C	LCL	P	T
	MEN'S DIVISION					
	White-collar					
3	Clerk, clerk-stenographer	8	7	2	3	3
1	Chief clerk	1				1
1	Storekeeper	2			2	
1	Supervisor of shops	3			5	
6	Total white-collar men	14	7	2	10	4
	Blue-collar					
1	Blacksmith's helper	1			1	
2	Carman, car painter	8	6	6	4	
1	Machinist's helper	1			1	
1	Shop foreman	1			1	
8	Signalman, signal helper	18	2	1	13	46
2	Signal shopman	3	1		3	
1	Stores helper	2			3	
16	Total blue-collar men	34	9	7	26	46
2	Position unidentified	7			19	
	WOMEN'S DIVISION					
	White-collar (family member of)					
3 (0)**	Wife of clerk, daughter of clerk	5			8	
1 (0)	Wife of supervisor of shops	5			8	
4 (0)	Total women, white-collar family	10	0	0	16	0
	Blue-collar (family member of)					
1 (0)	Wife of blacksmith's helper	1			1	
1 (1)	Wife of carman	2			10	
1 (1)	Wife of engineer	3			4	1
1 (0)	Wife of machinists' helper	1			1	
1 (0)	Wife of shop foreman	3			3	

TABLE 4-2
(*continued*)

Number Reporting business	Position	Number of reports	Reported business*			
			C	LCL	P	T
6 (1)	Wife of signalman, signal helper	23			82	
1 (1)	Wife of signal shopman	4			8	
1 (1)	Wife of stores helper	2	—	—	9	—
14 (5)	Total women, blue-collar family	39	0	0	118	1
2 (2)	Wife of (position unidentified)	2			3	

*C, carload freight; LCL, less-than-carload freight; P, passenger; T, tip. All reported business figures are probably understated significantly, as in instances where number of passengers or shipments was not recorded (66 of 106 instances) the minimum possible number (1) was inserted.
**The number in parentheses is the number of women (none of whom were employees) whose husband or father is not included as a contributor in the Men's Division summary. To prevent double counting, the number of employees contributing (on their own or through family members) is found by adding the total in parentheses to the Men's Division total.

Finally, the tables indicate that Cincinnati and Zanesville CTP results were not heavily dependent upon a few consistently prolific producers. The seven-month ratio of reports to reporting employees for Cincinnati was 1.46; the twelve-month ratio for Zanesville was 2.97. In other words, the protean efforts of Mrs. S. E. Cupp notwithstanding (she reported traffic secured in eleven of the twelve months), the Zanesville average was just under three reports per reporting employee per year. For Cincinnati the maximum annual rate, possible only if previous contributors continued to produce at their previous rate and no additional employees reported traffic, would have been 2.50 reports per reporting employee. Were such a figure typical of the system, the systemwide monthly active participation rate of 2.8 percent would amount to an annual rate of over 13.4 percent—13.4 percent of all B&O and Alton employees reporting traffic secured within a given year. Against a reasonable standard, that would be an entirely respectable figure.

Since the CTP had established itself as a modest but steady success, were other railroads rushing to copy it? Not exactly. The B&O, after all, was not encouraging them to do so. As the tangible half of the program's purpose was the diversion of traffic from other carriers, rail as well as highway, to encourage emulation by the competition would have been substantially self-defeating. The CTP was not the deepest of secrets, but neither was it publicized beyond the B&O–Alton system. The company did not even talk about the program to *Railway Age*. It was not so much as mentioned in the pages of that journal until June 1939, when a summary of a prior article from *Baltimore & Ohio Magazine*, detailing the program's five-year accomplishments, was published.[52]

However, in an industry as interdependent as railroading, general information about interesting developments usually spreads through informal channels with a modicum of speed and accuracy. It is reasonable to assume that within a year of the CTP's develoment, at least a few people of influence at the other major carriers in the B&O's region had heard something about it. The more aggressive and optimistic among them probably tried to move their roads in a similar direction; a few of those achieved marginal success. The best example of an eastern district railroad that appears to have followed the B&O in this way was the Norfolk & Western. By early 1936 the N&W had set up a string of organizations called Better Service Clubs at twenty-one major points across the system. The function of the clubs was to provide opportunities for employee social interaction, to encourage employees to do their jobs in friendlier and more efficient fashion, and to encourage employees to solicit N&W patronage—the CTP functions with a dash of Cooperative Plan thrown in. Organizationally, the clubs seem to have been given at least the appearance of an autonomy reminiscent of the PRR Mutual Beneficial Association, not surprisingly as the Pennsylvania was a major N&W stockholder. The program was active for a couple of years, then faded into obscurity. Beyond that its level of success and ultimate disposition are unclear.[53]

On the PRR itself, CTP imitation was noticeable but not very energetic or coherent. At the start of the Depression, the Pennsylvania was doing basically the same thing that the B&O was doing: encouraging employee traffic solicitation and publishing the names of successful employees in the company paper, the twice-monthly *Pennsylvania News*. Further encouragement was provided occasionally by the MBA's *Mutual Magazine*. For a year and a half after the CTP was started, the PRR did nothing more. Then, in an action strikingly parallel to their establishment of the Bureau of New Ideas, the company's management organized a PRR variant of the B&O predecessor program. Beginning in May 1935, large rallies were conducted across the railroad for the purpose of generating enthusiasm for an expanded employee traffic solicitation campaign. It was unprecedented, for the Pennsylvania; *Mutual Magazine* told glowingly of the "monster get-together" at central region headquarters in Pittsburgh, attended by all of six hundred people, all officers and supervisors. A couple of months later, out in the hinterlands, the company did better. At

Logansport, Indiana, the main shop town and division point on the PRR's Panhandle lines, the sales rally drew five hundred (including wives and children); blue-collar workers were invited this time. Internal publicity on the campaign, through both the *Pennsylvania News* and *Mutual Magazine,* was substantial for a few months, giving prominence to "stirring appeals" by employees and their family members to promote the company's services to friends, neighbors, and local merchants.[54] And that was it.

In attempting to secure the benefits of a CTP adaptation, PRR management was careful to distill away any traces of the warmer and more open B&O corporate culture. Thus the PRR campaign differed from the CTP in four primary respects. First, as there was no intangible company-family-building objective for the campaign, it was not integrated with employee social activities. Still usually sponsored by the MBA and the PRRYMCA, those were rebounding after some early-Depression cutbacks; during 1935, for example, the central region MBA picnics at Conneaut Lake Park and a PRRYMCA bowling league were restored. Second, the campaign had no full-time staff; it was conducted by traffic department officials as part of their regular duties. Third, there was no local committee structure; everything was tightly controlled through regular hierarchical channels. Somewhat decentralized, occasionally ad hoc local organizing was a B&O tendency, not the practice of the Pennsylvania. Fourth, the campaign was not intended to have a long-run existence. It was to help the railroad out of its temporary doldrums, and then, presumably, to end.[55]

This list of differences might as well be a list of reasons why the PRR campaign flopped; these were critical elements in the CTP's success. Results in terms of measurable traffic increases evidently were deemed insufficient to justify the effort of continuing the campaign, and it coasted to a stop. To the extent that it was replaced, it was by reliance on the general industry advertising campaign begun in the summer of 1936 by the Association of American Railroads (AAR, successor to the ARE), supplemented by occasional reminders in company publications to sell PRR services specifically. Organized employee traffic solicitation on the Pennsylvania was for all practical purposes dead. In a speech to the 1938 MBA General Assembly, PRR president Martin W. Clement, who succeeded General Atterbury in 1935, spoke at length about the need for political pressure from PRR employees to secure regulatory equity for the railroads; he said not a word about a need for them to try to sell Pennsy services.[56]

The Pennsylvania basically was rejoining the pack. Throughout the middle and late 1930s, most railroads followed a group approach to the problem of low sales volume. Beyond the normal activities of their traffic departments, most roads confined their individual efforts to small points such as reciprocity stickers. Big pushes generally were regional and national in scope; employees then were urged to support the industry campaign through their personal contacts. The usual medium for such urging was the company magazine, which most major roads had begun publishing before 1930. For example, the Santa Fe's most visible attempt to involve its employees in traffic solicitation centered upon the western district's 1935 joint advertising campaign. The Santa Fe's participation in the campaign was announced in a two-page article in *Santa Fe Magazine* accompanied by a brief appeal to all employees to "back it up to the extent of our ability in order to make it succeed." [57]

There was little or no organizational follow-up to these campaigns and appeals, and results seem to have been marginal. On some roads they were nearly nil. Successful employee traffic solicitation was so rare on the Chesapeake & Ohio, for example, that when engineman Burley Mullins of Danville, West Virginia, secured a passenger to Marion, Ohio, the company magazine gave the accomplishment a two-column-inch story.[58] Many roads did somewhat better, but it does not appear that any of them tried so hard or did so well as the B&O.

Why? We ask the same basic question posed in regard to the Cooperative Plan, and elements of the same answer apply to the CTP. First, there is the necessary but not sufficient factor of economic pressure: in this instance, the B&O's debt, pressing it harder than many other roads were pressed. Second, and again decisively, is the factor of leadership character. In the case of the CTP, that factor was translated into the four essential components cited as missing from the PRR program, and into a broader and deeper phenomenon that energized and bonded all aspects of the program: employee spirit, carefully cultivated by Daniel Willard for over twenty years. The CTP helped to build the B&O's sense of company family, but it also was built by it. A CTP cannot be built from scratch overnight, without the necessary preconditions and foundations. On the N&W, the PRR, the Santa Fe, the C&O, and the rest of the American railroad industry, one or more of these elements was weaker than on the B&O, or was missing altogether.

While the Cooperative Traffic Program was rolling along steadily, how was the original Cooperative Plan doing? Not so well. In the mechanical department, shop conferences continued to be held monthly, but the level of activity at those conferences was markedly lower than it had been back in the 1920s. As noted in chapter 3, through the end of 1926, the Cooperative Plan had generated an average of 529 suggestions per month, and the monthly average from January of 1927 through December of 1933 was 190. During the next four years, the average number of suggestions per month was fifty-two, barely more than one per shop.[59]

As a result, shop meetings tended either to be short or to be devoted largely to matters other than shop efficiency. At the October 1938 meeting at Ivorydale, for example, the main agenda items were a discussion of the company's financial illness, a consideration of ways to boost the CTP, a discussion of local advertising alternatives, and remarks by superintendent F. L. Hall, the same gentleman who led the Ivorydale meetings in 1925, on the plight of the American railroads.[60] System meetings in Baltimore were on average not much different. The meetings of January and April 1938 lasted seventy and ninety-five minutes, respectively. A dozen suggestions, most of them deferred from prior meetings, were discussed at each; the balance of the time was spent talking about layoffs, poor traffic, and the company's four new diesel passenger locomotives. Of system meetings of the last half of the decade, only the October 1937 meeting bears much resemblance to the meetings of the midtwenties, and that is somewhat superficial. The meeting lasted for over three hours, and twenty-one suggestions were reviewed. Closing general discussion was mostly germane to shop operations and cooperation, including a suggestion from the federation's acting president, Harry Doyle (interim and eventually long-term successor to William McGee), that local cooperative committees be reminded to discuss the CTP. However, a major reason for the meeting's length and purposefulness was the fact that the prior quarter's meeting had been cancelled. Moreover, only two of the twenty-one suggestions on the agenda were reported to be completed, and one of those—repair of the floor and pits at the Willard, Ohio, roundhouse—dated from November 1931. Of the remaining proposals, four were in the process of completion, one was officially held in abeyance for lack of funds, and fourteen were deferred pending investigation and identification of low-cost solutions.[61] This was not the Plan at its best.

The Plan as applied to the transportation and maintenance of way departments was losing steam similarly. From its beginning through the end of 1933, suggestions averaged sixty-eight per month; the average for the subsequent four years was thirty. Perhaps more critically, the suggestion acceptance rate fell even more drastically; whereas the acceptance rate in the mechanical department stayed fairly steady, well above 80 percent, the CT/MW acceptance rate dropped from an average of 67 percent through the end of 1933 to 15 percent over the next four years.[62] Budgetary constraints were the principal culprit; when those were relieved by financial recovery in 1939 and 1940, the acceptance rate actually exceeded 100 percent for a time, as the backlog of suggestions held in abeyance was worked down.[63] Even so, workers could not have found having their ideas sit in limbo for months or years very encouraging.

The Cooperative Plan still was functioning as a means of communication between labor and management in the late thirties, but much of its vitality was gone. The reasons for the continuing decline appear to be the same factors mentioned previously: exhaustion of the more obvious ideas for improvement, worn-off novelty, lower morale, and the discouraging impact of severe budgetary constraints on suggestion implementation, plus management's preoccupation with the CTP. It even had lost some of its commanding superiority over the Pennsylvania's Bureau of New Ideas. The BNI was generating almost as many suggestions per month as the Cooperative Plan. Because of the BNI's still much lower acceptance rate (consistently around 30 percent) and the PRR's much larger employment base (nearly three times the B&O's), the Plan's "constructive participation rate" was more than seven times that of the BNI. But that was down from a factor of more than 32 ten years before.[64]

The ongoing decline of the Plan was accompanied during this period by the first signs of weakness in the company's overall relations with organized labor. Collective bargaining on the B&O had been almost always smooth and free of rancor throughout the Cooperative Plan years. After the 1922 Shopmen's Strike, Willard never had to face a walkout by his people; it appears that the 1929 misunderstanding over the shopcrafts' five-cent raise was as close as he had come, and that was not very close. Through Charles Galloway, he resisted any wage requests that would have put the B&O at a competitive disadvantage, but he was amenable to negotiating anything that did not. The unions, for their part, did not really press him. Nor did they really press anyone else all that hard. During the twenties the normal pattern was for a union to negotiate a reasonable settlement with the carrier or carriers whose contracts expired first, and for the other carriers (whether dealing with real or company unions) then to fall more or less into line. During the thirties the trend was toward industrywide collective bargaining, for the sake of simplicity and immediate uniformity, but there still was no serious rupture in relations, even over something as painful as the 1932 wage cuts. Some railroads, notably the Pennsylvania, had to cope with union representational hassles; the B&O did not face even that kind of disagreement. It was a remarkably placid state of affairs—and it almost was grievously upset in 1937–1938.

Two observations can be made about the unions as the Depression dragged on: they were losing patience and they were gaining strength. The 1932 wage deductions had been restored by stages in 1934 and 1935, but rail unionists nonetheless were increasingly restive about their failure to make real progress. At the same time, the national labor movement in general was emboldened by a series of prolabor government actions (especially the outlawing of company unions in 1934 and the passage of the National Labor Relations Act in 1936); the AFL was stronger, and thus more able and willing to encourage assertiveness in its railway department, than it ever had been. So in March 1937 the national unions of both operating and nonoperating employees presented all of the railroads with demands for pay increases averaging about 20 percent. Negotiating teams for the carriers and the unions failed to reach agreement, and strike votes were authorized. The National Mediation Board, functioning under the Railway Labor Act, intervened and averted a strike by mediating an agreement raising wages by roughly a quarter of the amount demanded. Then in May 1938 the railroads, citing the recent downturn in traffic, announced their intent to cut selected wages by 15 percent; the unions responded with a strike call. This time a Presidential Emergency Board had to be created; the board reported in favor of the employees, the carriers canceled the planned cuts, and the strike was called off.[65]

So the B&O was not struck, but it came closer than it had since 1922. Willard's moderating presence simply was not felt in these disturbances. Why not? Perhaps his energy failed him, or perhaps hard-liners on both sides were in no mood to be moderate. Whatever the case, the confrontations were unfortunate. They placed B&O union members in a position that divided their loyalty; some may have felt like part of an increasingly distant branch of the B&O family. Despite the counterefforts of the CTP, the corporate culture may have begun to erode among some segments of the blue-collar work force. The combined effects of the decline of the Cooperative Plan and the reappearance of adversarial collective bargaining may have caused some workers to wonder whether the B&O was just another big corporation after all.[66]

The period between the 1938 discord and Willard's retirement as president in June 1941 was an interlude of calm on the labor front, marked by a reassuring sign: the slippage of the Cooperative Plan in the shops stopped, at least in quantitative terms. Primarily because of the recall of furloughed employees and increased levels of shop activity, suggestion submissions increased slightly, from a monthly average of fifty-two to fifty-three.[67] In the CT and MW departments, however, the trend was negative, and seriously so. Despite the flurry of suggestion acceptances, suggestion submissions plummeted by nearly two-thirds, averaging a mere twelve per month for the forty months ending in April 1941. The CT/MW program, always relatively high in cost and low in benefits, was nearing the point of ineffectiveness. There are no known documents indicating that the program did not survive the summer of 1941, but neither are there any to indicate that it did. It seems simply to have disappeared.[68]

With the recovery of industrial production and railroad traffic, discernible changes were taking place within the CTP as well. From a near-disastrous 1938, B&O railway operating revenues jumped 20 percent in 1939 and another 11 percent in 1940; by 1941 they almost had regained their level of 1929. With business easier to secure, the immediate effect upon the CTP was a significant increase in reported numbers in all categories.[69] The longer-term effect, though, was a shift in emphasis; the company community or social dimension of the program gradually gained importance at the expense of the business dimension. As the recovery proceeded, business meetings became shorter and entertainment became more elaborate. The inclination of some committees not to hold meetings during the summer, except for the annual picnic, became general practice. Business was up, and the pressure was off. Reflecting the decreased need for intensive effort, multiple committees at single sites frequently were merged; by November 1940 the original 368 B&O–Alton committees had declined to 250.[70]

Nonetheless, the CTP still could pack a meeting room. On the evening of November 6, 1940, a crowd estimated at six thousand people jammed the Baltimore Coliseum for the Baltimore Terminals annual CTP rally. O. S. Lewis was to be the speaker for the evening; he was to be followed by the entertainment, provided as always mostly by employees and their children, then by a dance. In fact, Lewis never spoke that evening. Just before the 8:15 start of the program, Daniel Willard had arrived at the hall, with three of his four grandchildren in tow, and had taken a seat toward the front of the audience. Of course, he was invited to the podium, to a standing ovation, and he delivered the evening's address. It was probably not the best speech he ever gave; he was less than three months short of his eightieth birthday, and some of the energy of his earlier years was gone. It was a good speech, though, full of do-unto-others philosophy and urgings to please the customer and praise for CTP workers.[71] It was one of Willard's last major public appearances.

What of Daniel Willard during the last few years of his presidency? Little has been said of him in this chapter; was he similarly less prominent in the running of his railroad? In certain respects it appears that he was. Not in matters of general policy or corporate relations: there, as always, he seems to have been firmly in command. With respect to many day-to-day decisions and details, though, it appears that more were delegated than had been earlier in his tenure. It is difficult to tell for certain, because surviving commentary and correspondence tend to treat him with a certain reverent refusal to acknowledge his age, but the impression remains that Willard had become more head of state than prime minister. He still put in long hours working in the home office and touring the railroad, but Charles Galloway was increasingly visible on the pages of *Baltimore & Ohio Magazine,* especially when the contextual issue or decision was only of moderate importance. In discussions with lenders and the federal government concerning the shoring up of the B&O's financial position, Willard was present for the formal and general discussions, but his surviving son, Daniel, Jr. (his older son, Harold, had died of influenza in 1918), who was the B&O's assistant general counsel, worked out most of the behind-the-scenes details.[72] Willard always had delegated; now he delegated more.

As befits that of a senior corporate head of state, some of Willard's correspondence took on a more broadly reflective quality than it had earlier in his career. Some of it provides interesting insights into the way he saw his job and the world. On matters of general railroad industry labor relations, for example, he still took deep offense at workers who demanded and got something for nothing. When the regional Mediation Board at Chicago handed down a series of decisions expanding the scope of "arbitraries"—special-case bonus payments like the one Willard ordered to be paid in the "Pullman 10" incident discussed in chapter 3—Willard was disturbed. At the same time, though, he saw the matter philosophically. Perhaps, he wrote to Otto Beyer, it was an inevitable working of Emerson's (Ralph Waldo, not George or Harrington) law of compensation. Railroad managements had done many unfair things to their workers in the past, and it was their turn to be treated unfairly by their men. It was his hope, however, that once labor had had its compensatory justice across the industry, workers and managers could forget past inequities and deal with each other "more in harmony with the spirit that should obtain under existing conditions."[73]

More generally, his belief in the central role of morality in determining the course of human events is nicely illustrated in a series of letters that he and Beyer exchanged late in 1937. Beyer had sent him a copy of Woodward's *New American History,* a work heavily shaded with economic determinism. Willard vigorously objected to that quality in the book, in particular its assertion that the Civil War was fought over economic differences, not the moral issue of slavery. Willard argued that although deeply held moral convictions about slavery may have motivated only a minority, they were a very influential minority, and "they furnished the animus that was necessary to bring the two sections into a contest of arms." He further asserted that if a half-dozen people on each side, such as William Lloyd Garrison in the North and Robert Toombs in the South, had not taken on the roles they did, then the war might never have happened. Economic friction may have been a necessary condition, but it was not sufficient. A second condition also was required: existence of morally committed abolitionist leaders and their southern antagonists.[74] Economic forces and individual moral character: those are the same factors that, it is argued, led to the creation of the B&O's cooperative programs.

Did Willard see the creation of his company's programs in those terms? To a degree he did. Modesty was a fundamental Willard trait, so he did not try to glorify himself as the great man of moral courage, in this instance or in any other. He firmly believed in the importance of the B&O's cooperative programs, but he gave most of the credit to Beyer and William Johnston from the very beginning. The Cooperative Plan, he stated again and again, probably never would have been born had they not come to his office to suggest it. It was, he said, "a case where I, so to speak, was kicked upstairs and got credit for having landed on my feet at the top."[75] Beyer and Johnston were the men of courage, he allowed, not he. But that is not to say that he considered himself irrelevant to the accomplishment. A private action here is probably more revealing than public words. Back in 1934 on a visit to Beyer's new government office in Washington, Willard had noticed a photograph of the CN's Sir Henry Thornton on the wall. A few days later Beyer received a similar photograph of Willard, along with his note expressing the hope "that perhaps you might also be glad to include me in your list of those who have at least been willing to try to bring about a better relationship between employers and employees."[76] Beyer and Johnston may have deserved first and second place on the list of the worthy, but Willard was not going to concede third place, even to his friend Sir Henry.

Willard was entitled to hope for his share of the credit. Beyer certainly realized that; he acknowledged the fact that Willard was not only indispensable to the cooperative movement, but unique in the extent of his contributions to railroad labor-management relations generally.[77] The best ideas in the world are of little practical value unless someone of power and influence puts them to use. Willard's role was to be that someone: the implementer. As his long career wound to its end, he certainly deserved to look back on it with the satisfaction that he had made a difference.

With the entry of the United States into World War II at the end of 1941, the B&O's needs changed dramatically. The railroad was deluged by wartime traffic; its operating revenues reached $306 million in 1942, more than double their 1938 level, and exceeding those of the prior record year of 1926 by almost $50 million. The company basically had no need for traffic solicitation by anyone. The CTP and its local committees carried on enthusiastically, but their direction was reoriented toward general morale building and win-the-war efforts.[78]

For eight years the CTP had been the focal point of management efforts to promote employee involvement in the life of the company. Was it worth that level of attention? What had the Cooperative Traffic Program really accomplished? By some standard quantitative corporate measures, it had not accomplished a great deal. As noted previously, the CTP probably increased revenues by just over 1 percent per year. Market share, the most common simple measure of sales and marketing success, scarcely budged until the general economic recovery began in earnest in 1940, the program's seventh year.

TABLE 4-3
Market Share
(Percentage of Railway Operating Revenues)
Eastern District Class I Line-haul Steam Railroads and Subsidiaries

	Pennsylvania R.R.	Baltimore & Ohio R.R.	All Other Eastern District
1932	23.39	8.88	67.73
1933	23.38	9.45*	67.17
Avg. 1932–1933	23.39	9.19	67.45
1934	23.55	9.29	67.16
1935	23.95	9.23	66.82
1936	24.69	9.45	65.86
1937	25.15	9.35	65.50
1938	24.44	9.13	66.43
1939	24.97	9.33	65.70
1940	26.35	9.76	63.89
Avg. 1934–1941	24.82	9.39	65.79
1942	27.38	10.00	62.62

*The anomalous increase in 1933 B & O market share is due almost entirely to a doubling of iron ore traffic.

Sources: *B & O Annual Reports* (B & O); *Moody's Investment Manual, Steam Railroads* (PRR); Interstate Commerce Commission, *Statistics of Railways in the U.S.* (Eastern District).

Table 4-3 suggests that the B&O's share of eastern district rail traffic moved more closely with gross national product (GNP) changes than with CTP efforts. Although market share was higher during the first four years of the CTP than it was during the two years before the startup of the program, it actually fell below pre-CTP levels as the economy slipped back into deep depression in 1938. It increased rapidly thereafter, moving upward with the general economic recovery and the particular expansion of war-related heavy industry. With its strategic position in the upper Ohio River Valley—shared with the Pennsylvania, whose market share moved along a similar cycle—the B&O was blessed, or cursed, with a larger share of basic industrial traffic than were some of its competitors. Its traffic mix was heavy on highly cyclical coal, iron ore, and steel, and light on more stable general merchanise. In good economic times basic industry boomed, and so did the B&O. In bad times basic industry substantially shut down, and so did major portions of the B&O. Such cyclicality tended to overwhelm any other factor, such as the CTP, which might have had an impact upon market share.

Distortions associated with the business cycle can be reduced appreciably if long-term averages are used to level economic peaks and valleys. Table 4-4, using revenues rather than market share for the sake of simplicity, does so. The key element in that table is the comparison of average revenues for the first eight years of the CTP (1934–1941) with the averages for the preceding eight years (1926–1933). The average CTP-period revenue index number for the B&O was 0.767, while that of the PRR was 0.797; this indicates, more authoritatively than does table 4-3, that the B&O actually lost ground to its principal competitor during the period. A reasonable conclusion is that on the average, a superior physical plant beats superior employee commitment, given the time-sensitive nature of most traffic. However, it also should be noted that the B&O's 0.767 was greater than the average revenue index number of 0.756 recorded by the composite of all other eastern Class I railroads; the B&O, then, gained ground on the remaining competition. A reasonable conclusion here is that when sophistication and location of physical facilities are at least loosely comparable, superior employee commitment can be the decisive factor.

The number of instances in which CTP efforts directly or indirectly were the decisive factor in a routing decision may have been small, but it was not insignificant. The significance of the CTP's small numbers becomes apparent in light of the B&O's financial situation in 1938. The company had fallen slightly below the break-even point again in 1937, losing $0.7 million. Then in 1938, with the serious resumption of the Depression, the B&O lost $13.1 million. Its liquid assets already were terribly thin, and default on the interest payments on its debt was imminent. In an attempt to avoid receivership, Willard's financial officers and board of directors devised a debt modification plan, the critical elements of which were extension of maturity dates on $166 million of debt, and easing of immediate interest charge pressure by assigning 36 percent of annual interest charges contingent status—payable if earned and deferred if not earned.[79]

The modification plan was a sensible means of preventing the upheaval of bankruptcy proceedings, but not all of the B&O's bondholders were both willing and legally able to give their assent. Accordingly, it became necessary to amend the Federal Bankruptcy Act to allow the B&O to proceed despite the objecting minority. For a railroad led by anyone other than Daniel Willard, to secure such legislation might have been next to impossible; for Willard's B&O, it was merely difficult. Willard was a staunch Republican, but his personal integrity and his openness to organized labor had won him many friends among Democrats as well as members of his own party. By drawing upon his nearly three decades' worth of accumulated goodwill, he was able to win passage of the Chandler Bill, which provided for the necessary amendment with such restrictions as to make it applicable almost uniquely to the B&O.[80] The

TABLE 4-4
Railway Operating Revenues, Indexed
(Base: 1926–1933)
Eastern District Class I Line-haul Steam Railroads and Subsidiaries

	Pennsylvania R.R.	Baltimore & Ohio R.R.	All Other Eastern District
Bases (1926–1933)	1.000	1.000*	1.000*
1934	0.627	0.631	0.645
1935	0.671	0.660	0.675
1936	0.806	0.786	0.774
1937	0.832	0.788	0.781
1938	0.658	0.629	0.644
1939	0.787	0.749	0.746
1940	0.872	0.834	0.804
1941	1.121	1.059	0.979
Average 1934–1941	0.797	0.767	0.756
1942	1.531	1.425	1.262

*1926–1931 Revenues have been adjusted to include the Buffalo, Rochester, & Pittsburgh Railway and the Buffalo & Susquehanna Railroad with the Baltimore & Ohio, as the BR&P and the B&S were merged into the B&O on January 1, 1932. Otherwise, the B&O index base would be misleadingly low and its 1934–1942 index numbers would be too high.

Sources: *B&O Annual Reports* (B&O); *Moody's Investment Manual, Steam Railroads* (PRR, BR&P, and B&S); Interstate Commerce Commission, *Statistics of Railways in the U.S.* (Eastern District).

debt modification thereupon was put into effect, and the company avoided bankruptcy. Secondarily, but of great future importance, under the terms of the modification the company established a sinking fund with which to eliminate $100 million of its bonded indebtedness.[81] There is some irony in the fact that Willard's last major action as president of the Baltimore & Ohio was to accomplish, under duress, that which might have been properly among his first.

The company was saved from receivership, but the matter had hung so delicately in the balance that had the B&O been financially any weaker, the matter might not have been so felicitously resolved. Without the CTP, the B&O would have been just a bit weaker; without it, then, Willard might not have succeeded. So the CTP, despite its relatively small numbers, might have played a critical role in the prevention of a major financial disaster and in the relief of future financial burdens. That alone would have made the CTP worth the effort.

But even beyond such matters of measurable dollars and cents, there were the CTP's long-term intangibles. Was the CTP more successful as a builder of enduring company spirit than as a direct generator of traffic? It probably was. In an article entitled "I Located That Family Spirit *Everywhere,*" published in *Baltimore & Ohio Magazine* in April 1944, the magazine's new field editor, Inez M. DeVille, practically gushed about what a lively and loyal community she had found the B&O to be in her first year on the job.[82] Surely there were those who did not share the spirit; the strains of the Depression may have increased their number. But it appears that a majority of B&O employees at least to some degree still did have it, past layoffs and increasingly assertive unions notwithstanding. Throughout the 1930s and 1940s, the B&O enjoyed a widespread reputation for being the best in the East with respect to passenger service variables that were especially dependent upon employee conscientiousness—particularly timekeeping, courtesy, attentiveness, cleanliness, and food quality. Such a reputation bespeaks high employee morale and sense of commitment. The CTP certainly played a major part in building those qualities.[83]

The Cooperative Traffic Program, then, was of considerable significance to the Baltimore & Ohio Railroad. Was it of significance to anyone else? By itself, probably not much—it clearly lacks the ground-breaking independent historical import of the Cooperative Plan. But it should not be viewed by itself, because it was not by itself. It was an extension of, and closely entwined with, the more seminal Plan and prior welfare work. It was perhaps more significant as an effect than as a cause, a demonstration of the good things that could result from nearly three decades of consistently cultivating mutual respect and commitment, not just three members of the sales staff organizing local committees to persuade other employees to drum up business for the railroad. It may not have been notably innovative, but it was progressive; like its predecessors, it viewed all employees as possessing initiative and desire to improve their well-being while improving that of the company. That quality is the cord that held Daniel Willard's package of management programs together. The package surely was historically significant, and the CTP was part of the package.

5

1 9 4 2 – 1 9 6 3

AFTER WILLARD

Willard's progressive programs and the corporate culture that they molded suffered further erosion in the years following his semiretirement and subsequent death. Given the low likelihood of finding a successor of equal stature, that should not be unanticipated. What is remarkable is not the continuing decline of the programs and culture, but their continuing strength. They declined, they stabilized, they declined some more: they lingered for a very long time before they died. The CTP and at least the partial shell of the Cooperative Plan outlived Willard by two decades, and traces of the B&O spirit were detectable even longer. In light of the various stresses to which they were subjected, their staying power was singular, and an impressive testimony to the depth of Willard's imprint upon the company.

An overview of that imprint is presented at the beginning of this chapter, with particular attention to its similarity to the postwar management practices of the typical large Japanese corporation. Then the administrations of Willard's successors are discussed, with respect to leadership character, state of the Willard programs, and general company performance. Finally, the end of the B&O is briefly chronicled, from its acquisition by the Chesapeake & Ohio in 1963 to its official disappearance into CSX Corporation in 1987.

Daniel Willard celebrated his eightieth birthday and the beginning of his thirty-second year as president of the Baltimore & Ohio Railroad in January 1941. It was time for the board of directors to entertain seriously his offer to resign. A special committee of the board was named to conduct a search for a new president; in April they settled upon Roy B. White, the president of West-

Daniel Willard receiving an honorary doctor of laws degree from Isaiah Bowman, president of Johns Hopkins University, June 3, 1941. (Courtesy of the B&O Railroad Museum)

ern Union Telegraph Company and a former B&O official. On June 1 Willard assumed the newly created position of chairman of the board, and White succeeded him as president.[1]

Willard was characteristically gracious in giving way to his successor, but to be so must have required some effort at times. He continued daily to go to the office—now a much smaller and less elegant office than his old one—to answer his mail and to confer occasionally with officers and visitors, but he was no longer at the center of the action. The situation caused him considerable sadness and frustration; more than once he quietly complained to friends and long-time colleagues of how disappointing it was to be "on the shelf."[2]

As confined as his new job was, he still preferred it to ten more years of life with no job at all. That was the choice that his doctor laid before him seven months into his chairmanship. His heart condition was worsening; essentially, his alternatives were to retire altogether or to die. Willard chose spending a short time handling his correspondence and talking to people at his plain little office over spending a long time staring out the window at his Connecticut farmhouse. Four and a half months later he was hospitalized by another heart attack, and six weeks after that, on July 6, 1942, he passed away.[3]

Daniel Willard had been brought to Baltimore in 1910 as an operating man, to build up the property and to run it efficiently. In that regard he did not disappoint the directors who hired him, or their successors. The railroad that he turned over to Roy White was, despite the depredations of the Depression, in far better shape physically than it was when he arrived. The B&O was still the third-place eastern railroad, but it ran a considerably closer third than it had three decades before. By some measures of operating efficiency, it ran first. Among the eastern Big Three, the B&O had the best transportation ratio (transportation expenses divided by railway operating revenues) in 77 of the 120 months of the 1930s; the Pennsylvania's ratio was best for 29 months, and the New York Central's for only 14. In 1939 the B&O recorded a transportation ratio of just 35.40 percent, compared to 36.00 percent for the PRR and 37.27 percent for the NYC.[4] The B&O's reputation for gracious passenger service, noted in the preceding chapter, was firmly established; its punctuality was exemplary. The company even had acquired a bit of reputation as an innovator, having been a pioneer among eastern roads in air-conditioning, streamlining, and dieselization of passenger trains.[5]

Nonetheless, it was in the realm of human relations that Willard's legacy was most significant and enduring. Nearly five decades after his death, retired B&O employees vigorously and almost unanimously insist that their company enjoyed better labor-management relations and greater general camaraderie throughout their careers than did competing lines, and they trace this phenomenon to the presidency of Daniel Willard.

Why is this the case? What was the essence of his approach to his people, the defining quality of his management style that his counterparts on other railroads could not or would not match? Scholars in the field of comparative management systems would note in Willard's approach a substantial measure of the Japanese concept of *wa,* the company as harmonious community. Differences between that important governing principle of the typical postwar Japanese corporation and Willard's abiding concern for the development of B&O family spirit are difficult to distinguish. Similarities between Japanese and Willardian approaches to management can be perceived as well at more specific levels; the parallel between Japanese quality circles and B&O Cooperative Plan committees already has been discussed. Even some of the smallest details of the way things were done on Willard's B&O, such as the use of a company song at employee gatherings, are characteristic of corporate Japan.

Prompted by the preoccupation of the American business community during the 1980s with Japanese managerial success, one might ask how closely Willard's philosophies and actions correspond to a comprehensive list of the basic qualities of "the Japanese management system." That term is itself problematic; there is no one management system followed by all Japanese business. The term as it is understood in the United States refers to qualities that for the most part are found only among large Japanese corporations, not among small businesses. Even in the corporate sector, those cited qualities do not apply to the management of most women and part-time employees, and the strength of adherence to particular principles varies somewhat from company to company. So "Japanese management" is not a unitary concept.[6] That point being understood, it is still an interesting concept, and the question remains worth asking: To what degree were there parallels between this postwar Japanese "system" and the prewar B&O?

As the concept of the system itself is somewhat abstracted and idealized, it is reasonable to work from an idealized list of its qualities. The best known of such lists, overstated as to degree but substantively correct, is that of William Ouchi. According to Ouchi, the typical Japanese corporation is governed by the following principles:

1. Lifetime employment
2. Slow evaluation and promotion
3. Nonspecialized career paths
4. Little emphasis on detailed, quantifiable, short-run objectives
5. Collective decision making
6. Collective responsibility
7. Concern for total well-being of the employee[7]

The record of Willard's B&O with respect to some of these points does not consist of extensive and compelling evidence, but it suggests some similar tendencies. Lifetime employment, albeit with frequent layoffs among junior blue-collar workers, was the norm on the B&O; this was true of other railroads, but Willard made efforts to minimize layoffs that exceeded those of his competitors. Evaluation and promotion of employees inevitably were slow, as a result of the combination of lifetime employment and the lack of significant long-term company growth, as well as Willard's personal caution; Arthur Thompson was much more the exception than the rule. With respect to Ouchi's third point, nonspecialized career paths, the pattern of similarity is broken. Again as on other railroads, the typical B&O employee worked his way upward in the department in which he was hired; the careers of C. N. Fullerton, Helen Foreman, and G. P. Grimsley were unusual. Similarity seems to reappear on the fourth point: the B&O's only detailed and clearly stated quantitative objectives or constraints were in the form of departmental budgets, but detailed objectives were not much in vogue across American industry before World War II anyway.

Regarding point five, collective decision making, the B&O did make a conscious and moderately successful effort that tended to correspond to the Japanese pattern. The Cooperative Plan entailed fairly broad-based group participation in lower-level decisions, subject to the ratification of upper management; at upper levels Willard himself evidently relied heavily on staff meetings and on the advice of subordinates to shape his decisions. These are not examples of "democratic" leadership in any sense, but neither is that of the Japanese corporation of which Ouchi writes. Both approaches might be called "group-centered, moderately authoritarian"; Ouchi well might have used such a term instead of *collective*, with its implication of communal participation in all decisions. On the other hand, *collective* accurately describes both the Japanese and Willardian notions of who is responsible for the performance of the company and its parts: every employee holds shared responsibility. A central element of both the Cooperative Plan and the CTP was the sharing of suggestions and mutual aid across departmental lines. In neither case was an individual incentive offered; all employees would benefit or none would. With respect to the seventh point, an all-encompassing concern for the employee, the B&O's stance corresponded to the Ouchi model from the establishment of the Welfare Bureau in 1916.

In summary it might be concluded that Willard's management style was at least for its time unusually close to Ouchi's model of mid- to late-twentieth-century Japanese management along three of the seven dimensions (numbers 5, 6, and 7), close but not unusually so for its industry along another three (numbers 1, 2, and 4), and dissimilar along the remaining one (number 3). Such a record does not qualify Willard to be called the "first Japanese manager," but it might add interesting information to the discussion of the real origins of an approach to management widely assumed to be essentially Oriental.

To Daniel Willard all of this would be somewhat bemusing and substantially beside the point. He did not consider himself a particularly creative thinker, and he never displayed any serious interest in grand and elaborate theories of management style. As he often stated, his notion of what constituted proper management was reducible to the eleven words of the Golden Rule. The term *management style* itself seems not to fit him; style is too shallow and artificial a concept to describe the way in which he led his company. He did not act as he did because, like many American managers today, he had heard that someone had come up with a great new theory that could be used to ma-

Resolution presented to Daniel Willard by the B&O General Chairmen's Association, Baltimore, October 30, 1941. (Courtesy of the B&O Railroad Museum)

nipulate workers into being more productive. He acted as he did because of what he believed to be right.

If Willard's philosophy of management can be summarized in a single maxim, then perhaps his day-to-day practice of management can be summarized in a single incident. The following story was told by Dr. Isaiah Bowman, president of Johns Hopkins University, at a testimonial dinner held in Willard's honor on December 4, 1941:

Years ago, one of his men was dismissed from his job of engine hostler in the B&O roundhouse at Frederick because it was alleged that he had burned out the crown sheet of an engine [a serious and dangerous act of negligence, causing major damage to the firebox of a steam locomotive by allowing the water level in its boiler to fall too low]. Let the man himself tell the story as it was related to me by one of his employers who is here tonight.

"I didn't burn no crown sheet out of no damned engine, and I went home and told my old woman that I didn't burn no crown sheet out of no damned engine, and I says, 'It ain't fair,' and she says, 'Bill, 'tain't right, but there ain't no use your arguing about it. You go to Baltimore and see Mr. Willard and tell him what happened.'

"I was scared when I walked into that big office, and I says to myself, 'Bill, you're a damn fool. It won't do you no good to go in here.' But in I went, and there was Mr. Willard setting at a big desk. He knowed my name and he stood up and shuck hands and said, 'Bill, have a seat, and tell me what's on your mind.'

"I sat down there and told him I was fired for burning the crown sheet out of an engine, and I said, 'Mr. Willard, that ain't right. I ain't never burned no crown sheet out of no engine, and there's politics in that shop. Another man burned the crown sheet out of that engine and I got fired for it, and it ain't fair.'

"Mr. Willard said, 'Bill, I think I see your point. Now you go back home, and I'll look into this matter.'

"I went back to Frederick feeling pretty blue, but at eight o'clock that night the call boy come for me and I went back where I was fired from that morning and hostled engines the same as I had always done. The man that burned the crown sheet out of the engine got fired, and so did the foreman that covered it up. No sir, there ain't nobody fooling Mr. Willard for very long."[8]

The hostler and Dr. Bowman might have added, "There ain't nobody with a legitimate complaint being ignored by Mr. Willard for very long."

Willard's personnel programs—the safety campaign, the Welfare Bureau, the CTP and its predecessors, and especially the Cooperative Plan—may be understood simply as extensions of the basic moral principles evident in Bowman's story. Two such principles stand out: an uncompromising insistence upon thorough and conscientious work, and a deep respect and compassion for even the lowliest worker. Those two principles might seem to be in tension, with adherence to one limiting adherence to the other. But Willard, more than most men of his or any other time, was able to adhere firmly to both. In his funeral eulogy at the small community church in North Hartland, Alfred Rodman Hussey, Willard's long-time pastor at First Unitarian Church of Baltimore, referred to his ability to embrace both principles by calling him a "Puritan liberal."[9] That is probably as good a two-word description of his moral philosophy as one can offer. And, to return to the original question of why he was able to leave such an enduring legacy of goodwill on the Baltimore & Ohio Railroad, that philosophy, rigorously practiced as a matter of faith, was both the source of his vision and the determinant of his actions. Beyond his native intelligence and his broad experience, it was the reason for his success.

Having to go outside the company to find a new president is often an indication that something is amiss. At the least it suggests that the retiring president did not take care to groom an adequate successor. Willard may have been liable to such criticism; he may have been, despite his offers to resign, too reluctant to begin relinquishing his central position in the company. Still, it can be argued that Willard should not be judged too harshly in this matter. The logical internal successor to Willard, the person with the broadest experience and responsibility within the company, would have been operations vice president Charles Galloway, but Galloway had suffered a fatal heart attack in December 1940, at the age of seventy-two. Galloway's successor, C. W. Van Horn, had barely settled into his new office when the search for a new president began; Van Horn was not really prepared for the presidency. Given the advanced age of other B&O officers—senior vice president and chief financial officer George M. Shriver was seventy-three in 1941—Willard may be faulted for allowing something of a gerontocracy to develop. But it would have been inappropriate for him to ask Galloway to step aside for a younger man; the company's operating and transportation ratios indicate that Galloway was doing a fine job, and besides, Galloway was eight years Willard's junior.

More significantly, Roy White was not really an outsider. He came to the B&O presidency via the presidency of Western Union, but in fact he was a twenty-five-year B&O veteran. He began his career in 1900 as a telegraph operator at Dana, Illinois, on what later became the B&O's Indianapolis Division. In 1901 he was promoted to the position of train dispatcher at Indianapolis; he then became, in succession, chief train dispatcher, chief clerk to the B&O general superintendent in Cincinnati, superintendent of the Illinois Division, superintendent of the Indiana Division, superintendent of the Philadelphia Division, and superintendent of the Baltimore Division. In 1921 he became general superintendent of the Maryland District, and in 1923 he was made general manager of the B&O's New York properties. He ended his direct employment by the B&O when in 1926 he was elected senior vice president of the Central Railroad of New Jersey, the indirectly controlled (through the B&O's partial ownership of the Reading Company) line over which the B&O's trains entered the New York metropolitan area. Before the year was over, he was elected president of the Jersey Central. He held that position until 1933, when he assumed the Western Union presidency.[10]

Given his long familiarity with the B&O and the general reverence with which his predecessor was viewed around the company, White made no major changes early in his administration. He professed himself a firm supporter of Willard's labor policies, and "SUGGESTIONS ARE ALWAYS IN ORDER" continued to appear on the editorial page masthead of *Baltimore & Ohio Magazine* for a time.[11] The Cooperative Plan actually underwent something of a revival, at least in terms of the companywide attention focused upon it. With wartime traffic pushing the limits of B&O capacity, the railroad's rolling stock was subjected to a punishing rate of utilization, and the efficiency and creativity of shop forces once more became critical concerns. As a result, to publicize and to reinvigorate the Plan in the shops, beginning in November 1942 the company magazine began running a pictorial page featuring local cooperative committees and various innovations implemented as a result of their discussions.

The new "shop achievements" page tended to focus on relatively inventive time- and labor-saving devices suggested by individual workers through the committees, usually looking past matters of working conditions or of parts and materials availability. For example, the December 1942 page featured Glenwood machinist W. B. Gallegher and the fifty-ton hydraulic press that he had adapted for use in locomotive stoker maintenance, along with Mount Clare general foreman J. A. Finnegan and his portable link trunion bracket boring machine. Similarly, the page in August 1943 pictured Cumberland Back Shop electrical foreman W. P. Yarnall and five devices that he had designed, one of which was a train control receiver ventilator; in addition, the Ivorydale cooperative committee was shown seated at their conference table. In October 1943 the page contained photographs and descriptions of a vise bench fabricated from scrap superheater tubes by Clarksburg boilermaker A. W. Seward, an oil immersion tank for riveting hammers suggested by Glenwood general car foreman J. J. McGuirk, and a small swinging boom crane suggested by Tenth Street (Pittsburgh) electrician J. Ohara and carman C. Martin, primarily for use in loading used batteries onto trucks for disposal.[12]

Despite his commendable showcasing of Cooperative Plan successes, though, there are grounds upon which one might question whether White's commitment to the Plan and its underlying premises was as deep as Willard's. For one thing, conspicuous support of the Plan was the politic posture for White to take, without respect to his attitude toward union men. Labor-management production committees were being touted by the War Production Drive headquarters as a vital means of ensuring proper patriotic efficiency in war-related industries. In August 1942, three months before the Plan page began appearing in *Baltimore & Ohio Magazine*, the *Saturday Evening Post* published a lengthy and laudatory article entitled "It Worked for the B&O," describing the Cooperative Plan as a model for such committees, one that should be followed by all firms involved in the war effort. The article was

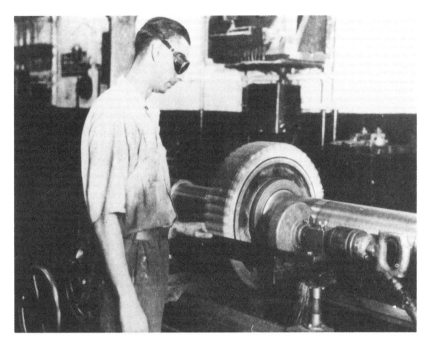

Mount Clare machinist W. E. Griffith and his improved journal polishing device. From *Baltimore & Ohio Magazine*, November 1942. (Courtesy of the B&O Railroad Museum)

reprinted by the U.S. Government Printing Office and given wide distribution beyond the *Post*'s readership. Under the circumstances, for White not to publicize the program in-house might have seemed at least curious.[13]

Adding more substance to suspicions about White's commitment was his apparent reluctance to implement the Cooperative Plan when he was president of the Jersey Central. In December 1930, early in the discussion of setting up separate maintenance of way cooperative committees on the B&O, Bert Jewell wrote to Otto Beyer that after a preliminary conference with Willard, he should take up the matter with White, "looking toward the inauguration of this program on the C. R. of N.J." Jewell hoped to use a successful MW pilot program to entice White into support of a full Jersey Central version of the Cooperative Plan, and to increase the membership of the federated shopcrafts unions in the process: "[Inaugurating a cooperative program] would thus afford you an opportunity to make a demonstration to Mr. White of the advantages occurring to management from such cooperative relations with a bona fide organization, and thus we [the Executive Council] hoped to secure his active cooperation, instead of just his policy of non-opposition in organizing those eligible to membership in these six federated trades." [14] There is no known evidence that White ever formally discussed the issue with Beyer or with any other union representative, or that the Cooperative Plan was ever formally extended to the CNJ—its partial ownership by the B&O notwithstanding.

Simply and obviously, Roy White was not Daniel Willard. Willard's general image among his employees was that of kindly and gentle "Uncle Dan"; White generally was viewed as tougher, more intimidating, and less accessible. [15] His approach to his job often seemed to reflect the quasi-military mindset of the traditional railroad officer. In fact, he pronounced himself entirely comfortable when opportunity arose for him to appear at the office in military uniform. [16] He had several such opportunities, the first at the end of December 1943, when a threatened nationwide rail strike led to the temporary seizure of the railroads by the federal government; [17] White and six other railroad presidents were given commissions as colonels in the army, with authority to run their own and neighboring roads as units of the War Department. Similar actions, in response to the increasingly militant stance of the national leadership of the operating brotherhoods, were taken by President Truman briefly in 1946 and for somewhat longer periods in 1948 and 1950. During at least three of the four periods (the record regarding the 1946 instance is not clear), Colonel White appeared in public only in his carefully tailored army uniform. Presumably such deference to military protocol was expected of him by the War Department. But the uniformed display was somewhat out of keeping with the established "B&O family" atmosphere—employees commonly responded by saluting each other and by indulging in other forms of light, good-natured mockery, such as chalking sergeant's stripes on their coat sleeves—and White appeared to be not much concerned. [18] He gave no noticeable indication that he was apprehensive about the impact of military administration, and the labor strife that prompted it, upon the B&O's reservoir of internal goodwill. That reservoir was large, and it would not be drained by a few nationwide strikes or by a somewhat daunting president who was pleased to play colonel for a few weeks every two or three years. However, he personally added little goodwill to the reservoir; at his best he simply maintained what was already there. Not surprisingly, he was not widely known as "Uncle Roy."

None of the preceding observations should be taken to mean that White was in any way hostile to Willard's cooperative programs. The commentary devoted to them in the company's 1948 annual report suggests that he was quite pleased with them. But it appears that he liked them simply because they worked, not because they were the right thing to do in any normative sense. White was a nominal Presbyterian, but evidence that religion had much of an

Col. Roy B. White (center) with military staff during the federal takeover of the railroads, August 1950. (Courtesy of the B&O Railroad Museum)

impact on the manner in which he managed his company is scarce. As long as
the Cooperative Plan improved efficiency in the shops and as long as the CTP
generated new traffic, they were fine with him.

And the two programs basically still were doing those things. The Cooperative Plan had nowhere near the vitality that it had during its early years,
but it still was producing suggestions, at a slightly higher rate than it had in the
last years of Willard's presidency. The average number of suggestions per
month had reached a low of fifty-two during the 1934–1937 period; for the
period beginning in January 1938 and ending in March 1942, the average increased marginally to fifty-five. Presumably because of the Plan's increased
visibility and the restoration of a full work force (total B&O employees—
excluding those of the Alton, which was lost to bankruptcy in 1942—exceeded
sixty-four thousand by 1944[19]), the average number of suggestions per month
rose a little more, to sixty-eight, during the period from April 1942 through
December 1948.[20]

The Cooperative Traffic Program could claim at least equal success. Direct and immediate traffic solicitation was unnecessary while the war continued, but the sustenance of employee morale and the development of goodwill among future customers remained essential; in those realms the CTP did
its job well. Regular CTP meetings stressed hard work and conscientious ser-

vice as a matter of patriotic duty. Major CTP rallies and entertainment, such as the Baltimore committees' "Red, White and Blue Revue" of October 1943, helped in somewhat lighter fashion to sustain employee morale, patriotism, and pride in the company.[21] CTP special representatives John Bliss, Mildred Drechsler, and C. N. Fullerton (who had returned to the B&O after a year of government service when "Doc" Grimsley retired early in 1940), almost continuously on the road, made themselves available for speaking at functions such as blood donor drives, war bond rallies, and Red Cross campaign meetings, as well as regular CTP gatherings. Members of the CTP women's division were prominently active in local hospitals, station canteens for military personnel, the USO, and the Red Cross.[22] The CTP thus contributed substantially both to reinforcing employee enthusiasm and to polishing the B&O's image as a good corporate citizen—resources for the company to draw upon in the event that traffic levels should slacken.

Of course, traffic did drop off considerably after the end of the war. From their 1944 peak of $395 million, B&O revenues fell 7 percent in 1945 and another 15 percent, to $311 million, in 1946. The CTP was again needed to serve its original purpose of direct traffic solicitation. White committed himself to support of the program, issuing an appeal for renewed interest in the CTP and its business-generating function in November 1946.[23] He became somewhat more visible at CTP events, and his statements about the program seemed increasingly to indicate an appreciation of the Willard-era view of its benefits. At the CTP dinner held as part of the B&O Day celebration in New Castle in June 1948, White (attired in his colonel's uniform) included in his speech the following comments:

> Important as the business solicitation objective of the Cooperative Traffic Program has been, however, it has had another important result. The CTP has been a most useful agency on our line for expanding and further developing the B&O family spirit.
>
> You employees have put in for the Company work that you have done, I believe, because you have liked to do it, and work that, therefore, reflects the good feeling that exists so generally among us. So, you see, this good feeling which is so manifest here tonight and also among the CTP as a whole, is an extremely valuable thing, to us as members of the railroad family and to all the other interests connected with the Baltimore & Ohio Railroad. It is my hope that this good feeling will increase and become more and more real in coming years. It is fundamental in the satisfaction of working for the B&O, and in the success of our joint enterprise.[24]

In the company's 1948 annual report, White devoted considerable space to describing and praising the CTP, the Cooperative Plan, and the various other employee-centered programs of the B&O. In that year, the eighth of his presidency, an observer might have gained the impression that the B&O had shaped White more than White had shaped the B&O.

Although in some cases lower in vitality, all of the major elements of the Willard personnel policy and program were still in place in 1948. The Co-operative Plan and CTP were alive and well, and the safety committees had been successful in bringing under control an employee injury rate that had increased during the war. Activities begun by the Welfare Bureau remained at many locations, in particular the athletic and musical groups at the larger B&O centers of activity. The Mount Clare Band was gone, but the Men's Glee Club and the Women's Music Club were more successful than ever. Each numbered over one hundred voices, and in 1948 they gave separately or together over one hundred concerts, including two nationwide broadcasts over the ABC radio network. *Baltimore & Ohio Magazine* had been instrumental in starting the B&O Junior Railroaders Club for B&O children in 1945; by 1948 the club had sixteen hundred members. The magazine had been cut in half from its late-1920s peak, to sixty-four pages, but it still won first prize as the best human interest publication in a contest conducted by the American Railway Magazine Editors Association. The pre-Willard Veterans' Association and its Ladies' Auxiliary remained active and healthy.[25] Professional women on the B&O still were a tiny minority, but there were more of them than on any other railroad in the country.[26]

Roy White surely deserves some credit for knowing when not to mess up a good thing. He may not have understood fully the wellsprings of the Willard heritage, but he did respect it.

An example both of the residual strength of that heritage and of White's somewhat passive willingness to let it to a certain point have its course was the "One Million New Customers" campaign. Begun in the summer of 1950 as a response to a 1949 traffic slump, it was essentially a direct-mail advertising campaign undertaken largely at employee expense. The company supplied postcards inviting prospective customers to try the B&O's services, and employees supplied postage and mailed the cards to friends and acquaintances. The campaign was proposed by Mount Clare machinist John A. Gribbin, who, interestingly, took the idea to his union lodge instead of the CTP or shops cooperative committee. The local machinists' chairman, W. E. Griffith, then took the proposal to shop superintendent C. H. Spence, who bounced it off his boss (A. K. Galloway, George Emerson's successor as superintendent of motive power and equipment) and J. W. Phipps, successor to O. S. Lewis as general freight traffic manager and official head of the CTP. Having secured management's blessing, Griffith presented the proposal successively to the local shopcrafts federation and to shopcrafts Federation No. 30, both of which endorsed it. The campaign was to be tested at Mount Clare; if successful, it was to be passed to the CTP and the Veterans' Association for systemwide implementation. Unfortunately, although more than seventy-five hundred postcards were mailed by Mount Clare employees during the first three weeks of the campaign, it did not spread. Primarily because traffic made a strong recovery on its own late in 1950 and through 1951, the campaign was shelved for three and a half years. Then in the spring of 1954, at the onset of a severe downturn in traffic, it was dusted off by John Bliss, run through channels again, and finally established across the railroad. More than sixty thousand postcards were distributed in roughly four months. The campaign, like the traffic solicitation postcard efforts of the 1920s, was a modest success—it was a good builder of B&O morale and public image—but machinist Gribbin never got his one million new customers.[27]

Roy White should be remembered as a fairly competent but generally uninspired administrator. Certainly he was not a leader of Daniel Willard's stature. However, he did allow Willard's personnel programs to continue, and he made some significant improvements to the B&O's physical property. The company made money in every year of his presidency, albeit in some years not much. With the boom years of the war included, the B&O's average annual return on equity during the White administration was 4.37 percent, somewhat better than the rate of return on a passbook savings account.[28] When he retired at the age of seventy in August 1953, he passed on to his successor Howard Simpson a railroad that was reasonably sound, if not especially well prepared to cope with the increasing competitive pressures of subsidized highway and air transportation, and that still possessed an unusually loyal and conscientious work force.

Howard E. Simpson began his career in railroading at the age of fifteen, when he dropped out of school to become a clerk in the passenger department of the Central Railroad of New Jersey. By 1925, at the age of twenty-eight, he was the Jersey Central's advertising agent. A year later he was division passenger agent at Newark, where he first came to the attention of Roy White. Simpson made a good impression, and by 1931 he was the road's assistant general passenger agent. From that position he moved to the parent company, as B&O's general passenger agent for New York and New England. He progressed upward through the B&O's passenger department, finally becoming traffic vice president in 1947, upon the retirement of Golder Shumate.[29]

Simpson was a hearty, outgoing, affable man. By all indications he was well liked by everyone who knew him—a true member of the B&O family, his Jersey Central origins notwithstanding. Unfortunately, his geniality was probably by a wide margin his most outstanding quality. He was not notably visionary or innovative, and he was not a particularly dynamic leader. Like

White he did not dismantle any of the Willard personnel programs, but neither did he add much to them, other than his occasional smiling presence. He clearly loved his job, and he worked hard at it, but nothing much seemed to happen under his direction. To the extent that good things were accomplished on the B&O during his presidency, they are more likely traceable to the efforts of his subordinates, and to remaining momentum from the Willard and White eras, than to his leadership.

Of all the Willard programs, the CTP usually was given the most attention during Simpson's time as president. Its budget and staff, the former more or less adjusted for inflation, stayed basically the same as they were in the late 1930s. The company continued to cover the costs of hall rental for major rallies or meetings; otherwise, the local committees were financially on their own. The program still had five full-time staff members: three special representatives, a clerk, and a secretary.

The venerable C. N. Fullerton had immediate charge of the CTP as senior special representative until his retirement, after fifty-two years of B&O service, in January 1955.[30] At that time Fullerton's leadership role was assumed by seventeen-year CTP veteran John Bliss, and William Howard moved over from other traffic department responsibilities to help Bliss with the men's division. Mildred Drechsler, who had supervised the women's division since 1943, continued to do so and to write the narrative for the "CTP Activities" pages of *B&O Magazine*. Aided by their clerk, who prepared the monthly *CTP Bulletin* from statistical summaries sent in by local committee chairmen, and by their secretary, the triumvirate of Bliss, Drechsler, and Howard ran the CTP for the remainder of its existence.[31]

They spent most of their time on the road, especially during picnic season in July and August and during Christmas party season in December. Their itineraries usually were determined by a balancing of three needs: to respond to local committee invitations, to visit each location with approximately equal frequency, and to minimize travel time. For example, if the women's committee in Flora wished Drechsler to attend their tea as guest and speaker, she would arrange to do so if she had not been there for a few months and if she could arrange to visit nearby points—perhaps St. Louis, or North Vernon or Washington, Indiana—on the same trip. During their visits they conferred with local committee officers and brought meeting attendees up to date, by speech and occasionally by film, on what was happening around the railroad. More broadly, they were cheerleaders, exhorting CTP participants to keep up the good work.[32]

And good work was generally what CTP participants were doing, although it did not measure up well against the work that was done during the program's early years. Business reported through the CTP committees in 1955 amounted to 5,016 freight carloads, 12,315 LCL shipments, and 17,186 passengers.[33] These numbers represented 23, 64, and 51 percent, respectively, of the annual averages for the years 1934 through 1938. The loss of the Alton might have caused a reduction in reported traffic of about 10 percent, but that loss would have been to some degree offset by higher employment on the B&O proper (despite productivity-related cuts in immediately preceding years, there were still 9 percent more B&O employees in 1955 than in 1937).[34] The fact was that the CTP was still generating traffic, but the numbers were down in comparison to those of the Willard era. There was little chance of significant underreporting; if anything, some of the numbers might have been a bit overstated. All solicited traffic still was self-reported, by the employee or family member through the local committee to the CTP office in Baltimore. The potential for abuse remained, and occasionally it was realized. For example, the women's chairman in Philadelphia was strongly suspected of routinely inflating her reported passenger traffic during this period. Neither Drechsler nor Bliss called her to account, though; it was considered critical to avoid embarrassing either the program or the chairman, given the outside possibility that her reports actually were accurate.[35]

The essence of the decline in tangible success of the CTP was less a dearth of effort by CTP participants than a dearth of CTP participants. In January 1955, for example, only 515 employees or family members reported traffic—less than two-thirds of the number for January 1934, before the program was in full operation, and not much more than one-third of the 1934–1938 average. Meeting attendance was generally lower than it was in the early years. Fewer meetings were being held; only fifty-two committees gathered with their memberships in January 1955.[36] The loyal and enthusiastic employees of the 1950s appear to have been a lesser percentage of the B&O family than they were in the 1930s. At some locations their number seems to have fallen below the critical mass necessary to make programs like the CTP work consistently and independently.

Some formerly flourishing CTP groups failed to meet for months at a time, until they were rebuilt or reenergized by the special representatives from Baltimore. In Zanesville, for example, by late 1956 the CTP was moribund: meetings were not being held, and traffic was not being reported. Then early in 1957, Bliss prevailed upon newly transferred ticket agent Paul Mobus to take on the CTP men's chairmanship and to engineer a turnaround. For four months, results were marginal. Then Mobus began offering small prizes for outstanding contributions, and posting lists of winners. Bliss helped by agreeing to have the CTP office pick up the cost of spouses' meals at the reinstituted annual dinners and dances. By the end of the year, the program was up and running again. B&O employment in Zanesville had dropped to about seventy

Howard Simpson (right) with Maryland governor Theodore McKeldin. Baltimore CTP
dinner dance, January 1956. (Courtesy of the B&O Railroad Museum)

with the 1956 transfer of signal shop activities to Cumberland; of those seventy roughly fifty resumed some form of active or passive CTP involvement.[37]
A similar cycle of decline, intervention from Baltimore, and revival was typical of local CTP activity throughout the decade.

    If fault for the CTP's decline is to be assigned, it likely should be placed
some levels higher in the hierarchy than the level of the CTP office. Fullerton,
Bliss, Drechsler, and Howard were all unusually energetic, positive, outgoing, articulate, and engaging people, possessing precisely the qualities necessary to enlist their peers in a volunteer effort. The problem is that many
employees never bothered to meet them. During the Willard era, one might
surmise that some skeptical employees were coaxed or led to their first CTP
meetings by a combination of gentle coercion and moral suasion, as well as
avuncular understanding, that emanated from the top of the company. Little of
such qualities emanated from the president's chair when it was occupied
by Howard Simpson. He was an affable fellow, but he lacked *gravitas*:
confidence-inspiring weight and dignity and purposefulness. Moreover, what
weight he did have, he did not much lend to the CTP. During his eight years as
president, he appeared at two major CTP functions: the twentieth-anniversary

dinner held in Cumberland the month after he took office, and the Baltimore women's division dinner dance in January 1956, at which Maryland governor Theodore McKeldin was the principal speaker.[38] Simpson had refused an invitation to speak at the latter meeting, but he was forced to attend anyway when McKeldin was invited in his place and accepted.[39]

The CTP suffered decline during the Simpson years, but it was not just coasting by any means. CTP leadership was responsible for the reintroduction and distribution of reciprocity cards in the spring of 1956, an effort repeated in the spring of 1958. In the fall of 1958 a campaign to increase LCL freight traffic was launched through the CTP. As the decade ended, with the B&O's financial condition rapidly deteriorating, CTP meeting attendance generally stabilized, with major social events continuing to draw much larger crowds than regular business meetings. In one instance attendance reached a number characteristic of the Willard era: the picnic and railroad open house jointly sponsored by the men's and women's committees of Salamanca (New York) in August 1959 drew more than fifteen hundred employees, plus their family members, from points all over the B&O's former BR&P lines. More typically, the Martinsburg dinner meeting of April 1960 drew 144 people, the Cumberland dinner dance of June 1960 drew 220, and the Baltimore picnic at Kurtz Beach later that summer was attended by approximately 800. The Baltimore dinner dance in March 1960, at which an editor of *Modern Railroads* magazine was the principal speaker, was attended by 400 people, an improvement over the 300 who attended that event four years earlier to hear Simpson and Governor McKeldin.[40]

Meanwhile, the Cooperative Plan had virtually disappeared from public view. The Cooperative Plan page had been dropped from *Baltimore & Ohio Magazine* in 1948, and the Plan was not mentioned in the company's annual report after that year. By the mid-1950s, people outside the company, and many of those inside, would not have known whether the Plan still existed without undertaking a pointed inquiry. A lengthy internal report on the organization and functions of the company's personnel department, issued the month that Simpson took office, made no reference to the Cooperative Plan. A booklet issued to participants in the B&O's technical graduate training course, also dating from the early part of the Simpson presidency, likewise said nothing of the Plan, although it did refer to quarterly systemwide motive power department management meetings. A page in the August 1956 company magazine, describing devices recently developed by Glenwood shop employees, contained no mention of the Cooperative Plan; neither did the record of a June 1956 luncheon conference between Simpson and the general chairmen of the various labor organizations on the B&O, including the shopcrafts unions. The 1958 edition of the company's new-employee handbook mentioned the CTP and the Veterans' Association, but not the Cooperative Plan. It contained instead a section on suggestions, headed by a cartoon showing an overalled employee and a business-suited manager in front of a sign reading "SUGGESTIONS ARE ALWAYS IN ORDER," urging employees to send their suggestions to the corporate secretary in Baltimore, who would have them evaluated by a management suggestion committee.[41]

Invisible as it may have been outside the shops, the Cooperative Plan survived into the Simpson years in much of its original outward form. Local meetings were held monthly in most shops on company time; the top manager at the facility, a stores department employee, and a few foremen usually represented management, and one member of each of the shopcrafts unions usually represented labor. System meetings were held quarterly in Baltimore, most often over lunch at a downtown hotel; management normally was represented by the company's chief mechanical officer, the car department superintendent, the regional motive power superintendents, one or two master mechanics, the purchasing agent, and the superintendent of the stores department.[42]

The matters under discussion likewise often bore some similarity to those of the program's early years. Many items considered at local cooperative meetings were much like those listed in chapter 2: lack of proper tools, insufficient locker space, poor lighting, drafty conditions in winter, and lack of toilet paper, as well as supervisory complaints about poor quality of workmanship. However, in comparison to those of the 1920s, local meetings tended to have shorter agendas and to be oriented more heavily toward small gripes; truly innovative suggestions were rare. The typical quarterly system meeting was more a forum for general discussions of conditions around the railroad than a decision-making conference for resolution of suggestions or complaints not resolved at the local level.[43]

Without visible attention, support, or publicity from the top of the company, the conduct of the Plan in the field apparently was left increasingly to the discretion of local management. If the shop manager was a true disciple of the B&O way of doing things, then the program still functioned to some extent as originally intended. On the other hand, if the supervisor had drifted away from (or never accepted) the Willardian culture, then the program tended to become a mostly meaningless shell. By the late fifties, instances of the latter seem to have been fairly numerous. At some locations the program, such as it was, was not even generally known as the Cooperative Plan, for the very good reason that there was not much cooperative about it. Local meetings might consist simply of the superintendent's calling the union people into his office, telling them what he wanted done, and then sending them out to do it.[44] That was not what Willard, Beyer, and Johnston had in mind back in 1923.

At best the Cooperative Plan had become a matter of unremarked routine, not only for management but also for the unions. In 1940 the Plan was a matter of some importance to shopcrafts labor; System Federation No. 30 had a standing committee on cooperation, and the 1940 biennial convention of the federation strongly endorsed both the Cooperative Plan and the CTP. Over the subsequent two decades, however, union interest in the Plan diminished considerably. This shift in attitude was not marked by any apparent sudden antipathy toward the notion of cooperation; the loss of union enthusiasm came gradually. At the 1950 convention of Federation No. 30, the committee on cooperation was no longer in existence, but addresses on cooperative matters by C. N. Fullerton and A. K. Galloway were generally well received, and the Gribbin One Million New Customer campaign was approved without major dissent. The 1952 convention was a shade more militant, pushing to impose more restrictive work rules on the company, but the assembly still voted to retain in the preamble to the federation bylaws a statement of intent to "bring about closer cooperation between management and employees." By 1960 the stance of the federation was noticeably adversarial. That year's convention accepted a revision of federation bylaws that removed the cooperation objective from the preamble, and the tone of some of the resolutions adopted by the body was distinctly hostile to management.[45]

The deterioration of relations between the shopcrafts unions and the B&O was paralleled, and probably accelerated somewhat, by increasing acrimony in railroad labor-management relations in general. In particular the operating brotherhoods—those of the engineers, firemen, conductors, and trainmen—seem to have reached the conclusion that railroad management was their enemy. More than highway competition or inequitable government policy or their own highly restrictive contractual work rules, railroad managers were blamed by union officers for the failure of their memberships to improve their relative economic positions. Their actions consequently were not to cooperate with management against the forces threatening their industry, but to fight them tooth and nail for every last penny that would be taken from them.[46]

By the liberal use of strikes or threats thereof, the brotherhoods were quite successful in their continuing battle. Wages of operating employees rose considerably faster in the postwar years than did railroad revenues. Perhaps more significantly, their militance enabled them to be amazingly successful at protecting their memberships against technological job loss. The diesel locomotive made the locomotive fireman obsolete, and radio communication reduced the need for a second brakeman on many freight trains. Nonetheless, the brotherhoods insisted, upon pain of strike, that those positions be maintained. At one point in 1950, the firemen's brotherhood even demanded that a second fireman be required on diesels, as if one man staring at the scenery or sleeping the miles away were not enough. That demand was not met, but smaller concessions on work rules were granted, in that instance and in others, and railroad payroll costs continued to spiral upward.[47]

Management for its part was increasingly angered by the waste that all of this entailed. The combination of "featherbed" manning requirements and short, nineteenth-century crew districts created situations in which ten people (two crews of an engineer, a fireman, a conductor, and two brakemen) would have to be paid to make a two-hundred-mile run—work that often could be accomplished easily by three people. Such circumstances reinforced the positions of rail managers who had held that the unions were the enemy all along. With both sides thus convinced, more or less, that the other side was the enemy, labor-management relations on the operations side of railroading degenerated into trench warfare. The struggle's long-term costs to both sides were high, as competing modes of transportation were not beset by similar bloodletting. Still, the brotherhoods, their militance aided by greater political clout than they had possessed a generation earlier, were making appreciable short-run gains. Shopcrafts union leaders could not help but notice this, and their estimation of the benefits of cooperation thus presumably was adjusted downward a notch or two.

In this context a number of changes specific to the B&O take on added significance to the loss of shopcrafts enthusiasm for cooperation. One irritant to the shopmen, of increasing aggravation during postwar employment cutbacks, was outside purchasing of parts and subcontracting of equipment repair, a practice that they viewed with some justification as being in violation of the spirit of the Cooperative Plan. Then there was the apparently growing ineffectuality of the Plan as a means of accomplishing nonroutine working condition improvements that earlier in its life it would have addressed more satisfactorily. During the last years of the White presidency and on through the Simpson administration, matters that formerly would have been resolved within the cooperative committee structure were being raised before the federation convention as resolutions, to be handled as bargaining points in contract negotiations with the company. Heating of the Martinsburg wash and locker room, leather jackets for welders, asbestos gloves for boilermakers working with hot firebox components, better ventilation to remove diesel fumes from roundhouses: these and many similar requests were no longer being granted through the cooperative committees.[48]

Compounding the unions' understandably negative response to such signs of management's diminished commitment to the Plan were changes in union organization and leadership. In 1948 the shopcrafts employees of the Western Maryland, like the Reading and the Jersey Central partially owned by the B&O but not participating in the Cooperative Plan, were folded into System Federation No. 30. By 1960 shopmen of the independent Akron, Canton, &

Youngstown had been added as well. The federation was no longer exclusively a part of the B&O family, and the Cooperative Plan no longer even
nominally applied to all of its members. Of at least equal importance was the
fact that none of the union leaders who had worked personally with Daniel
Willard in the development of the Plan was still in office. Bert Jewell had left
the presidency of the AFL's Railway Employees' Department in 1946, and
Federation No. 30 president Harry Doyle, who had succeeded William McGee
in 1932, had retired from his position in 1948.[49] Their successors did not
really know Daniel Willard, nor did they know William Johnston or Otto
Beyer. They were acquainted with Roy White or Howard Simpson or both,
and they knew the militant and powerful leaders of the operating brotherhoods. That they displayed an attitude toward union-management cooperation
somewhat different from that of their predecessors is not surprising.

So through the 1950s and into the early 1960s, the Cooperative Plan was
serving as little more than a means of limited labor-management communication, occasionally resolving local concerns of minor import. It was doing so
without the active encouragement or hindrance of either the president of the
B&O or the leadership of System Federation No. 30. By all indications the
program simply was running on its own diminishing momentum.

To a degree the whole company was running on momentum established in
prior years, and the results were not good. Jervis Langdon, who served as
B&O general counsel under Simpson and became president when Simpson
was eased out of office in 1961, observed that when he joined the company in
December 1956, it was "a failing enterprise . . . [with] most of the top people
waiting for retirement."[50] The consequence of this executive lassitude was a
financial near-disaster. The railroad's momentum carried it reasonably well
through 1956; total revenues that year were a record $473 million, and return
on equity was 4.40 percent. With the onset of recession late in 1957, though,
top management's inability to deal creatively with an increasingly hostile environment became progressively more obvious. Revenues fell to $392 million
in 1958, recovered marginally in 1959 and 1960, and fell again to $357 mil-
lion in 1961. The company turned less than 2 percent on equity in 1958 and
1959, barely broke even in 1960, and lost $31 million in 1961: a negative 5.53
percent ROE, leaving the company technically insolvent.[51]

Deferred maintenance on both road and rolling stock had been accumu-
lating throughout the period; the property was in increasingly poor shape, and
reliability was declining correspondingly. Symbolic of the company's sad
state, *B&O Magazine* was down to a mere twenty-four pages. The morale of
even the most loyal employees was low and getting lower. The need for an
executive change was abundantly clear. Simpson stepped aside as president in
favor of Jervis Langdon on June 1, 1961; he thereupon became board chair-

man and chief executive officer, the former position being passed to him by
the aging and ailing Roy White. In December he relinquished the CEO position as well, to Langdon.[52] Retaining only the ceremonial chairmanship, Howard Simpson, a pleasant fellow who was promoted beyond his competence,
was effectively removed from the management of the Baltimore & Ohio.

While Simpson's B&O was sliding toward insolvency, most of the rest of
the railroad industry to one degree or another also was suffering financial difficulty. Largely because of truck competition, reinforced by the commencement
of the Interstate Highway System in 1956, rails were battling a substantial and
accelerating erosion of their freight market share. The loss of passenger market
share to airlines and private automobiles was even greater; the passenger services of most railroads were failing by a fairly wide margin to cover their full
costs. Under serious pressure from rising costs and apparently helpless to do
much about stagnant or declining revenues, many railroads sought refuge in
the economies derivable from consolidation of facilities and staff. The result
was something of a scramble for merger partners, particularly in the railroad-
saturated northeastern quadrant of the country.

The weakening B&O naturally was caught up in this activity. Early in
1959 Alfred Perlman, president of the similarly weakening New York Central,
proposed to Simpson and officers of the still-strong Chesapeake & Ohio that
the three roads be merged. Perlman's thinking presumably was that the numerous parallel lines and duplicative terminals of the NYC and the B&O
could be consolidated, with associated capital costs partially underwritten by
the prosperous, coal-traffic-based C&O. The board chairman and president of
the C&O, Cyrus Eaton and Walter Tuohy, respectively, were not enamored
of the idea of bailing out two larger carriers and losing control of their own in
the process, so they launched their own unilateral bid to acquire the B&O. In
the subsequent war for the favor of B&O shareholders, the C&O beat the
NYC fairly handily. In February 1961 Tuohy announced that his company
held or controlled 61 percent of B&O common stock. Petition was made to the
Interstate Commerce Commission to sanction officially the C&O's acquisition
of the B&O. After a year and a half of hearings and deliberations, the ICC in
December 1962 announced its approval of the C&O petition. On February 4,
1963, the Chesapeake & Ohio officially took control of its older, larger
neighbor.[53]

When Jervis Langdon assumed the B&O presidency in June 1961, then,
he placed himself in a difficult position: he had to engineer a turnaround of a
failing company under the scrutiny of a group of outsiders who at some time
in the not-too-distant future might decide to replace him. By the end of the
year, the company's current liabilities exceeded current assets by over $24

million, and losses, although slowed somewhat, were continuing to mount. Langdon clearly had to cut costs substantially and promptly.[54] He instituted a "strict, weekly mancount" in all departments, with the requirement that all nonessential positions be eliminated.[55] It was Langdon's decision, but as he made it, he must have been aware that C&O officials in Cleveland were watching his performance.

Meanwhile, John Bliss had been invited in October 1961 to address the C&O's Better Service Conference (BSC) system meetings at that railroad's Greenbrier Hotel in West Virginia. Bliss assumed that his remarks on the CTP were to be the first step toward integrating his program with the acquiring company's BSC, a program of local meetings between shippers and traffic department employees that up to a point paralleled the CTP's traffic-generating function. He made his address and returned to Baltimore believing that the CTP would in some fashion survive the merger. Consequently, he was stunned when on March 9, 1962, Bliss's immediate superior in the traffic department, W. H. Schmidt, called him into his office and told him that he was dissolving the program. All local committees were to be disbanded, and any company funds that they held were to be returned by the end of the month. No more CTP events were to be held: Mildred Drechsler had to cancel the annual Baltimore dinner dance just three weeks before it was to take place. William Howard transferred to another job in the traffic department, and Bliss and Drechsler elected to take an early retirement. By April 1 the Cooperative Traffic Program no longer existed.[56]

Officers and members of the 194 CTP committees (153 in the men's division and 41 in the women's) still active when the decision was made were generally surprised and distraught. As Bliss put it many years later, "They all felt we had a wonderful family spirit on the railroad, and felt something very close to them was being taken away." [57] There was nothing they could do about it, though; the CTP was gone, the victim of departmental interpretation of Langdon's man count order. Langdon's recollection is that the issue of the CTP's termination never reached his office.[58]

The story of the disposition of the Cooperative Plan is considerably murkier. The Plan during the 1950s and early 1960s was virtually invisible, and whatever internal documentation did exist apparently has been destroyed. Cooperative committee meetings were more a habit than part of a grand and purposeful scheme of union-management cooperation, and no one cared enough to make a fuss about them one way or another. As a result, the specifics of the Plan's demise are unclear; all that is clear is that the Cooperative Plan did not continue in any formal fashion after the C&O gained effective control.[59]

The last vestiges of the programs that had shaped the B&O family, and

Daniel Willard's office mantel. (Courtesy of the B&O Railroad Museum)

that set the stage for the real innovation of the Cooperative Plan, disappeared along with the company's independence as the decade proceeded. The Glee Club managed to hang on into the C&O era, but not for long; most social and athletic events did not survive the death of the CTP. Langdon was able to run his own show for a time, but only for a time. In the fall of 1964 C&O management, possibly irritated by inroads made by a recovering and more aggressive B&O on the C&O's coal traffic, denied the B&O's request to build state-of-the-art coal dumpers at Baltimore and at Lorain, Ohio. Langdon resigned over the matter, and C&O president Walter Tuohy stepped into his position. From then on, except for a brief period in 1965–1966, the president of the C&O was also the president of the B&O.[60]

Although retaining its original corporate charter, the B&O suffered further loss of its identity in 1972, when the parent company decided to adopt for marketing purposes the name "Chessie System" for itself, the B&O, and the B&O's former partially owned subsidiary, the Western Maryland. Then in 1980 the Chessie System joined the Seaboard Coast Line rail system to form an entity called CSX Corporation, submerging the B&O even more deeply. Finally, on April 30, 1987, the B&O was officially consolidated into the parent corporate structure.[61] Its charter relinquished, the Baltimore & Ohio Railroad Company ceased to exist. Most of its trackage still was in place, some of it quite busy—but its name was gone, just as Daniel Willard, his personnel policies and programs, and his railroad family were gone.

CONCLUSION

At CSX corporate headquarters, the full record of Daniel Willard's presidency, aside from B&O annual reports, is a twelve-line listing of his work history: date of birth, job titles and dates of appointment, partial salary data, and date of death. Little more is known of Willard by the management of the successor company, and there is not much interest in adding to that knowledge. During the preparation of this book, the reactions of various CSX officials to the author's queries ranged from polite interest and helpfulness, to polite indifference, to open contempt for "those old B&O guys." [1]

Why should they care? What was so special about Daniel Willard, and what does it have to do with running a railroad or any other company today? A broad and simple answer to those questions is that better than any other man in his industry and in his time, and arguably as well as anyone in any industry and in any time, he showed how to lead a company. His appreciation of the dangers of financial leverage may not have been especially strong, and his expansion strategy of the early 1930s may not have been well timed, but those were almost inevitable manifestations of his intense belief in the importance of his company and its services, and his desire to build them up. He was determined that his railroad would provide the best services possible: that his customers would be well cared for, and that as a consequence, so would be his shareholders. Given his company's geographic disadvantages and hostile environment, his success was remarkable.

The means by which he achieved this success was as noteworthy as the success itself. How so? The quality that distinctively marked his leadership, and that secures his honorable position in the history of corporate management, was his deeply empathetic appreciation of what motivates employees.

183

He understood their needs, and he knew that the company that met those needs in a disciplined setting could have its employees' generally enthusiastic commitment. From that commitment would come corporate success.

What more specific lessons might the practicing manager learn from his story? Willard was fond of maxims, so it seems proper that at least the first effort to draw practical conclusions should be in that form. As a nod in the direction of originality, his personal favorites will not be used verbatim but will be paraphrased. The following is a fair list of neo-Willardian maxims:

1. Serve your customers; without them, your company and your job would not exist.
2. Respect your subordinates; without them, you would not be able to do your job.
3. Treat both customers and subordinates as you would want to be treated were you in their places.
4. Give your shareholders their due.
5. Keep your door open; be visible, and listen carefully.
6. Do not prejudge sources of ideas, information, or effort.
7. Search out that which is right and good; believe in it, and always act accordingly.

No doubt, many sophisticated folk would find these precepts banal and naive. Willard would not. He ran his company by them.

Simple truths can be powerful guides to action if they are taken seriously. If the reader has increased his or her appreciation of that point, then the author is pleased. However, there is more to be understood from this story, namely, the means by which those truths were translated into specific actions that in turn led to a particular set of desired results. We must return to the causal process argued in the introduction—leader to management program to corporate culture to corporate performance—and reconsider it in light of five chapters of historical details. To what extent has that pattern been affirmed? The final answer to that question is left to the reader's judgment. Still, in the hope of influencing that judgment, the following summary assessment is offered, moving backward through the process, from effect to cause.

First, the matter of results: the B&O's performance during the Willard administration clearly did improve in some respects relative to that of the competition. Return on equity increased markedly during the early years of the Cooperative Plan, and market share increased slightly during the prewar years of the CTP. By some measures of operating efficiency (for instance, the transportation ratio during the thirties), the railroad looked very good even when the company's bottom line did not. Such results are hardly overwhelming, but they have some significance in a troubled and tightly regulated industry where fixed plant is truly fixed and marketing options are closely circumscribed. Willard's company was able to post some excellent numbers during the good times and to avoid disaster during the bad.

To what can such results be attributed? Capital expenditures were central during the catch-up years of the teens, but thereafter B&O plant and equipment improvements were just proportionately equal to or less than those of the competition. The key factor distinguishing Willard's railroad from the rest of the industry at least from 1923 onward was personnel. B&O people cared more about doing their jobs well, on average, than did their competitors' people. Decades before it became fashionable for every company to claim, often cynically, to be a customer-oriented, caring family, the B&O was one. That was the essence of the firmly established B&O culture, and that was why the company succeeded as it did.

How can one be confident that the company's performance was traceable to culture, and not directly to the management programs that shaped that culture? Was culture really a necessary intermediary? The answer to the second question is yes, and the reason—the answer to the first question—is that none of Willard's programs (after some experimentation with shop piece rates during the teens) used direct, tangible incentives. B&O employees were not tangibly rewarded for performance; they were intangibly rewarded for conforming to a culture that encouraged performance. The PRR shopman who forwarded a good idea to the BNI received a cash bonus; the B&O shopman who sent a similar idea to his local cooperative committee received the approval of his colleagues, and an assurance that his proposal might in some small way contribute indirectly to his job security by helping the company in general. Viewing himself strictly as an isolated individual, he might not consider that to be enough incentive to participate. Viewing himself as part of a company family, though, subject to peer pressure to pitch in and help the family out, he might take the time to develop the idea and to send it in. His primary reward would be in the form of peer acceptance for having conformed to the corporate culture, reinforced by his own understanding that in moral terms it was the right thing to do. Similar observations can be made about the other programs and practices of the Willard era. Glee Club singers and baseball team members were not paid out of the advertising budget, nor were CTP contributors given sales commissions. Their rewards were indirect or intangible. The thrust of Willard's approach was to create a culture that would encourage people to perform better, not to purchase better performance directly.

That is admittedly the less certain approach. Cultures are hard to shape and a long time in the making, whereas cash is simple to dispense and effective immediately. The problem with cash is that it is strictly a short-run incentive; when the bonus stops, so does improved performance. A well-founded corporate culture, in contrast, tends to endure for the long run; it lingers, as on the B&O, even after its source has been cut off.

And what was its source on the B&O? There was no single all-encompassing determinant, but the most powerful one was the collective actions of the company's management. The causal process was not linear—simply from management action to culture—but more circular: action shaped culture, which influenced subsequent action, which further shaped culture, and so on. Thus, in the most important example, the Welfare Bureau shaped culture, which facilitated establishment of the Cooperative Plan, which further shaped culture—until the system was complete, and its full benefits could be derived. Each of Willard's progressive policies, carefully kept consistent with prior ones, built upon its predecessors, and in so doing reinforced and clarified the B&O way of doing things. They were all important, then: his acceptance of the unions, the safety committees, the company magazine, the Welfare Bureau, his limited adherence to scientific management, the cooperative claim prevention committees, his acceptance of women as more than clerical employees, the open division superintendents' meetings, the Cooperative Plan, the centennial celebration, and the Cooperative Traffic Program. They were parts of a whole, constructed step by step as a need or opportunity arose, and held together by Willard's open door policy and his visible personal example.

We thus are led back to the fundamental thesis of the book: that the sine qua non of all of this was Daniel Willard. Without him most of the B&O's progressive policies would have fizzled after a trial period or never would have been adopted at all. He was the central and essential figure. That is not to say that his stewardship of his company was flawless, a model of theoretical perfection. He made occasional mistakes; he did not have the presumed educational advantage of an MBA. His was not a great creative mind; the basic ideas behind his centerpiece programs came from others. But he knew his business thoroughly, and he had a great talent for recognizing good ideas and bringing them to fruition. He was not the brilliant entrepreneur, but he was the epitome of the capable administrator. As well as anyone, he understood how to lead the tens of thousands of employees of a sprawling, century-old company. He knew how to get things done.

Willard was blessed with and aided by his gently demanding manner and his modest personal magnetism; his personality had a quality that made people want to please him. The real reason for his success, though, is deeper than either knowledge or style. It is character: the profound essence of the human spirit. Willard was a man of genuine humility and real empathy for his employees, undergirded by a rigorous sense of morality. Those qualities in him, more than any techniques inherent in the programs themselves, explain the success of his progressive approaches. They also explain why he adopted them. Willard was not a man given to shallow expediency; he adopted and maintained his programs because he knew them to be right. Such moral commitment was absolutely essential to his accomplishments.

Those accomplishments, and this study of them, stand in categorical opposition to the notion that programs like Willard's can be applied manipulatively, in the manner of the latest "quick fix" management technique. Employees eventually will detect the sham, and the programs will not work. Thus managers who would lead people more effectively might spend more time examining their souls than lapping up the most recent book on improving style. The faddish adoption of mere techniques, or of programs without deep commitment to the values upon which they are based, is a waste of everyone's time. The integrity of the leader is vital—absolutely so. That is the core message of the story of Daniel Willard and his railroad.

NOTES

Introduction

1. J. M. Kouzes, D. F. Cladwell, and B. Z. Posner, "Organizational Culture: How It Is Created, Maintained, and Changed" (paper presented at OD Network National Conference, Los Angeles, Oct. 9, 1983); and T. E. Deal and A. A. Kennedy, *Corporate Cultures* (Reading, Mass.: Addison-Wesley, 1982), p. 4. See also Thomas Peters and Robert H. Waterman, *In Search of Excellence* (New York: Harper & Row, 1982), and Edgar H. Schein, "The Role of the Founder in Creating Organizational Culture," *Organizational Dynamics*, Summer 1985, p. 14.

Chapter 1

1. Fuller discussions of the state of the Baltimore and Ohio between 1890 and 1910 are available in John F. Stover, *History of the Baltimore & Ohio Railroad* (West Lafayette, Ind.: Purdue University Press, 1987), chaps. 10–11, and Edward Hungerford, *The Story of the Baltimore & Ohio Railroad* (New York: G. P. Putnam's Sons, 1928), vol. 2, chaps. 11–15.

2. Albro Martin, *Enterprise Denied: Origins of the Decline of American Railroads, 1897–1917* (New York: Columbia University Press, 1971), 1–95. Martin argues that railroad capital improvements in 1907 (and subsequently) were inhibited less by recession than by the deadening influence of government regulation, specifically the 1906 Hepburn Act's proviso that the Interstate Commerce Commission might prescribe maximum rail rates.

3. Baltimore & Ohio Railroad, *Annual Reports*, 1900–1909.

4. Martin, *Enterprise Denied*, p. 91.

5. Baltimore & Ohio Railroad, *Annual Reports*, 1901–1909. Net income here is defined as net after preferred dividends.

6. Stover, *History of the Baltimore & Ohio*, 209–10.

7. Alfred D. Chandler, Jr., *The Visible Hand: The Managerial Revolution in American Business* (Cambridge, Mass.: Belknap Press, 1977), 173–75; also Martin, *Enterprise Denied*, 18–21, 115–16. The other six groups (and their main components) were the Vanderbilt lines (New York Central system, Chicago & North Western), the J. P. Morgan roads (Erie, Southern, Atlantic Coast Line, Louisville & Nashville), the Gould roads (Wabash, Missouri Pacific, Denver

& Rio Grande), the Moore roads (Sante Fe, Rock Island), the Hill Lines (Great Northern, Northern Pacific, Burlington), and the Harriman lines (Union Pacific, Southern Pacific, Illinois Central).

8. Hungerford, *Story of the Baltimore & Ohio*, 240–42; Stover, *History of the Baltimore & Ohio*, 199–200.

9. Stover, *History of the Baltimore & Ohio*, 199, 213–18.

10. Edward Hungerford, *Daniel Willard Rides the Line: The Story of a Great Railroad Man* (New York: G. P. Putnam's Sons, 1938), chaps. 3–8; Stover, *History of the Baltimore & Ohio*, 216–17; *Baltimore & Ohio Magazine*, August 1942, 5–7; and Richard C. Overton, *Burlington Route* (Lincoln: University of Nebraska Press, 1965), 281.

11. Baltimore & Ohio Railroad, *Annual Report*, 1910.

12. Baltimore & Ohio Railroad, *Annual Reports*, 1910–1915.

13. Hungerford, *Daniel Willard Rides the Line*, 273–74.

14. Ibid., 11.

15. Ibid.

16. "The Women behind President Willard," *Baltimore & Ohio Magazine*, May 1935, 5–8.

17. Hungerford, *Daniel Willard Rides the Line*, 13, 19–21.

18. Ibid., 13–18.

19. Ibid., 19–31, and *Baltimore & Ohio Magazine*, August 1942, 5.

20. Hungerford, *Daniel Willard Rides the Line*, 28–59; *Baltimore & Ohio Magazine*, December 1941, 11.

21. *Baltimore & Ohio Magazine*, August 1942, 5.

22. Hungerford, *Daniel Willard Rides the Line*, 73–89.

23. Ibid., 90–107.

24. "How the Chief Did It," *Baltimore & Ohio Magazine*, April 1941, 5–7.

25. Hungerford, *Daniel Willard Rides the Line*, 107–110.

26. Ibid., chap. 8; Overton, *Burlington Route*, 281, 286; Keith L. Bryant, *History of the Atchison, Topeka, and Santa Fe Railway* (Lincoln: University of Nebraska Press, 1974), 233.

27. Ibid., 137–40, 153–60; and Baltimore & Ohio Railroad, *Annual Reports*, 1910–1911.

28. "Collective Bargaining: A Right Freely Acknowledged by the B&O Nearly 30 Years Ago," *Baltimore & Ohio Magazine*, February 1938, 5–7; and Hungerford, *Daniel Willard Rides the Line*, 164–65. Willard was at this stage in his career no great booster of unionism, but his amicable tolerance of the brotherhoods differed noticeably from the attitudes of even some of the more worker relations–oriented railroad presidents of the time, such as Edward P. Ripley of the Santa Fe (Bryant, *History of the Atchison*, 238).

29. *Baltimore & Ohio Employes Magazine*, October 1913, 5, 23.

30. Ibid., 5–14, 23–37.

31. Ibid., 12.

32. Ibid., 11.

33. Ibid., 24.

34. Baltimore & Ohio, *Safety Bulletin No. 6*, 1912, reported in *Baltimore & Ohio Employes Magazine*, November 1912, 4.

35. *Baltimore & Ohio Employes Magazine*, December 1912, 12.

36. Ibid.

37. *Baltimore & Ohio Employes Magazine*, October 1912, 22.

38. Stover, *History of the Baltimore and Ohio*, 256; and *Baltimore & Ohio Magazine*, February 1927, 11. See also *Baltimore & Ohio Employes Magazine*, July 1915, 9–12.

39. Daniel Nelson, *Managers and Workers: Origins of the New Factory System in the United States, 1880–1920* (Madison: University of Wisconsin Press, 1975), 101–6.

40. Ibid., 106–21; see also David Brody, "The Rise and Decline of Welfare Capitalism," in Braeman, Bremner, and Brody, *Change and Continuity in 20th Century America: The 1920s* (Columbus: Ohio State University Press, 1968), 147–78.

41. John T. Broderick, "Welfare Work," paper read at the Annual Convention of the Baltimore & Ohio Association of Railway Surgeons, Philadelphia, Pa., June 7, 1916; reprinted in *Baltimore & Ohio Employes Magazine,* June 1916, 33–36.

42. *Baltimore & Ohio Employes Magazine,* October 1912, 25, 38; April 1916, 10; July 1916, 33; September 1916, 5; November 1916, 47–49; December 1916, 47–48; May 1917, 21–22.

43. *Baltimore & Ohio Employes Magazine,* July 1915, 55–59; July 1916, 63; September 1916, 45–47; March 1918, 40; May 1918, 16.

44. *Baltimore & Ohio Employes Magazine,* September 1916, 50–51; October 1916, 69; January 1917, 47–56; March 1917, 49–50, 57; May 1917, 49–54.

45. *Baltimore & Ohio Employes Magazine,* April 1916, 31–32; January 1917, 38; March 1917, 19–20, 43–45; December 1917, 28–31.

46. *Baltimore & Ohio Employes Magazine,* August 1916, 45–48; September 1916, 71–72; October 1916, 28–29; January 1917, 42–44; March 1917, 65–66.

47. Don L. Hofsommer, *The Southern Pacific, 1901–1985* (College Station: Texas A&M University Press, 1987), 111–13; Bryant, *History of the Atchison,* 236–38; Overton, *Burlington Route,* 286; Stover, *History of the Baltimore & Ohio,* 157–59; George H. Burgess and Miles C. Kennedy, *Centennial History of the Pennsylvania Railroad Company* (Philadelphia: Pennsylvania Railroad, 1949); Ralph W. Hidy, Muriel E. Hidy, and Roy V. Scott, *The Great Northern Railway: A History* (Boston: Harvard Business School Press, 1988), 144; *Railway Age* 100, no. 7, (Feb. 15, 1936): 291.

48. Bryant, *History of the Atchison,* 237–38; Hofsommer, *Southern Pacific,* 112; Hidy, Hidy, and Scott, *Great Northern,* 144.

49. *Santa Fe Employees' Magazine,* March 1912, 87–88, and July 1912, 75–76; *The Mutual Magazine* (publication of the Mutual Beneficial Association of Pennsylvania Railroad Employes, Inc.), July 1915, 13–14; August 1915, 18–21; November 1915, 22–31; December 1915, 13–17.

50. Hofsommer, *Southern Pacific,* 112; Hidy, Hidy, and Scott, *Great Northern,* 166; Maury Klein, *History of the Louisville & Nashville Railroad* (New York: Macmillan, 1972), 433; E. F. Striplin, *The Norfolk & Western: A History* (Roanoke, Va.: Norfolk & Western Railway Co., 1981), 170; Louise Lee Outlaw, *History of the Mutual Beneficial Association of Penn Central Employees, Inc.* (Philadelphia: Mutual Beneficial Association of Penn Central Employees, 1970), 4–5; *Railway Age* 81, no. 11, (Sept. 11, 1926): 456.

51. *Mutual Magazine,* July 1915, 13–14; August 1915, 18–21; Outlaw, *History of the Mutual Beneficial Association,* 6–18.

52. Ibid., 4, 15.

53. Letter from Daniel Willard to Seth Low, 13 Feb. 1913 (Low Library, Columbia University: Low Manuscripts, Box 93), cited in Stephen J. Scheinberg, "The Development of Corporation Labor Policy" (Ph.D. diss., University of Wisconsin, 1966), 39.

54. Hungerford, *Daniel Willard Rides the Line,* 194.

55. K. Austin Kerr, *American Railroad Politics, 1914–1920* (Pittsburgh: University of Pittsburgh Press, 1968), 33–34; Stover, *History of the Baltimore & Ohio,* 230–31.

56. Hungerford, *Daniel Willard Rides the Line,* 190–97; Kerr, *American Railroad,* 34; Stover, *History of the Baltimore & Ohio,* 230–31.

57. For a full discussion of the attitudes of organized labor toward scientific management, see Milton J. Nadworny, *Scientific Management and the Unions* (Cambridge, Mass.: Harvard University Press, 1955). Union opposition to the movement generally diminished during the 1920s,

as practitioners beame more sensitive to the need to cushion workers from its potential negative impact on their jobs.

58. Martin, *Enterprise Denied,* 206–14.

59. Emerson's firm also performed a small piece of work for the B&O, a standard time study at the Martinsburg switch shop, in 1911. Letter from Harrington Emerson to J. M. Davis, 30 Oct., 1916, Pattee Library, Pennsylvania State University, Harrington Emerson Papers, B&O Railroad reports, bk. 3, pt. B.

60. Martin, *Enterprise Denied,* 220; Nelson, *Managers and Workers,* 70–71.

61. "A Resume of the Work of the Emerson Company on the Baltimore & Ohio Railroad," ca. November 1916; "Crooks, Labor, and Efficiency Troubles," report from Harrington Emerson to Daniel Willard, 14 June 1915; letter from Harrington Emerson to J. M. Davis, 30 Oct. 1916, all Pattee Library, Pennsylvania State University, Harrington Emerson Papers, B&O Railroad reports, respectively, bk. 3, pt. A, bk. 4, pt. 1, and bk. 3, pt. B; see also, e.g., *Baltimore & Ohio Employes Magazine,* June 1916, 65–68.

62. An interesting side issue to the general subjects of scientific management and cooperative management programs is why they tended to be applied more often in manufacturing (in this case, equipment and right-of-way construction and maintenance) settings than elsewhere. To hazard a simple answer, the key determinants seem to be scale and repetitiveness of tasks. If one has large numbers of people doing similar, routine tasks in a single location, then the possibility of discovering an optimal technique or method, whether by consultant or cooperative committee, is much increased, with benefits easily and greatly multiplied across the large number of workers. Unfortunately, that does not explain why such programs were not applied in some clerical settings (e.g., paper-processing departments such as car service) that met those criteria.

63. *Baltimore & Ohio Employes Magazine,* March 1917, 58; August 1917, 47–51; November 1917, 32–37; January 1918, 23–25; June-July 1918, 26–27; November 1918, 25.

64. Stover, *History of the Baltimore and Ohio,* 229–43; and *Baltimore & Ohio Employes Magazine,* June-July 1918, 7–10; August 1918, 6; December 1918, 36; July 1919, 47–49.

65. *Baltimore & Ohio Employes Magazine,* June-July 1918, 7–10; for a full discussion of the politics of railroad control during the USRA period, see Kerr, *American Railroad,* esp. chaps. 4–8.

66. Baltimore & Ohio Railroad, *Annual Report,* 1920, 5–13.

67. *Baltimore & Ohio Employes Magazine,* September 1917, 21.

68. Stover, *History of the Baltimore & Ohio,* 237; and *Baltimore & Ohio Employes Magazine,* February 1918, 23; March 1918, 14–20; December 1918, 34–35.

69. *Baltimore & Ohio Magazine,* July 1920, 43; August 1920, 28; September 1920, 34–35; September 1921, 29; June 1922, 20.

70. *Baltimore & Ohio Magazine,* September 1920, 32; April 1921, 30; May 1921, 34; August 1921, 34, 39–42; September 1921, 30–32.

71. *Baltimore & Ohio Magazine,* April 1921, 30, 62; July 1921, 37; September 1922, 55; December 1922, 45.

72. Stover, *History of the Baltimore & Ohio,* 249.

Chapter 2

1. Sud Ingle, *Quality Circles Master Guide* (Englewood Cliffs, N.J.: Prentice-Hall, 1982). An earlier summary version of material contained in the first part of this chapter is David M. Vrooman, "The Ancient Samurai Secret of Daniel Willard: Quality Circles and the Baltimore &

Ohio Railroad Cooperative Plan of 1923," *Essays in Economic and Business History* 6 (1988): 55–71.

2. A full discussion of the subject is Rodney Clark, *The Japanese Company* (New Haven: Yale University Press, 1979).

3. *Japan Quality Control Circles* (Tokyo: Asian Productivity Organization, 1972), 5, 55. See also C. P. Alexander, "Learning from the Japanese," *Personnel Journal* 60 (August 1981): 616–19; H. Takeuchi, "Productivity: Learning from the Japanese," *California Management Review* 23 (Summer 1981): 5–19; G. Munchus, "Employer-Employee-Based Quality Circles in Japan: Human Resource Policy Implications for American Firms," *Academy of Management Review* 8 (April 1983): 255–61; H. J. Bocker and H. O. Overgaard, "Japanese Quality Circles: A Managerial Response to the Productivity Problem," *Management International Review* 22, no. 2 (1982): 13–19; Edward E. Lawler and S. A. Mohrman, "Quality Circles after the Fad," *Harvard Business Review* 63 (January–February 1985): 64–71; and M. O'Donnell and R. J. O'Donnell, "Quality Circles: Latest Fad or a Real Winner?" *Business Horizons* 27 (May–June 1984): 48–52.

4. *Railway Age,* 75, no. 21 (Nov. 24, 1923): 956. See also 76, No. 7 (Feb. 16, 1924): 407; and 76, no. 10 (Mar. 8, 1924): 543–45.

5. *Railway Age,* 76, no. 7 (Feb. 16, 1924): 407–8; and 76, no. 10 (Mar. 8, 1924): 543–45.

6. Ibid.

7. *Baltimore & Ohio Employes Magazine,* October 1912, 22–40; July 1919, 11–15; August 1919, 5–6; *Baltimore & Ohio Magazine,* October 1920, 8–9, 18–20, 41–42; March 1921, 16–17.

8. *Baltimore & Ohio Employes Magazine,* October 1917, 23–24; December 1917, 32; January 1918, 26; February 1918, 39; April 1918, 27; *Baltimore & Ohio Magazine,* July 1920, 27–28; August 1920, 56.

9. *Baltimore & Ohio Magazine,* April 1921, 18.

10. Louis Aubrey Wood, *Union-Management Cooperation on the Railroads* (New Haven: Yale University Press, 1931), 2–4, 298–300. For broader discussions of the origins and further development of cooperative approaches to employee-management relations, see Ernest Richmond Burton, *Employee Representation* (Baltimore: Williams & Wilkins Co., 1926); Sumner Slichter, *Union Policies and Industrial Management* (Washington, D.C.: Brookings Institution, 1941); and John Simmons and William Mares, *Working Together* (New York: Alfred A. Knopf, 1983).

11. K. Austin Kerr, *American Railroad Politics, 1914–1920* (Pittsburgh: University of Pittsburgh Press, 1968), 75, 91–97.

12. Ibid., 160–78.

13. Wood, *Union-Management,* 80–81.

14. Ibid., 81–82, and William L. Chenery "Arsenal Employes' Organization," *Survey,* 8 May 1920, 205–7.

15. Wood, *Union-Management,* 82–84.

16. Ibid., 84, and American Federation of Labor, Railway Employes' Department, *Official Proceedings,* Fifth Biennial Convention, Kansas City, Mo., April 1920, 132–34.

17. Wood, *Union-Management,* 85.

18. Memorandum from O. S. Beyer to William H. Johnston, with cover letter dated 15 Nov. 1921, Library of Congress, Manuscript Division, Otto Beyer Papers, box 95.

19. Wood, *Union-Management,* 86.

20. Ibid.

21. Ibid.

22. Letter from O. S. Beyer to WIlliam H. Johnston, 20 Apr. 1922, Library of Congress, Manuscript Division, Otto Beyer Papers, box 95.

23. Daniel Willard, remarks before the National Civil Federation, New York City, 17 Feb. 1927, in *Industrial Management* 73, no. 5 (May 1927): 260–63.

24. Robert H. Zieger, *Republicans and Labor, 1919–1929* (Lexington: University of Kentucky Press, 1969), 118–21, 192.

25. Wood, *Union-Management,* 70–76.

26. Ibid., 75–76; *Railway Age* 73, no. 6 (Aug. 5, 1922): 247–48.

27. Zieger, *Republicans,* 120–21, 129–36.

28. Ibid., 120, 130; *Railway Age* 73, no. 6, (Aug. 5, 1922): 248; 73, no. 10, (Sept. 2, 1922): 421.

29. *Railway Age* 73, no. 6, (Aug. 5, 1922): 248.

30. Zieger, *Republicans,* 130–38.

31. Ibid., 138; *Railway Age* 73, no. 10 (Sept. 2, 1922): 417–21; 73, no. 12, (Sept. 16, 1922): 503–4; 73, no. 13 (Sept. 23, 1922): 567–69; 73, no. 14 (Sept. 30, 1922): 605.

32. *Railway Age* 73, no. 15 (Oct. 7, 1922): 649; Zieger, *Republicans,* 138–39.

33. *Railway Age* 73, no. 13 (Sept. 23, 1922): 549.

34. *Industrial Management* 73, no. 5 (May 1927): 262.

35. Ibid., 261.

36. Ibid., 261; Wood, *Union-Management,* 87–88.

37. Wood, *Union-Management,* 88.

38. Ibid., 89.

39. Philip M. Wagner, "It Worked for the B&O," *Saturday Evening Post,* Aug. 22, 1942, 22, 81–82 (reprinted by U.S. Government Printing Office, 1942).

40. Otto S. Beyer, Jr., address on the Glenwood experiment, published in *Proceedings, Fifth Convention of Division No. 4, Railway Employees' Department of the American Federation of Labor,* Montreal, P.Q., March 1924, 29. Also Wood, *Union-Management,* 89, and Wagner, "It Worked."

41. Letter from Otto S. Beyer, Jr., to William H. Johnston, July 26, 1923, Labor-Management Documentations Center Archives, Cornell University, AFL Railway Employees' Department Collection, box 87. For further commentary by Beyer on the background and early results of the Glenwood experiment, see O. S. Beyer, Jr., "The Employee Morale Problem of Our Railroads," *Railway Age* 75, no. 15 (Oct. 13, 1923): 656–58, and "B&O Engine 1003," *The Survey* 51, no. 7 (Jan. 1, 1924): 311–17.

42. Beyer, "Employee Morale Problem"; Wood, *Union-Management,* 90; Wagner, "It Worked."

43. *Industrial Management* 73, no. 5 (May 1927): 261.

44. Economic evidence was more compelling to higher officers than to lower ones. An example of a lower-level supervisor who clung stubbornly to his personal power was a Glenwood boiler foreman by the name of Stapleton: nineteen months after the start of the cooperative program his arbitrary and abusive behavior still was undermining it. Letter from Boilermakers District 31 chairman P. D. Harvey to O. S. Beyer, August 12, 1924, Library of Congress, Manuscript Division, Otto S. Beyer Papers, box 94.

45. Letter from Daniel Willard to Otto S. Beyer, October 14, 1923, Library of Congress, Manuscript Division, Otto S. Beyer Papers, box 94. *Railway Age* 76, no. 7 (Feb. 16, 1924): 407–8; 76, no. 10 (Mar. 8, 1924): 543–45.

46. *Railway Age* 76, no. 10 (Mar. 24, 1924): 545.

47. *Baltimore & Ohio Magazine,* May 1924, 12–13.

48. *Railway Age* 77, no. 19 (Nov. 8, 1924): 839–41.

49. *Baltimore & Ohio Magazine,* March 1931, 10.

50. *Railway Age* 76, no. 10 (Mar. 8, 1924): 543.

51. Wood, *Union-Management,* 249; letter from Daniel Willard to Otto S. Beyer, May 21,

1924, Library of Congress, Manuscript Division, Otto S. Beyer Papers, box 103; and *Industrial Management* 73, no. 5 (May 1927): 262.

52. *Railway Age* 80, no. 7 (Feb. 13, 1926): 426.

53. Ibid., 426.

54. Memo from the secretary-treasurer of Railway Employes' Department, American Federation of Labor, to the Executive Council of Railway Employes' Department, Feb. 14, 1924, Labor-Management Documentation Center Archives, Cornell University, AFL Railway Employees' Department Collection, box 88.

55. Letter from B&O motive power chief George H. Emerson to AFL Railway Employees' Department president Bert M. Jewell, June 3, 1925; letter from Bert M. Jewell to Baltimore Federation of Labor president Henry F. Broening, June 9, 1925; letter from IAM president William Johnston to Henry F. Broening, June 5, 1925; letter from Bert M. Jewell to members of the executive council of AFL Railway Employees' Department, June 9, 1925; letter from Bert M. Jewell to George H. Emerson, June 12, 1925; letter from System Federation No. 30 president William H. McGee to Daniel Willard, June 12, 1925; letter from Bert M. Jewell to System Federation No. 30 secretary H. L. Alberty, June 23, 1925, George Meany Memorial Archives, Railway Employees Department records, reel 58.

56. Letter from R. E. Reynolds, secretary of B&O local shopcrafts federation, to H. L. Alberty, secretary of B&O System Federation No. 30, June 30, 1925, with attached circular, dated (misdated?) July 7; letter to H. L. Alberty from Bert Jewell, president, Railway Employees' Department, AF of L, July 29, 1925, Labor-Management Documentation Center Archives, Cornell University, AFL Railway Employees Department Collection, box 87.

57. Copy of letter from C. G. Watson, secretary of Lodge 212, International Association of Machinists, to J. Howe, superintendent of Cumberland Shops, July 23, 1925, with cover letter to IAM president William Johnston, George Meany Memorial Archives, Railway Employees Department records, reel 58.

58. Letter from Thomas E. Carroll, IAM Gand Lodge representative, to William Johnston, July 25, 1925; telegram from Bert Jewell to H. L. Alberty, July 25, 1925; telegram from H. L. Alberty to Bert Jewell, July 25, 1925; letter from C. N. Fullerton, IAM District 29 general chairman, to C. G. Watson, July 26, 1925; letter from C. N. Fullerton to H. L. Alberty, July 26, 1925; letter from H. L. Alberty to Bert Jewell, July 27, 1925; letter from George Beisser, shopcrafts Local Federation No. 7 president, to H. L. Alberty, July 28, 1925; letter from H. L. Alberty to William Johnston, July 29, 1925; letter from H. L. Alberty to George Beisser, July 29, 1925, all Labor-Management Documentation Center Archives, Cornell University, AFL Railway Employees Department Collection, box 88; letter from boilermakers' Local 332 committee chairman L. R. Ambrose to Bert M. Jewell, Sept. 9, 1925; letter from William J. McGee to Brother Scott, Aug. 13, 1925; letter from Bert M. Jewell to members of the executive council of AFL Railway Employees' Department, August 22, 1925; letter from the blacksmiths' union president, James W. Kline, to Bert M. Jewell, Aug. 29, 1925; letter from Bert M. Jewell to James W. Kline, Sept. 4, 1925, George Meany Memorial Archives, AFL Railway Employees Department Collection, box 88.

59. "Eliminating Railroad Unionism," *Industrial Pioneer* (January 1924): 8; "Railroad Labor at the Crossroads" and "The Campaign for Class Collaboration," *Labor Herald* (January 1924): 9 and 13, respectively; cited in letter from Otto S. Beyer to Daniel Willard, January 28, 1924, Library of Congress, Manuscript Division, Otto S. Beyer Papers, box 103.

60. Letter from Daniel Willard to Otto S. Beyer, Feb. 11, 1924; letter from Otto S. Beyer to Daniel WIllard, Feb. 27, 1924, Library of Congress, Manuscript Division, Otto S. Beyer Papers, box 103. More generally, see Milton Nadworny, *Scientific Management and the Unions* (Cambridge, Mass.: Harvard University Press, 1955), 126, and Sanford M. Jacoby, "Union-

Management Cooperation in the United States: Lessons from the 1920's," *Industrial and Labor Relations Review* 37, no. 1 (October 1983): 26.

61. Baltimore & Ohio Railroad, Motive Power Department, Minutes of Meeting Covering the Plan of Co-operation between Employees and the Management, Ivorydale, Ohio, Shops, Jan. 7, 1925, Labor-Management Documentation Center Archives, Cornell University, AFL Railway Employees Department Collection, box 88.

62. Ibid.

63. Baltimore & Ohio Railroad, Motive Power Department, Minutes of Meeting Covering the Plan of Co-operation between Employees and the Management, Ivorydale, Ohio, Shops, Jan. 21, 1925; also Feb. 4, 1925; Feb. 18, 1925; and March 4, 1925, Labor-Management Documentation Center Archives, Cornell University, AFL Railway Employees Department Collection, box 88.

64. Ibid.

65. Ibid. For details of the resolution of the Sunday-holiday time-and-a-half issue, see letter from O. S. Beyer to Daniel Willard, Aug. 28, 1926; letter from Daniel Willard to O. S. Beyer, Aug. 30, 1926; memorandum from F. E. Blaser (assistant to operations vice president Galloway) to all division superintendents, shop superintendents, master mechanics, and division engineers, Sept. 2, 1926, Library of Congress, Manuscript Division, Otto S. Beyer Papers, box 103.

66. Baltimore & Ohio Railroad Company, Minutes of Meeting Covering the Plan of Cooperation between Employees and the Management, Flora, Illinois, Shop, Jan. 7, 1925, Labor-Management Documentation Center Archives, Cornell University, AFL Railway Employees Department Collection, box 88.

67. Ibid.

68. Ibid.

69. Baltimore & Ohio Railroad Company, Minutes of Meeting Covering the Plan of Cooperation between Employees and the Management, Flora, Illinois, Shop, Jan. 7, 1925; also Feb. 4, 1925; Feb. 18, 1925; and Mar. 4, 1925, Labor-Management Documentation Center Archives, Cornell University, AFL Railway Employees Department Collection, box 88.

70. Ibid.

71. Ibid.

72. Wood, *Union-Management*, 91.

73. *Railway Age* 77, no. 22 (Nov. 29, 1924): 994–95; 79, no. 11 (Sept. 12, 1925): 493; and Wood, *Union-Management*, 92–97.

74. Wood, *Union-Management*, 97–99, and letter from Otto S. Beyer, Jr., to John Scott, secretary-treasurer of the Railway Employees' Department, American Federation of Labor, Mar. 30, 1925, Labor-Management Documentation Center Archives, Cornell University, AFL Railway Employees Department Collection, box 88.

75. Wood, *Union-Management*, 99–101.

76. The Seaboard discussed the matter with Beyer and the AFL at some length, and adopted some of its tenets, but never signed a formal comprehensive agreement; see Labor-Management Documentation Center, Cornell University, AFL Railway Employees Department Collection, box 89, folder 5.

77. *Baltimore & Ohio Magazine*, February 1925, 7–9; and Wood, *Union-Management*, 276–88. Wood incorrectly dates the start of the CT/MW cooperative program as early 1924, not early 1925; he apparently was using as his source *Railway Age*: 78, no. 8 (Feb. 21, 1925): 453–54, which reproduced the *B&O Magazine* article, and which by typographical error identifies that article as from the February 1924 issue.

78. *Baltimore & Ohio Magazine*, February 1925, 8.

79. Wood, *Union-Management*, 281–88.

80. Otto S. Beyer, "The Employee Morale Problem of Our Railroads," *Railway Age* 75, no.

15 (Oct. 13, 1923): 656–58; "B&O Engine 1003," 51, no. 7 (Jan. 1, 1924): 311–17; "Railroad Union-Management Cooperation," *American Federalist* (August 1925): 2; "Three Years of the B&O Plan," *New Republic,* Aug. 4, 1926, 298.

81. Daniel Willard, "The Labor Policy of the Baltimore & Ohio," *Railway Age* 77, no. 19 (Nov. 8, 1924): 839–41; William H. Johnston, "Cooperation—Organized Labor's Contribution," *Railway Age* 75, no. 21 (Nov. 24, 1923): 954–75. The cited Willard speeches were given in February and March 1927 and were reprinted in *Industrial Management* 73, no. 5 (May 1927): 260–63, and *Machinists' Monthly Journal* 39, no. 5 (May 1927): 259–63.

82. Francis Westbrook, "Unions and Management," *Outlook,* Apr. 14, 1926, 566; George Soule, "Engineering versus Revolution: The Story of the B&O Labor Plan, *Independent,* July 5, 1924, 12–14; Whiting Williams, "Let's Try Goin' Along with 'Em," *Collier's,* July 5, 1924, 11; *Nation* (March 1927): 253.

83. During this period at least one major scientific management recommendation was implemented in the context of the Cooperative Plan. Partially traceable to the firm of Harrington Emerson, the "spot system" of heavy repairs at the Mount Clare locomotive shop (a major change in shop layout and work flow) was established during the winter of 1925–1926. See spot system procedure manual, Nov. 3, 1925, Library of Congress, Manuscript Division, Otto S. Beyer Papers, box 100; letter from Daniel Willard to Harrington Emerson, Oct. 29, 1930, Pattee Library, Pennsylvania State University, Harrington Emerson Papers–B&O Railroad reports, box 1, file 7; Chester B. Lord, "Three a Day," *American Machinist,* July 24, 1930, 149–54; July 31, 1930, 199–202; Aug. 7, 1930, 231–35.

84. *Bulletin of the Taylor Society* 11, no. 1 (February 1926): *Railway Age* 80, no. 7 (Feb. 13, 1926): 423–28.

85. Eisuke Daito, "Railways and Scientific Management in Japan, 1907–1930," *Business History* 31, no. 1 (January 1989): 1–28; miscellaneous correspondence of Harrington Emerson, especially a letter from Emerson to the Japanese Minister of Railways, H. Ogawa, Dec. 26, 1928, Pattee Library, Pennsylvania State University, Harrington Emerson Papers, box 10, file 9. Even though Emerson apparently was not under contract to the B&O at this time, he stayed in personal contact with Willard; see, for example, a letter from Willard to Emerson, Dec. 28, 1928, Harrington Emerson Papers, box 1, file 6.

86. Jacoby, "Union-Management Cooperation," 27–28; Nadworny, *Scientific Management,* 135–41. See also Sumner H. Slichter, *Union Policies and Industrial Management* (Washington, D.C.: Brookings Institution, 1941). All three authors also identify two cooperative schemes that predated the B&O Plan, both in the clothing industry.

87. Letter from Sumner H. Slichter to Otto S. Beyer, Sept. 29, 1926, Library of Congress, Manuscript Division, Otto S. Beyer Papers, box 95.

88. *Industrial Management* 73, no. 5 (May 1927): 262.

89. Wood, *Union-Management,* 190.

90. Baltimore & Ohio Railroad, *Annual Reports,* 1922–1926; and *Moody's Investment Manual: Steam Railroads* (New York: Moody's Investors Services, 1924 and 1930).

91. Net income here is defined as net income to common equity; preferred stock dividends have been treated as an interest charge deducted from the bottom line of the *Annual Report* income statement.

Chapter 3

1. For a fuller discussion, see John F. Stover, *History of the Baltimore & Ohio Railroad* (West Lafayette, Ind.: Purdue University Press, 1987), 1–183; and Herbert H. Harwood, Jr.,

Impossible Challenge: The Baltimore & Ohio Railroad in Maryland (Baltimore: Barnard, Roberts, & Co., 1979).

2. See *Official Guide of the Railways* (New York: National Railway Publication Co., 1926). The city pairs in question are New York–Chicago (PRR advantage), Philadelphia-Chicago (PRR), Baltimore–Chicago (PRR), Washington–Chicago (B&O), Washington–St. Louis (B&O), New York–Pittsburgh (PRR), Philadelphia-Pittsburgh (PRR), Baltimore–Pittsburgh (PRR), Washington–Pittsburgh (B&O), Pittsburgh–Chicago (close, but PRR), Pittsburgh–St. Louis (PRR), New York–Cincinnati (PRR), Philadelphia–Cincinnati (PRR), Baltimore–Cincinnati (B&O), Washington–Cincinnati (B&O), Pittsburgh–Cincinnati (PRR), Cincinnati–Chicago (PRR), Cincinnati–St. Louis (B&O), Cincinnati–Detroit (B&O), New York–Detroit (PRR), Philadelphia–Detroit (PRR), Baltimore–Detroit (PRR), Washington–Detroit (B&O), and Pittsburgh–Detroit (PRR).

3. *Baltimore & Ohio Magazine,* March 1940, 7.

4. Opinion of the Railroad Labor Board censuring the Pennsylvania Railroad for its refusal to obey Board Decision no. 218, requiring a free election to determine shopcrafts representation, *Railway Age* 74, no. 25 (June 23, 1923): 1514.

5. A. J. County (Pennsylvania Railroad vice president), "Improving Human Relations in the Transportation Industry," address before the Ninth Annual Conference on Human Relations in Industry, Industrial Department of the YMCA, Silver Bay, N.Y.; reprinted in *Railway Age* 81, no. 11 (Sept. 11, 1926): 455–59.

6. Remarks of W. W. Atterbury at the Pennsylvania Railroad Chicago General Office Association, May 1, 1934, reported in *Railway Age* 96, no. 18 (May 5, 1934): 666–67.

7. *Railway Age* 97, no. 16 (Oct. 20, 1934): 485.

8. Ibid., 83, no. 19 (Nov. 12, 1927): 956, and 84, no. 24 (June 16, 1928): 1412.

9. Ibid., 92, no. 21 (May 21, 1932): 865, 877–78.

10. Ibid., and Baltimore & Ohio Railroad, *Annual Report,* 1925; George H. Burgess and Miles C. Kennedy, *Centennial History of the Pennsylvania Railroad Co.* (Philadelphia: Pennsylvania Railroad, 1949), 807.

11. For examples, see *Baltimore & Ohio Magazine,* March 1928, 28, 48–49; January 1929, 28–29; August 1929, 18.

12. *Baltimore & Ohio Magazine,* October 1927, 7; December 1927, 4, 28, 38, 64–65; April 1929, 47–51; July 1929, 18–21.

13. Louis Aubrey Wood, *Union-Management Cooperation on the Railroads* (New Haven: Yale University Press, 1931), 119.

14. *Baltimore & Ohio Magazine,* December 1927, 30; October 1928, 36–37.

15. Ibid., April 1929, 31; July 1929, 32; August 1929, 18.

16. Ibid., May 1927; May 1928; June 1929; June 1950, 2.

17. Ibid., January 1921, 35; June 1929; June 1947, 22–23; April 1951, 14. Also *New York Times,* Dec. 22, 1940, and Mar. 1, 1951; and *Baltimore Evening Sun,* Feb. 28, 1951.

18. Adelaide Handy, "Woman Designer of Bridges Has Enhanced Rail Travel," *New York Times,* Dec. 22, 1940.

19. Summarized in *Baltimore & Ohio Magazine,* July 1929, 6–7. For specifics, see, e.g., October 1912, 12; April 1920, 38; December 1922, cover; June 1923, 5; February 1927, 13; October 1927, 13; January 1928, 21; August 1929, 6; December 1930, 8.

20. *Railway Age* 87, no. 18 (Nov. 2, 1929): 1042.

21. *Baltimore & Ohio Magazine,* November 1926, 18.

22. *Railway Age* 87, no. 22 (Nov. 30, 1929): 1269.

23. Stover, *History of the Baltimore & Ohio,* 275. *Wall Street Journal,* June 2, 1932.

24. For examples, see *Baltimore & Ohio Magazine*, August 1926, 12–13; November 1926, 28–29.

25. Baltimore & Ohio Railroad Company, *Annual Reports*, 1926 and 1927.

26. Letter from Florence C. Thorne, of the *American Federationist*, to Bert M. Jewell, Mar. 17, 1927; letter from H. L. Alberty to Bert M. Jewell, Mar. 26, 1927, George Meany Memorial Archives, Railway Employees Department records, reel 58.

27. Letter from C. W. Galloway to W. J. McGee, July 26, 1927; letter from Bert M. Jewell to W. J. McGee, Aug. 1, 1927; letter from Bert M. Jewell to H. L. Alberty, Aug. 11, 1927; letter from Bert M. Jewell to W. J. McGee and H. L. Alberty, Aug. 20, 1927, George Meany Memorial Archives, Railway Employees Department records, reel 58.

28. Walter H. Dunlap, "Stability of Railroad Employment," *Monthly Labor Review* (August 1928): 19–27.

29. Baltimore & Ohio Railroad Company, *Annual Report*, 1928; letter from Otto S. Beyer to Bert M. Jewell, June 12, 1928; letter from Bert M. Jewell to Otto S. Beyer, June 16, 1928, George Meany Memorial Archives, Railway Employees Department records, reel 58.

30. Beyer, Jewell, and McGee had found it necessary on at least two prior occasions to appeal to Willard to get around Emerson's objections to their proposals regarding the Sunday overtime issue (e.g., letter from Bert M. Jewell to H. L. Alberty, Oct. 25, 1927, George Meany Memorial Archives) and the creation of a joint committee to resolve seniority problems (letter from Otto S. Beyer to Bert M. Jewell, Apr. 24, 1926, George Meany Memorial Archives, Railway Employees Department records, reel 58.

31. Letter from Bert M. Jewell to William J. McGee, Aug. 7, 1928; letter from H. L. Alberty to Bert M. Jewell, Aug. 20, 1928, George Meany Memorial Archives, Railway Employees Department records, reel 58.

32. Ibid.

33. Wood, *Union-Management*, 277.

34. Memorandum from H. L. Alberty to membership of System Federation No. 30, Jan. 28, 1929; letter from William J. McGee to Bert M. Jewell (including text of telegram from McGee to Daniel Willard, Feb. 13, 1929), Feb. 17, 1929, Library of Congress, Manuscript Division, Otto S. Beyer Papers, box 103.

35. Letter from H. L. Alberty to Bert M. Jewell, July 24, 1928, George Meany Memorial Archives, Railway Employees Department records, reel 58.

36. Letter from H. L. Alberty to Bert M. Jewell, July 24, 1928; letter from H. L. Alberty to Bert M. Jewell, Nov. 7, 1928; letter from Otto S. Beyer to H. L. Alberty, Apr. 11, 1929; letter from Bert M. Jewell to William McGee, May 1, 1929, George Meany Memorial Archives, Railway Employees Department records, reel 58. William Johnston was not a party to these discussions because he had retired from the IAM leadership in 1926.

37. Letter from Bert M. Jewell to Otto S. Beyer, May 20, 1927; letter from H. L. Alberty to Otto S. Beyer, Sept. 25, 1929; letter from Bert M. Jewell to William J. McGee, Dec. 12, 1929, George Meany Memorial Archives, Railway Employees Department records, reel 58.

38. Letter from William J. McGee to John Howe, May 4, 1933 (expressing the system federation's appreciation of Howe's efforts), George Meany Memorial Archives, Railway Employees Department records, reel 58.

39. *Baltimore & Ohio Magazine*, December 1929, 9–11. Willard was involved in other Cooperative Plan–boosting activities as well during the year; for example, he was a principal speaker at the labor conference sponsored by B&O system labor organizations in January (see minutes of *Railroad Labor Conference*, Baltimore, Jan. 19–20, 1929; sponsored by the Association of General Chairman, Baltimore & Ohio Railroad [American Federation of Labor, 1929]).

40. *Baltimore & Ohio Magazine,* February 1930, 5–19.
41. Letter from O. S. Beyer to William Green, Dec. 13, 1929; letter from William Green to O. S. Beyer, Dec. 18, 1929; letter from O. S. Beyer to Bert M. Jewell, Dec. 26, 1929; telegram from J. M. Burns to Bert M. Jewell, Dec. 30, 1929, George Meany Memorial Archives, Railway Employees Department records, reel 58.
42. *Baltimore & Ohio Magazine,* February 1930, 5, 19.
43. Ibid., 15.
44. Ibid., 9, 12, 14, 16.
45. Ibid., 16–17; also letter from Daniel Willard to Bert M. Jewell, Jan. 15, 1930, George Meany Memorial Archives, Railway Employees Department records, reel 58.
46. *Baltimore & Ohio Magazine,* December 1929, 6.
47. *Monthly Labor Review,* April 1930, 66; *Business Week,* Mar. 19, 1930, 9; letter and attached graph from H. L. Alberty to O. S. Beyer, Sept. 25, 1929, George Meany Memorial Archives, Railway Employees Department records, reel 58; joint memorandum signed by George Emerson, F. E. Blaser, and William McGee, Feb. 10, 1930, Library of Congress, Manuscript Division, Otto S. Beyer Papers, box 98.
48. Otto Beyer reported early in 1931 that the B&O successfully pressured an outside car builder into hiring 160 B&O carmen to work on the boxcar body order (Otto S. Beyer, "Keeping at the Job," *Survey* (Mar. 1, 1931): 601–4, 621). In a letter to William McGee dated Mar. 26, 1931, Beyer stated that only 75 B&O men had begun working at the plant in question (Standard Steel Car Co., in Baltimore), with another 18 recalled by the B&O and 47 placed elsewhere (Library of Congress, Manuscript Division, Otto S. Beyer Papers, box 101). See also *Railway Age* 89, no. 17 (Oct. 25, 1930): 869, and *Baltimore & Ohio Magazine,* November 1930, 5.
49. Beyer, "Keeping at the Job," 604.
50. Baltimore & Ohio Railroad Company, *Annual Reports,* 1929–1932; *Baltimore & Ohio Magazine,* August 1942, 7.
51. Baltimore & Ohio Railroad Company, *Annual Reports,* 1929, 1931, 1932; joint memorandum signed by George Emerson and William McGee, Sept. 27, 1932, Library of Congress, Manuscript Division, Otto S. Beyer Papers, box 98; statement of Daniel Willard, annual meeting of Baltimore & Ohio Railroad stockholders, Baltimore, Nov. 21, 1932, 8–9, Maryland Historical Society Archives, Baltimore & Ohio Railroad Collection.
52. Wood, *Union-Management,* 289.
53. Letter from Bert M. Jewell to Otto S. Beyer, Dec. 5, 1930; letter from Otto S. Beyer to Daniel Willard, Dec. 22, 1930; letter from Otto S. Beyer to Bert M. Jewell and Fred Fljozdal, president of the Brotherhood of Maintenance of Way Employees, Mar. 4, 1931, Labor-Management Documentation Center Archives, Cornell University, AFL Railway Employees Department Collection, box 88.
54. Report by Otto S. Beyer on the Cooperative Program for the Maintenance of Way Department, Baltimore & Ohio Railroad Company, Washington, D.C., June 19, 1931, Labor-Management Documentation Center Archives, Cornell University, AFL Railway Employees Department Collection, box 88.
55. Ibid.
56. Letter from Bert M. Jewell to O. S. Beyer, June 26, 1931, Labor-Management Documentation Center Archives, Cornell University, AFL Railway Employees Department Collection, box 88.
57. Letter from O. S. Beyer to Bert M. Jewell, July 20, 1931, Labor-Management Documentation Center Archives, Cornell University, AFL Railway Employees Department Collection, box 88.
58. Sanford M. Jacoby, "Union-Management Cooperation in the United States: Lessons from the 1920's," *Industrial and Labor Relations Review* 37, no. 1 (October 1983): 31; Milton Nad-

worny, *Scientific Management and the Unions* (Cambridge, Mass.: Harvard University Press, 1955), 141. The program on the Canadian National also apparently stayed alive through the Depression.

59. Nadworny, *Scientific Management,* 141.

60. *Baltimore & Ohio Magazine,* October 1931, 64.

61. *Mutual Magazine,* July 1930, 22; September 1930, 21–23; September 1935, 21; letter from Daniel Willard to Otto S. Beyer, July 27, 1931, Library of Congress, Manuscript Division, Otto S. Beyer Papers, box 103.

62. Letter from William McGee to the Local Federation No. 10 secretary, H. W. Reilly, July 25, 1931; letter from Daniel Willard to Otto S. Beyer, July 27, 1931, Library of Congress, Manuscript Division, Otto S. Beyer Papers, boxes 100 and 103, respectively; *Baltimore & Ohio Magazine,* October 1931, 64.

63. *Baltimore & Ohio Magazine,* August 1942, 31; letter from Daniel Willard to William McGee, Apr. 27, 1932, Library of Congress, Manuscript Division, Otto S. Beyer Papers, box 98.

64. For example, see letter from IAM Lodge 478 (Chicago/Garfield Park) secretary G. Henriksson to Sheet Metal Workers Local 367 secretary Harry Ditberner, Aug. 31, 1929; and letter from shopcrafts Local Federation No. 16 (Parkersburg, West Virginia) secretary Robert C. Cabell to William McGee, Sept. 5, 1931, Library of Congress, Manuscript Division, Otto S. Beyer papers, box 100.

65. Letter from C. W. Galloway to William McGee, Nov. 24, 1931; joint memorandum signed by shop superintendent F. S. Stewart and local shopcrafts committee president G. A. Tschudy, July 6, 1931; letter from F. E. Blaser to William McGee, Nov. 10, 1931, Library of Congress, Manuscript Division, Otto S. Beyer Papers, box 98.

66. Memorandum by Stewart and Tschudy, July 6, 1931; letter from Blaser to McGee, Nov. 10, 1931.

67. Letter from Balser to McGee, Nov. 10, 1931.

68. Letter from Galloway to McGee, Nov. 24, 1931.

69. Letter from Bert Jewell to Daniel Willard, Dec. 7, 1931, Library of Congress, Manuscript Division, Otto S. Beyer Papers, box 98.

70. Letter from Daniel Willard to Bert Jewell, Dec. 11, 1931, Library of Congress, Manuscript Division, Otto S. Beyer Papers, box 98.

71. Letter from Charles Galloway to William McGee, Dec. 15, 1931; memorandum from William McGee to Bert Jewell, Otto Beyer, and all System Federation No. 30 chairmen, undated, but apparently written after Dec. 15, 1931, Library of Congress, Manuscript Division, Otto S. Beyer Papers, box 98.

72. Stover, *History of the Baltimore & Ohio,* 264; Edward Hungerford, *Daniel Willard Rides the Line: The Story of a Great Railroad Man* (New York: G. P. Putnam's Sons, 1938), 293; collected speeches of Daniel Willard (with accompanying list, including references to speeches not in the file), Library of Congress, Manuscript Division, Otto S. Beyer Papers, box 103.

73. Daniel Willard, "The Wharton School: Its Field in a Changing World," address before the Wharton School of Finance and Commerce, University of Pennsylvania, Mar. 27, 1931.

74. Letter from Daniel Willard to Otto S. Beyer, Oct. 11, 1933; letter from Otto S. Beyer to Daniel Willard, Oct. 24, 1933; letter from Daniel Willard to Otto S. Beyer, Oct. 25, 1933, Library of Congress, Manuscript Division, Otto S. Beyer Papers, box 103. Willard carried the ball on this play, but Beyer, as he usually did, got it moving. Willard was pleased with and proud of the Plan, but Beyer was its primary promoter: it was the center of his career at this point (see, for example, letter from Otto S. Beyer to *Baltimore & Ohio Magazine* editor Robert M. Van Sant, Apr. 30, 1931, Otto S. Beyer Papers, box 100).

75. Stover, *History of the Baltimore & Ohio,* 277–79; Hungerford, *Daniel Willard Rides,* 277–87; *Baltimore & Ohio Magazine,* August 1942, 7. *Railway Age* 91, no. 25 (Dec. 19, 1931):

925, 937–38; 91, no. 26 (Dec. 26, 1931): 983; 92, no. 6 (Feb. 6, 1932): 232–34; 93, no. 12 (Sept. 17, 1932): 413.

76. Statement of Daniel Willard, annual meeting of Baltimore & Ohio Railroad stockholders, Baltimore, Nov. 21, 1932, 9, Maryland Historical Society Archives; Stover, *History of the Baltimore & Ohio,* 278; John F. Stover, "150 Years of the B&O," *Railway Age* (Apr. 25, 1977): 53.

77. Data derived from *Industrial Management* 73, no. 5, (May 1927): 262, and *Baltimore & Ohio Magazine,* April 1934, 17. The suggestion decline appears to have been fairly steady, as the following table indicates:

	Number of Suggestions				
Period	Beneficial to employees	Beneficial to management	Beneficial to both	From employees	From management
1927 July 6– Sept. 14	84	322	223	535	94
1929 July 3– Sept. 4	47	202	116	335	30
1931 July 1– Sept. 2	26	114	59	182	17

It is interesting to note that the percentage of suggestions exclusively benefiting employees stayed exactly constant (at 13 percent) through the decline, while the percentage of suggestions from employees increased (from 85 to 92 percent). Baltimore & Ohio Railroad Motive Power Department Cooperative Plan summary reports, Library of Congress, Manuscript Division, Otto S. Beyer Papers, box 97.

78. At this particular meeting, J. F. McGrath of the stationary firemen and oilers' union occupied a seat normally occupied by the blacksmiths' general chairman. The stationary firemen belonged to Federation No. 30, but they were not a part of the original Cooperative Plan organization.

79. Minutes of the system cooperative meeting between representatives of the Baltimore & Ohio Railroad Company and the General Committee of the Federated Shop Crafts, Baltimore, Jan. 4, 1933, George Meany Memorial Archives, Railway Employees Department records, reel 58.

80. Ibid.

81. In the mechanical department committees 8,789 meetings had been held, with 34,001 suggestions offered and 27,816 of them adopted; in the transportation and maintenance of way departments, the corresponding data were 735 meetings, 7,332 suggestions, and 4,938 adoptions. The shop committee at Flora, Illinois, had held 182 meetings; five other shop committees (Bailey's Car Shop, Maryland; Brunswick, Maryland; Cumberland Roundhouse, Maryland; Cumbo, West Virginia; and Somerset, Pennsylvania) each had held 180. Willard, Ohio (formerly Chicago Junction), led all committees in total suggestions with 1,651, followed by the Cum-

berland Back Shop with 1,471 and Mount Clare with 1,461. Somerset boasted an adoption rate of 96.8 percent, followed by Cumbo with 95.7 percent; Connellsville, Pennsylvania, was third with 92.3 percent, barely ahead of Zanesville, Ohio's, 92.2 percent, *Baltimore & Ohio Magazine,* April 1934, 17–18.

82. Figures derived from Baltimore & Ohio Railroad Company, *Annual Reports,* 1927–1941, and *Moody's Investment Manual: Steam Railroads* (New York: Moody's Investors Services, 1930–1941).

83. Ibid.

84. Stover, *History of the Baltimore & Ohio,* 284–86; Hungerford, *Daniel Willard Rides,* 235–39; *Baltimore & Ohio Magazine,* December 1931, 7, 15.

85. Ibid.

Chapter 4

1. Charles C. Kindleberger, *The World in Depression, 1929–1939* (Berkeley: University of California Press, 1973), 231.

2. Interstate Commerce Commission, *Statistics of Railways in the United States,* (Washington, D.C.: USGPO, 1923–1933).

3. There was also a third aspect of the B&O's survival efforts: pursuit of government assistance. Most notably, in November 1932 the B&O arranged a loan of over $31 million from the Reconstruction Finance Corporation to aid in refinancing its debt. Baltimore & Ohio Railroad, *Annual Report,* 1932.

4. An earlier version of some of the material contained in this chapter is David M. Vrooman, "The Cooperative Traffic Program: Employee Participation on the Baltimore & Ohio Railroad, Phase 2," *Essays in Economic and Business History* vol. 7.

5. Data derived from Baltimore & Ohio Railroad Company, *Annual Reports,* 1932–1933; *Moody's Investment Manual: Steam Railroads* (New York: Moody's Investors Services, 1934); and Interstate Commerce Commission, *Statistics of Railways in the United States* (Washington, D.C.: USGPO, 1933). The eastern district debt ratio excludes proprietary and lessor lines.

6. *Railway Age* 92, no. 19 (May 7, 1932): 782, 785; 91, no. 3 (July 18, 1931): 107; 91, no. 25 (Dec. 19, 1931): 951; 92, no. 6 (Feb. 6, 1932): 260.

7. Remarks by C. N. Fullerton, at Newark, Ohio, CTP dinner, Nov. 5, 1934, in *Baltimore & Ohio Magazine,* December 1934, 19; remarks by Daniel Willard, at Baltimore Terminals CTP dinner, Nov. 6, 1940, in *Baltimore & Ohio Magazine,* December 1940, 10; "The Story of Your Cooperative Traffic Program," pamphlet published by the Baltimore & Ohio Railroad, May 1, 1956, collection of William C. Howard.

8. *Baltimore & Ohio Employes Magazine,* August 1915, 42–43; November 1915, 55–57.

9. *Baltimore & Ohio Magazine,* December 1920, 24–25; January 1921, 30; February 1921, 6; July 1923, 12.

10. Ibid., January 1921, 30; February 1921, 5–8; March 1921, 5–7; April 1921, 5.

11. Ibid., April 1921, 5–6.

12. Ibid., May 1921, 5–9; June 1921, 5–7; July 1921, 26–37; August 1921, 11–14.

13. Ibid., and September 1921, 9–11; October 1921, 7–9; November 1921, 9–11; December 1921, 27.

14. Ibid., July 1923, 12; January 1924, 8–9; November 1926, 38–41; October 1928, 24–27; Baltimore & Ohio Railroad Company, *Annual Report,* 1924; see also *Baltimore & Ohio Magazine,* June 1928, 8; July 1928, 5–7, 15, 23. The shopcrafts federation in Chillicothe, Ohio, ran a "Cooperative Page" in the local newspaper, endorsing local merchants who patronized the B&O (*Scioto News,* Aug. 10, 1925, 3).

15. *Baltimore & Ohio Magazine,* July 1928, 32–35. The summary statistics for freight shipments and routing orders may understate the actual totals, as numbers were not specified in five instances, and the author inserted conservative estimates.

16. Ibid., April 1932, 18–19, 84–85.

17. Ibid., November 1926, 21–22; March 1934, 9.

18. "The Story of Your Cooperative Traffic Program," pamphlet published by the Baltimore & Ohio Railroad, Jan. 5, 1956, collection of William C. Howard; *Cooperative Traffic Program Bulletin,* December 1933, collection of John W. Bliss.

19. *Cooperative Traffic Program Bulletin,* December 1933, collection of John W. Bliss.

20. *CTP Bulletin,* January 1934; March 1934. Reported in *Baltimore & Ohio Magazine,* April 1934, 12; July 1934, 10.

21. *Baltimore & Ohio Magazine,* June 1934, 26–27.

22. Interview of retired CTP director John W. Bliss, by the author, Towson, Maryland, July 28, 1988.

23. *Baltimore & Ohio Magazine,* July 1934, 5, 7.

24. Ibid., 5; *Baltimore & Ohio Magazine,* December 1934, 19; March 1935, 10–12.

25. *Baltimore & Ohio Magazine,* March 1934, 9–10; December 1934, 10; March 1935, 12.

26. Letter from Bert M. Jewell to William McGee, Jan. 21, 1930, Labor-Management Documentation Center Archives, Cornell University, AFL Railway Employees Department Collection, box 87.

27. *Baltimore & Ohio Magazine,* July 1935, 21, and subsequent issues through 1962; interviews of retired CTP director John W. Bliss and retired CTP special representative William C. Howard, by the author, Towson, Maryland, July 28, 1988.

28. Report of R. T. George, correspondent for *Baltimore & Ohio Magazine,* December 1934, 18–19.

29. *Baltimore & Ohio Magazine,* December 1935, 8–9; September 1935, 28–29, 56; January 1936, 28; March 1936, 26; October 1935, 26; February 1936, 25.

30. Reports by Theresa Naughton in *Baltimore & Ohio Magazine,* December 1935, 20; February 1936, 20; report by Mrs. J. L. Cole in *Baltimore & Ohio Magazine,* December 1935, 20.

31. Report by Roy Collins in *Baltimore & Ohio Magazine,* March 1936, 28; report by Theresa Naughton in *Baltimore & Ohio Magazine,* April 1936, 24; unsigned report in *Baltimore & Ohio Magazine,* April 1936, 24.

32. Specific figures for total CTP credited traffic were not published year by year after 1934; the $1-million-plus figure is the author's estimate, based upon local committee reports and the five-year (1934–1938) CTP revenue totals given in O. S. Lewis's report to Daniel Willard in February 1939, summarized in *Baltimore & Ohio Magazine,* March 1939, 5–6. The comments on CTP costs are taken from interviews of retired CTP director John W. Bliss and retired CTP special representative William C. Howard, by the author, Towson, Maryland, July 28, 1988.

33. Baltimore & Ohio Railroad Company, *Annual Reports,* 1929–1936.

34. Letter from Bert M. Jewell to Daniel Willard, Aug. 9, 1935; letter from Daniel Willard to Bert M. Jewell, Aug. 10, 1935, George Meany Memorial Archives, Railway Employees Department records, reel 58.

35. *Baltimore & Ohio Magazine,* August 1942, 13, 40; interviews of John W. Bliss and William C. Howard, by the author, Towson, Maryland, July 28, 1988.

36. *Baltimore & Ohio Magazine,* December 1938, 37; March 1936, 28.

37. Ibid., June 1936, 20–21, 68.

38. Interviews of Bliss and Howard; interview of retired CTP special representative Mildred L. Drechsler, by the author, Towson, Maryland, Nov. 14, 1988.

39. Report by V. P. Travers in *Baltimore & Ohio Magazine,* December 1937, 40.

40. Report of general freight traffic manager O. S. Lewis to Daniel Willard, Feb. 18, 1939; summarized in *Baltimore & Ohio Magazine*, March 1939, 5–6, 11, and in *Railway Age* 106, no. 24 (June 17, 1939): 1051.

41. *Baltimore & Ohio Magazine*, November 1938, 48.

42. Interviews of Bliss, Howard, and Drechsler.

43. *Baltimore & Ohio Magazine*, March 1939, 5–6, 11; Baltimore & Ohio Railroad Company, *Annual Reports*, 1934–1938; "Business-Getting Employees," *Baltimore & Ohio Magazine*, July 1931–June 1932. The carload revenue estimate is O. S. Lewis's (108,000 carloads times average carload revenue of $50.00); the LCL estimate is the author's (95,877 shipments times an average shipment revenue of $8.17, derived from the average value of employee-solicited LCL shipments for the second half of 1931 and the first half of 1932, adjusted for 1934–1938 average rate charges), as is the passenger estimate (167,062 passengers times 1934–1938 average revenue per passenger of $2.62).

44. Baltimore & Ohio Railroad Company, *Annual Reports*, 1937–1938.

45. Report by Mrs. R. C. Koechlin, *Baltimore & Ohio Magazine*, December 1937, 41.

46. Reports by Mrs. C. H. Sortman, V. P. Travers, and M. C. Humpert, *Baltimore & Ohio Magazine*, December 1937, 41; December 1937, 40; January 1938, 42, respectively.

47. Report by R. H. Gohlke, *Baltimore & Ohio Magazine*, September 1939, 19–20; *Baltimore & Ohio Magazine*, December 1938, 34.

48. The data under examination here (tables 4-1 and 4-2) are from CTP reports by L. A. Hightshoe, Edith Hormann, and E. J. Dennedy (Cincinnati and Ivorydale) and C. B. L. Hahn, Mrs. R. C. Koechlin, Mrs. H. R. Barton, and Mrs. John Roberts (Zanesville), published in *Baltimore & Ohio Magazine*, January 1938–December 1938.

49. In 1937 the B&O (not including the Alton) reported to the ICC total employment of 42,492: 572 executives (white-collar), 7,162 professional and clerical employees (white-collar), 7,293 maintenance of way workers (nearly all blue-collar), 11,711 maintenance of equipment workers (nearly all blue-collar), and 15,754 transportation employees (mostly blue-collar, but including some lower-level supervisors).

50. Interviews of Bliss and Howard.

51. Report by C. B. L. Hahn, *Baltimore & Ohio Magazine*, December 1938, 35.

52. *Railway Age*, 106, no. 24 (June 17, 1939) 1051. An alternative explanation for the journal's silence was that the editors knew about the CTP all along, but simply were not much impressed by it.

53. *Railway Age* 100, no. 7 (Feb. 15, 1936): 291; also 102, no. 5 (Jan. 30, 1937): 234.

54. *Mutual Magazine*, September 1930, 15; June 1935, 33–34; August 1935, 23–25.

55. Ibid., June 1935, 33–34; August 1935, 23–25; September 1935, 21; December 1935, 27.

56. Ibid., August 1936, 8–9; November 1937, 38–39; October 1938, 8.

57. *Santa Fe Magazine*, June 1935, 33–34.

58. *The Rail* (magazine of the Chesapeake & Ohio and Pere Marquette Railways), January 1936, 26.

59. *Baltimore & Ohio Magazine*, February 1938, 5.

60. Ibid., November 1938, 48.

61. Baltimore & Ohio Railroad, Minutes of Quarterly System Cooperative Meeting, Oct. 19, 1937; also Jan. 11, 1938, and Apr. 26, 1938, Library of Congress, Manuscript Division, Otto S. Beyer Papers, box 101.

62. *Baltimore & Ohio Magazine*, April 1934, 17–18; February 1938, 5.

63. This is the only assumption under which the end-of-1937 figures can be reconciled with the Cooperative Plan summary sheet of April 1941 (Library of Congress, Manuscript Division, Otto S. Beyer Papers, box 97) other than error in one or both sets of numbers.

64. *Mutual Magazine*, March 1938, 7.

65. Baltimore & Ohio Railroad, *Annual Reports*, 1937–1938.

66. There is some possibility that these factors contributed to the below-average CTP participation rates of blue-collar employees.

67. 1934–1937 Average (*Baltimore & Ohio Magazine*, Februay 1938, 5) against January 1938–August 1941 average (Baltimore & Ohio Railroad Company, Motive Power Department: summary of suggestions discussed at cooperative meetings . . . to Sept. 3, 1941, Library of Congress, Manuscript Division, Otto S. Beyer Papers, box 97).

68. Cooperative Plan summary sheet, April 1941, Otto S. Beyer Papers. The retired B&O conductor and local union official George Stanton, interviewed by the author in Fairmont, West Virginia, on Oct. 8, 1988, stated that Cooperative Plan meetings in the conducting transportation department no longer were being held when he was hired by the B&O in 1941.

69. Baltimore & Ohio Railroad Company, *Annual Reports*, 1938–1941; memorandum from O. S. Lewis to Daniel Willard, Dec. 14, 1939, Library of Congress, Manuscript Division, Otto S. Beyer Papers, box 103.

70. *Baltimore & Ohio Magazine*, December 1940, 10.

71. Ibid., 10–12.

72. *Baltimore & Ohio Magazine*, June 1940, 13–15.

73. Letter from Daniel Willard to Otto S. Beyer, Mar. 7, 1938, Library of Congress, Manuscript Division, Otto S. Beyer Papers, box 103.

74. Letter from Daniel Willard to Otto S. Beyer, June 28, 1937; letter from Willard to Beyer, Sept. 14, 1937; letter from Beyer to Willard, Sept. 25, 1937, Library of Congress, Manuscript Division, Otto S. Beyer Papers, box 103.

75. Letter from Daniel Willard to Otto S. Beyer, Nov. 23, 1941, Library of Congress, Manuscript Division, Otto S. Beyer Papers, box 103.

76. Letter from Daniel Willard to Otto S. Beyer, Apr. 13, 1934; letter from Beyer to Willard, Apr. 24, 1934, Library of Congress, Manuscript Division, Otto S. Beyer Papers, box 103.

77. Draft of letter from Otto S. Beyer to Daniel Willard, ca. Mar. 30, 1938, Library of Congress, Manuscript Division, Otto S. Beyer Papers, box 103; also Beyer to Willard, Sept. 25, 1937.

78. Baltimore & Ohio Railroad Company, *Annual Reports*, 1938–1942; address by Roy B. White to Baltimore Terminals CTP rally, reported in *Baltimore & Ohio Magazine*, March 1942, 13.

79. Baltimore & Ohio Railroad Company, *Annual Reports*, 1938–1939.

80. Ibid., and John F. Stover, *History of the Baltimore & Ohio Railroad* (West Lafayette, Ind.: Purdue University Press, 1987), 293–94.

81. Baltimore & Ohio Railroad Company, *Annual Report*, 1938.

82. *Baltimore & Ohio Magazine*, April 1944, 3, 62.

83. For example, see a survey conducted by *Sales Management* magazine and summarized in *Baltimore & Ohio Magazine*, October 1936, 5; and Virginia Tanner, "B&O's Remarkable On-Time Record," *Baltimore & Ohio Magazine*, March 1946, 4–5, 57; also interviews of Drechsler, Bliss, and Howard and letter from retired B&O president Jervis Langdon, Jr., to the author, Aug. 27, 1988 (author's collection).

Chapter 5

1. Open letter from Daniel Willard to all Baltimore & Ohio employees, May 19, 1941; printed in *Baltimore & Ohio Magazine*, May 1941, 4.

2. *Baltimore & Ohio Magazine*, August 1942, 13, 50–51. Willard's spirits generally

were lowered during the last two years of his life by the death by heart attack of Daniel, Jr., in May 1940.

3. Ibid., 13–14.

4. "Operating Revenues, Operating Expenses, and Net Railway Operating Income," monthly reports issued by the Baltimore & Ohio vice president and comptroller, J. J. Ekin, 1930–1940; summarized and reported in *Baltimore & Ohio Magazine*, March 1940, 5, 7.

5. For examples of B&O's timekeeping achievements, see *Baltimore & Ohio Magazine*, September 1929, 5; September 1930, 21; March 1946, 4, 5, 57. For a fuller discussion of B&O's technical innovations, see John F. Stover, *History of the Baltimore & Ohio Railroad* (West Lafayette, Ind.: Purdue University Press, 1987), 282–83, 287–88.

6. For an introduction to the subject of Japanese management, see Mansel G. Blackford, *The Rise of Modern Business in Great Britain, the United States, and Japan* (Chapel Hill: University of North Carolina Press, 1988), esp. chaps. 5–8. For more detailed discussions, see Rodney Clark, *The Japanese Company* (New Haven: Yale University Press, 1979), R. T. Pascale and A. G. Athos, *The Art of Japanese Management* (New York: Simon & Schuster, 1981). Works that focus on the historical development and cultural context of Japanese management are Andrew Gordon, *The Evolution of Labor Relations in Japan: Heavy Industry, 1853–1955* (Cambridge, Mass.: Council on East Asian Studies, Harvard University, 1985); Vladimir Pucik, Schon Beechler, and Kiyohiko Ito, "American Organizational Theory in Japan: Western Concepts, Japanese Spirit," *Sociology and Social Research* 71, no. 1 (October 1986): 20–26; Peter Drucker, "Behind Japan's Success," *Harvard Business Review* (January–February 1981): 83–90; and Charles Y. Yang, "Demystifying Japanese Management Practices," *Harvard Business Review* (November–December 1984): 172–82.

7. William G. Ouchi, *Theory Z: How American Business Can Meet the Japanese Challenge* (Reading, Mass.: Addison-Wesley, 1981).

8. *Baltimore & Ohio Magazine*, January 1942, 12.

9. Ibid., August 1942, 40–41.

10. Ibid., May 1941, 4–6.

11. Ibid., 6; December 1941, 6.

12. Ibid., December 1942, 17; August 1943, 34; October 1942, 6.

13. Philip M. Wagner, "It Worked for the B&O," *Saturday Evening Post*, Aug. 22, 1942, 22, 81–82; reprinted and distributed by the War Production Drive Headquarters (Washington, D.C.: Government Printing Office, 1942).

14. Letter from Bert M. Jewell to O. S. Beyer, Dec. 5, 1930, Labor-Management Documentation Center Archives, Cornell University.

15. Interview of retired CTP special representative Mildred L. Drechsler, by the author, Towson, Maryland, Nov. 14, 1988.

16. Interview of Col. Roy B. White by Louis Azrael, broadcast May 12, 1948, over WBAL-TV, Baltimore; reported in *Baltimore & Ohio Magazine*, July 1948, 5.

17. The 1943 strike-averting seizure was one of a string of increasingly nasty confrontations between the railroads and the operating unions, extending back through a near-strike in the summer of 1941 to the near-strikes of 1938 and 1937, and forward through the federal seizures of the railroads in 1946, 1948, and 1950.

18. Baltimore & Ohio Railroad Company, *Annual Reports*, 1943, 1946, 1948, 1950; Stover, *History of the Baltimore & Ohio Railroad*, 309–10, 324–25; *Baltimore & Ohio Magazine*, January 1944, 1, 4; July 1948, 5, 61; October 1950, 13.

19. Baltimore & Ohio Railroad Company, *Annual Report*, 1951.

20. *Baltimore & Ohio Magazine*, February 1938, 5; June 1942, 6; and Baltimore & Ohio Railway Company, *Annual Report*, 1948.

21. Program, "Red, White and Blue Revue," all-B&O-employee song-and-dance show sponsored by the Baltimore CTP committees, Oct. 4, 5, and 7, 1943, collection of John W. Bliss.

22. "The Story of Your Cooperative Traffic Program," pamphlet published by the Baltimore & Ohio Railroad, Jan. 5, 1956, collection of William C. Howard.

23. Open memo from R. B. White to all CTP participants, reprinted in *Baltimore & Ohio Magazine*, January 1947, 36.

24. *Baltimore & Ohio Magazine*, August 1948, 30.

25. Baltimore & Ohio Railroad Company, *Annual Report*, 1948. The report incorrectly states that 1913 was the year in which the Veterans' Association was founded.

26. Interview of Mildred Drechsler.

27. *Baltimore & Ohio Magazine*, September 1950, 6–7, 51; April 1954, 1; May 1954, 2; Minutes of the Convention of System Federation No. 30, AFL, Lord Baltimore Hotel, Baltimore, June 11–12, 1952, Labor-Management Documentation Center Archives, Cornell University.

28. Baltimore & Ohio Railroad Company, *Annual Reports, 1942–1952.*

29. *Baltimore & Ohio Magazine*, September 1953, 8–11.

30. Ibid., March 1955, 8–9, 31.

31. Interview of the retired CTP senior special representative John W. Bliss and the retired CTP special representative William C. Howard, by the author, Towson, Maryland, July 28, 1988; interview of the retired CTP special representative Mildred L. Drechsler by the author, Towson, Maryland, Nov. 14, 1988.

32. Interviews of Bliss, Howard, and Drechsler.

33. "The Story of Your Cooperative Traffic Program," 6.

34. Baltimore & Ohio Railroad Company, *Annual Reports*, 1960 and 1937.

35. Interview of Mildred Drechsler.

36. *Baltimore & Ohio Magazine*, March 1955, 16.

37. Letter from the retired Zanesville ticket agent and CTP chairman Paul F. Mobus, to the author, Feb. 10, 1989, author's collection, and *Baltimore & Ohio Magazine*, May 1957, 25.

38. *Baltimore & Ohio Magazine*, November 1953, 16–17, 48; March 1956, 4–5, 46.

39. Interviews of Bliss, Howard, and Drechsler.

40. *Baltimore & Ohio Magazine*, March 1956, 7; March 1958, inside back cover; October 1958, inside back cover; November 1959, 10, 22; June 1960, 8; July 1960, 10; April 1960, 12–13; March 1956, 4–5.

41. Statement of personnel department organization and functions issued by the office of the vice president-personnel, Baltimore & Ohio Railroad, Sept. 1, 1953; introductory program booklet, technical graduate training course, Baltimore & Ohio Railroad, issued between Sept. 1, 1953, and Feb. 4, 1954, Labor-Management Documentation Center Archives, Cornell University; *Baltimore & Ohio Magazine*, March 1948, 42; July 1948, 48; *Baltimore & Ohio Magazine*, August 1956, 4, 15; "Welcome to the B&O," new-employee handbook issued by the Baltimore & Ohio Railroad, 1958, Labor-Management Documentation Center Archives, Cornell University.

42. Letter from retired B&O assistant car department superintendent Albert W. Gibson, to the author, Dec. 19, 1988, author's collection.

43. Ibid.

44. Interview of CSX Cumberland car shop superintendent Russell DeVore, by the author, Cumberland, Maryland, Oct. 7, 1989. DeVore was originally hired by the B&O as a carman at Keyser, West Virginia, in 1958.

45. Minutes of the Convention of System Federation No. 30, AFL, Fort Pitt Hotel, Pittsburgh, May 22–23, 1940; Minutes of the Convention of System Federation No. 30, AFL, Sinton Hotel, Cincinnati, June 7–8, 1950; Minutes of the Convention of System Federation No. 30, AFL, Lord Baltimore Hotel, Baltimore, June 11–12, 1952; Preamble to the Constitution and Bylaws of Sys-

tem Federation No. 30, AFL, as revised in June 1952; Preamble to the Constitution and Bylaws of System Federation No. 30, AFL, as revised in 1960; resolution submitted on behalf of System Federation No. 30 by president Oscar A. Anthony, to the Twelfth convention of the Railway Employees' Department, AFL, Chicago, Apr. 25, 1960; letter and attachments from System Federation No. 30 president Oscar A. Anthony to AFL Railway Employees' Department president Michael D. Fox, Mar. 9, 1960, Labor-Management Documentation Center Archives, Cornell University, Railway Employees Department collection.

46. For discussions of the general issue of postwar railroad labor relations, see Harold M. Levinson, Charles M. Rehmus, Joseph P. Goldbey, and Mark L. Kahn, *Collective Bargaining and Technological Change in American Transportation* (Evanston, Ill.: Northwestern University Transportation Center, 1971); Robert C. Lieb, *Labor in the Transportation Industries* (Washington, D.C.: U.S. Department of Transportation, 1973); and Jacob J. Kaufman, "Procedures versus Collective Bargaining in Railroad Relations Disputes," *Industrial and Labor Relations Review* (October 1971): 53–70.

47. Baltimore & Ohio Railroad Company, *Annual Reports,* 1946–1954; Martin J. Levine, "The Railroad Crew Size Controversy Revisited," *Labor Law Journal* (June 1969): 373–86.

48. Minutes of the Convention of System Federation No. 30, AFL, Sinton Hotel, Cincinnati, Oct. 10–11, 1946, Labor-Management Documentation Center Archives, Cornell University; Minutes of 1950 Federation No. 30 convention; Minutes of 1952 Federation No. 30 convention; letter and attachments from Oscar Anthony to Michael Fox, Mar. 9, 1960.

49. Minutes of the Convention of Western Maryland System Federation No. 24, AFL, Hagerstown, Maryland, Sept. 2, 1948, Labor-Management Documentation Center Archives, Cornell University; Bylaws of Federation No. 30; Minutes of 1946 Federation No. 30 convention; Minutes of 1948 Federation No. 30 convention.

50. Letter from retired B&O president Jervis Langdon, Jr., to the author, Aug. 27, 1988, author's collection. Langdon came to the B&O from the chairmanship of the Association of Southeastern Railroads. Before that he served in the legal departments of the C&O, the New York Central, and the Lehigh Valley (*Baltimore & Ohio Magazine,* January 1957, 38; John F. Stover, *History of the Baltimore & Ohio Railroad* [West Lafayette, Ind.: Purdue University Press, 1987], 356).

51. Baltimore & Ohio Railroad Company, *Annual Reports,* 1956–1961.

52. Stover, *History of the Baltimore & Ohio,* 356–58.

53. Ibid., 357–63; Baltimore & Ohio Railroad Company, *Annual Reports,* 1960–1963.

54. Baltimore & Ohio Railroad Company, *Annual Report,* 1961.

55. Letter from Jervis Langdon, Jr., to the author, Dec. 15, 1988, author's collection.

56. Letter from John Bliss to the author, Dec. 16, 1988, author's collection; interview of Mildred Drechsler.

57. Letter from John Bliss to the author, Dec. 16, 1988, author's collection.

58. Letter from Jervis Langdon, Jr., to the author, Dec. 15, 1988, author's collection.

59. Letter from Albert W. Gibson to the author Dec. 19, 1988, author's collection.

60. Letter from Jervis Langdon, Jr., to the author, Dec. 15, 1988, author's collection. Stover, *History of the Baltimore & Ohio,* 363–64.

61. *Trains,* November 1972, 8–10; Stover, *History of the Baltimore & Ohio,* 365–66; *Trains,* July 1987, 11.

Conclusion

1. The Willard work history sheet was provided by D. R. Shawley, manager of employee services, CSX Distribution Group, Baltimore (with cover letter dated Mar. 2, 1988).

Index

Adams, William, 62
Adamson Act, 26
Akron, Canton, & Youngstown Railroad, 178–79
Akron, Ohio, 30
Alberty, H. L., 58, 93–94
Allegheny Mountains, 6, 13, 79
Alton Railroad, 113–15, 124, 125–27, 136, 168, 173
Altoona, Pa., 24
Amalgamated Sheet Metal Workers' International Alliance. *See* AFL, shopcrafts unions
American Federationist, 70, 90
American Federation of Labor
  executive council, 39, 96, 167
  rail unions other than shopcrafts, 68, 96, 100–102
  shopcrafts unions. *See also* Baltimore & Ohio Railroad
    System Federation No. 30
    B&O traffic solicitation, 127–28
    demise of Cooperative Plan, 105–6, 177–79
    involvement in development of Cooperative Plan, 35–36, 39, 41–44, 52
    1922 strike. *See* Shopmen's Strike of 1922
    operation of Cooperative Plan, 57–61, 93–94

American Society of Mechanical Engineers, 70
Ann Arbor Railroad, 115
Askew, W. R., 120
Association of American Railroads, 145
Association of Railroad Executives, 42, 45–46, 108
Atchison, Topeka, & Santa Fe Railway. *See* Santa Fe Railway
Atterbury, W. W., 24, 25, 42, 45–47, 78–81, 110, 145

Baltimore, Md., 11, 12, 20, 21, 22, 25, 29, 31, 46, 57, 61, 78, 83, 87, 92, 98, 103, 120, 122, 125, 127, 129, 131, 132, 134, 135, 147, 150, 159, 175, 181, 182
Baltimore & Ohio Magazine, 15, 17–18, 28, 36, 38, 86–88, 90, 95, 105, 109, 121–23, 127, 138, 144, 150, 156, 165, 170, 172, 175, 179
Baltimore & Ohio Railroad
  acquisition of Alton, BR&P, and B&S, 113–15
  acquisition by C&O, 180–82
  B&O Athletic Association, Parkersburg, 85
  B&O Orchestra, 21, 30
  Baltimore Division, 30, 164